The Simplest of Signs

The Simplest of Signs

Victor Hugo
and the Language of Images
in France: 1850–1950

Timothy Raser

Newark: University of Delaware Press

© 2004 by Rosemont Publishing & Printing Corp.

All rights reserved. Authorization to photocopy items for internal or personal use, or the internal or personal use of specific clients, is granted by the copyright owner, provided that a base fee of $10.00, plus eight cents per page, per copy is paid directly to the Copyright Clearance Center, 222 Rosewood Drive, Danvers, Massachusetts 01923. [0-87413-867-1 $10.00 + 8¢ pp, pc.]

Other than as indicated in the foregoing, this book may not be reproduced, in whole or in part, in any form (except as permitted by Sections 107 and 108 of the U.S. Copyright Law), and except for brief quotes appearing in reviews in the public press.

Associated University Presses
2010 Eastpark Boulevard
Cranbury, NJ 08512

The paper used in this publication meets the requirements of the American National Standard for Permanence of Paper for Printed Library Materials Z39.48-1984.

Library of Congress Cataloging-in-Publication Data

Raser, Timothy Bell.
  The simplest of signs : Victor Hugo and the language of images in France, 1850–1950 / Timothy Raser.
     p. cm.
Includes bibliographical references and index.
  ISBN 0-87413-867-1 (alk. paper)
  1. Hugo, Victor, 1802–1885—Criticism and interpretation. I. Title.
PQ2301.R34 2004
848'.709—dc22   2003026814

PRINTED IN THE UNITED STATES OF AMERICA

Contents

List of Illustrations	7
Acknowledgments	9
Introduction	13
1. Simple Signs in Hugo: Dates, Words, Names, and Facts	21
Hugo's Dates: The Functions of Chronology 21	
Limits of Performative Language in Hugo's Theater 29	
People, Places, and Apostrophe in "Tristesse d'Olympio" 40	
Quatrevingt-treize: Revolution and Æsthetics 49	
2. Hugo's Textual Systems: Antithesis, Inscription, Ekphrasis	61
Politics and Æsthetics of Race in *Bug-Jargal* 61	
The Discipline of Letters: *Le Dernier Jour d'un condamné* 74	
Reading and Refereince in *Notre-Dame de Paris* 87	
3. Literary Accounts of the Visual Arts: Narrative, Citation, and Attribution	105
Painting Pictures with Words 105	
Reading and Denotation 107	
Art Criticism's Narratives 123	
The End of Citation in Baudelaire's Art Criticism 134	
Claiming Painting for Literature: Fromentin and Claudel 150	
Sartre and Tintoretto: This Side of Words 163	
Epilogue	188
Notes	192
Works Cited	208
Index	215

Illustrations

1. *Faust in His Study*, Rembrandt Harmensz van Rijn   92
2. *Little Figure* of Rouen Cathedral, John Ruskin   96
3. *Ovid among the Scythians*, London, National Gallery, Eugène Delacroix   127
4. Pastel, Musée Eugène Boudin, Honfleur, Eugène Boudin   128
5. *Miracle of Saint Mark (Saint Mark freeing the Slave from Torture),"* Gallerie dell'Accademia, Venice, Jacopo Tintoretto   173
6. *St. George and the Dragon*, National Gallery, London, Jacopo Tintoretto   180
7. *Winter*, Louvre, Paris, Giuseppe Arcimboldo   190

Acknowledgments

"HUGO'S DATES: THE FUNCTIONS OF CHRONOLOGY," APPEARED originally in *Studies in Modern and Classical Languages and Literatures (IV)* Rollins College, 1992. "Limits of Performative Language in Hugo's Theater," first appeared in *Romanische Forschungen*, Vol. 105, Nos. 3 & 4 (1993). "*Quatrevingt-treize*: Revolution and Æsthetics" appeared originally as "Æsthetics and Revolution in Hugo's *Quatrevingt-treize*," in *L'Esprit créateur* XXIX, No. 2 (Summer 1989). "Politics and Æsthetics of Race in *Bug-Jargal*," first appeared in the *Romantic Review*, Vol. 89, No. 3 (May, 1998). "Claiming Painting for Literature: Fromentin and Claudel," first appeared in *Claudel Studies*, Vol. XXV, Nos. 1 & 2 (1988). Permission to reprint these articles in modified form is gratefully acknowledged.

To the Réunion des Musées Nationaux/Art Resource, NY, go thanks for permission to reproduce a photograph of Giusseppe Arcimboldo's "Winter" (Louvre, Paris); to SCALA/Art Resourse, NY, go thanks for permission to use a photograph of the "Miracle of Saint Mark (Saint Mark freeing the Slave from Torture)," (Accademia, Venice); to the National Gallery of London go thanks for permission to reproduce photos of "Saint George and the Dragon" and "Ovid among the Scythians"; to the Musée Eugène Boudin thanks for permission to reproduce a photograph of "Pastel—Nuages"; to the Fine Arts Museums of San Francisco go thanks for permission to reproduce a Rembrandt's "Faust in Study," from the Bruno and Sadie Adriani Collection, 1959.40.22. I thank too the University of Georgia Center for Humanities and Arts for their support in obtaining permissions and printing these images.

Éditions Gallimard receives thanks for permission to quote texts from the works of Jean-Paul Satre, Michel Foucault, and Paul Claudel; passages from Michel Foucault's works in English translation are used with permission of Vintage Books. Texts from the works of Roland Barthes are used with the permission of Éditions du Seuil (French) and Hill and Wang (English translations). Translations of Ferdinand de Saussure, Paul Claudel, and Jean-Paul Sartre's *L'Imaginaire* are used by permission of the Philosopher's Library; those of Sartre's *Situations II* are used by permission of Harvard University Press. Phaidon Publishing granted permission to reprint passages of Charles Baudelaire's *Art in Paris: 1845–1862* and *The Painter of Modern Life and Other Essays* and Eugène Fromentin's *Masters of Part Time*. To Flammarion and University of Chicago Press go thanks for permission to reprint passages of Jacques Derrida's *La Vérité en peinture*, in French and English translation respectively. And to Oxford University Press go thanks for permission to use passages of Alban Krailsheimer's translation of *Notre-Dame de Paris* and Martin Sorrel's translations of Paul Verlaine's "Art of Poetry" and "Feverish Dreams" in their entirety. I thank Yale University Press for permission to use passages of Marcel Proust's *On Reading Ruskin*.

But most importantly, I thank Chris Retz of Associated University Presses for her painstaking and insightful copy editing, and my family, Paul, Matthew, and Melinda, for their patience and support during the writing of this book.

The Simplest of Signs

Introduction

SINCE THE ROMANTIC PERIOD, THERE HAS BEEN A STRONG INTEREST among French authors in art commentary: Stendhal, Baudelaire, Zola, Huysmans, and others,[1] famous and not so famous, have tried their hand at depicting and assessing works of painting and sculpture. While many of these wrote commentaries that referred to real works, publishing them as criticism or appreciations, others still wrote commentaries of fictions and presented theories of writing or of beauty in the guise of descriptions of non-existent works of art.[2] This interest has not been the exclusive province of French authors: John Ruskin, Walter Pater, and Henry James made significant contributions to the "genre," if such it can be called, and certainly these three constitute only a small fraction of those in England or the United States who practiced it.

What is curious about such an interest is its apparently self-defeating quality: even in the case of fictions, the text literally demands that the reader stop reading, lift her eyes from the page, and look at the painting the author has just described. In the case of real works, those described perhaps in a "Salon" or a critical essay, the reader seeks corroboration of the text just read, or perhaps wishes to perceive what the text presents only dimly, or finally, wants to see instead of to read: in all cases, the text apparently requires a supplement, with all the ambiguities such a supplement implies. And of course, whatever the supplement is, it is *not* the text, and the appeal to one is in effect an appeal not to read. In the case of fictions, turning from the text hardly replaces reading, but the gesture itself is suggestive: the reader tries to "imagine" the text, to elaborate some sort quasi-perceptual allegory for it. What are these texts that want not to be read?

Much can be said about the intentions of authors who describe works of art; in all cases, however, it follows from what has just been noted that writing about pictures, sculptures, or monuments implies a desire to go "beyond" the text into some other mode of signification. That a new mode of signification is sought follows from the fact that the text describes art, a signifying system related to, but not the same as, writing. This new mode implies an inadequacy on the part of writing and a promise of fulfillment elsewhere, and in this respect the description of artworks is a quintessentially romantic phenomenon, for like protestations of immediacy, self-presence and "natural" understanding, it designates a limit to culture's understanding of itself and postulates the possibility of going beyond that limit.

One writer who is both manifestly romantic and well-known for his descriptions of works of art is Victor Hugo. Already a successful poet and dramatist in 1830, it was his novel about the Cathedral of Paris—*Notre-Dame de Paris*—that established him as a best-selling author, and certainly, this novel (with *Les Misérables*) is a principal reason he is read today.[3] What is also evident about Hugo is his desire to exceed limits: the sheer volume of his published works says as much, but so do his insistence on themes of excess (*démesure*) and his repeated denunciations of rules of prosody, denunciations which contributed significantly to the success of both his poetry and his theater. The strongest reason to invoke Hugo, however, is his rhetoric, which from the poet's earliest days has been considered his greatest innovation.

Thus it was that in 1829, his friend Pierre Leroux presented a theory in *Le Globe* of Hugo's novelty: it sprang, he declared, from his adoption of a new style, "le style symbolique" (Leroux 1829), one that characterized other romantic writers such as Chateaubriand, and one which differed from the style of such authors as Racine. An appreciation of his friend as well as a discourse on symbol, Leroux's article has since been lost among the vast number of writings on both subjects, and this is perhaps unfortunate. Hugo's symbolism, a term that does not come easily to students of French poetry, is a possibility that should be entertained, if only because it is so difficult to define Hugo, and because definitions of symbol fall so short when applied to him. Certainly, Leroux's description of symbol traces a figure different from anything one might know from Wordsworth or Hegel, to say nothing of the French Symbolist poets of the second half of the century, but for that very reason, it is of interest. Here is a concept opening access to a poet who, as Harold Bloom has stated, "remains absurdly unfashionable and neglected by his nation's most advanced critics" (Bloom 1979, 13).

If Hegel defined symbol as a form striving to express a content out of all proportion to its abilities, and if Wordsworth used images that enjoyed an organic relation to the idea they communicated (Abrams 1953, 290–91), Leroux defines Hugo's "symbols" as little more than shorthand: "this form of language consists in not developing the idea one wishes to compare to another, but in developing only this second idea, that is, the image. It is thus an intermediate form, between simile and allegory properly speaking, more rapid than simile and less obscure than allegory" (Leroux 1829, 1:330; author's translation).[4] If the classical style required the parallel development of the tenor and vehicle of the founding metaphor, in the "symbolic style," Leroux writes, the vehicle alone is developed, even at the expense of the explanatory tenor, but with a corresponding gain in speed. The reader is thus confronted with images detached from their meanings, and if understood, the style is rapid; if not, it is obscure: "suppose that a figure permitting the continuous substitution of images for abstract terms, vague and indeterminate expressions for proper meanings, is introduced into a language: consider its effect. Abstraction will disappear from the poetry of this people, and mystery will be born" (Leroux 1829, 1:330; author's translation). And thus, for Hugo as for Chateaubriand before him, the critical reception was hostile: "The critics of the period tore these great figures apart" (Leroux 1829, 1:332; author's translation).

Leroux's estimate of contemporary hostility for romanticism may be exaggerated; his analysis of its source, however, is telling. According to him, classical literary theory dictated the full expression of any figure based on analogy: the "just as" part would receive precisely the same development as the "so also." Lopsided figures, where an image alone is expressed with no explanation, are obscure, mysterious, and inviting; Joad's prophetic vision in *Athalie*, the only such figure in Racine's work, is an early example. By presupposing the reader's ability to decode such figures without authorial explanation, the new style builds on an acquired readerly competence, using a more economical, effective language. Instead of achieving meaning by pointing to a formulation of its tenor, this style skips a step and produces meaning more directly.

Even if such writing was better received than Leroux allows, instances of resistance are suggestive. One such hostile critic is John Ruskin, whose reaction to Hugo's *Notre-Dame de Paris* is worth recalling *in extenso:*

> I never was thoroughly ashamed of you and your radicalism till you sent me that ineffably villainous thing of Victor Hugo's. Did you ever read *The Hunchback of Notre Dame*? I believe it to be simply the most disgusting book ever written by man, and on the whole to have caused more brutality and evil than any other French writing with which I am acquainted.
>
> De Balzac is sensual, but he is an artist of the highest touch, and a philosopher even in his sensuality. Eugène Sue paints virtue as well as vice. Dumas is absurd and useless, but interesting. Béranger blasphemous, but witty. George Sand immoral, but elegant. But for pure, dull, virtueless, stupid, deadly poison, read Victor Hugo. . . .
>
> Truly yours, if you will utterly and for ever disclaim Victor Hugo. (Wedderburn 1903–12, 36:212)

What most appalls Ruskin is the absence in Hugo's writing of any reference to a moral system. All the other writers he mentions in this tirade possess a compensatory virtue, whether philosophy, interest, wit, or elegance. Hugo's writing fails Ruskin's test because it is, he claims, one thing and one thing only. Balzac, Dumas, Béranger, and Sand can be criticized, but the failings of their prose (sensuality, uselessness, blasphemy, immorality) spring from opposition to positive terms, and thus even when failing they imply a moral structure. Hugo's prose, however, is not conceived oppositionally; its meaning does not spring from systematic structures, but from a simple, one-way process of signification. It succeeds only, if it is possible to call its effect success, in designating evil without ever recognizing the good.

In this respect, there is a curious affinity between Leroux's observations and Ruskin's: they agree that Hugo has left something out of his formulations and that the key to his style, difficult as it might be to admit it, is not accumulation, but ellipsis. Further, this device relates him to other nineteenth-century authors to whom he is now rarely compared, but for whom he was, in the mid–1800s, a model: art critics. His presence on the *Comité pour la préservation des monuments historiques* gave him a fleeting authority as one of the foremost æstheticians of the day, along with Victor Cousin who was also a member of the committee. Hugo's interest in works of art is part of his romanticism.

Because of his comments on the plastic arts, Roland Barthes's seminal article, "La Rhétorique de l'image," is apposite here. In it, he decodes an advertisement for Panzani food products. Pictures produce their effect, Barthes argues, by presupposing the ability to read images:

> Les signifiés de ce troisième message sont formés par les objets réels de la scène, les signifiants par ces mêmes objets photographiés, car il est évident que dans la représentation analogique, le rapport de la chose signifiée et de l'image signifiante n'étant plus "arbitraire" (comme il l'est dans la langue), il n'est plus nécessaire de ménager le relais d'un troisième terme sous les espèces de l'image psychique de l'objet.... Autrement dit, le signe de ce message n'est plus puisé dans une réserve institutionnelle, il n'est pas codé, et l'on a affaire à ce paradoxe (sur lequel on reviendra) *d'un message sans code.* (Barthes 1982, "Rhétorique," 28)

> [The signifieds of this third message are formed by the real objects of the scene, the signifiers by these same objects photographed, for it is obvious that since in analogical representation the relation of the thing signified and of the signifying language is no longer "arbitrary" (as it was in speech), it is no longer necessary to insert the relay of a third term in the form of the psychic image of the object.... In other words, the sign of this message is no longer drawn from an institutional stock, it is not coded, and we are faced with the paradox (to which we shall return) of a *message without a code.* (Barthes 1985, "Rhetoric" 25)]

The postulation of a "message without a code" is scandalous: all signification relies on codes, at least for semiology, of which Barthes is one of the founding members. In fact, just a few lines later, Barthes goes on to say "pour 'lire' ce dernier... niveau de l'image, nous n'avons besoin d'autre savoir que celui qui est attaché à notre perception: il n'est pas nul, car il nous faut savoir ce qu'est une image (les enfants ne le savant que vers quatre ans) et ce que sont une tomate, un filet, un paquet de pâtes" (Barthes 1982 "Rhétorique, 29) ["in order to 'read' this last (or this first) level of the image, we need no other knowledge than what is involved in our perception: this knowledge is not nil, for we must know what an image is (children know this only at about the age of four) and what a tomato, a string bag, and a package of pasta are" (Barthes 1985, "Rhetoric," 25)]. But the "knowledge" (*savoir*) necessary to read images, and which Barthes acknowledges is not negligible, is absolutely crucial. To say that one "perceives" pictorial images is to ignore the training necessary to read them, for any reading presupposes a code. This code must be learned, and it takes years to learn it. No signification is natural, taking place via perceived analogies between an object and a two-dimensional form "representing" it: resemblance is an unsupported principle of pictorial analysis just as cratylism is a useless principle of etymology.

Although evaluating it differently and calling it by vastly different names, Leroux, Ruskin, and Barthes are designating a single, anomalous mode of signifying, one that exploits an ellipsis in the signifying process. Leroux calls Hugo's decision not to state completely both terms of an analogy "symbol" and qualifies it as an innovation; Ruskin labels Hugo's refusal to define vices by opposition to their corresponding virtues "poison," and qualifies it as a failing; Barthes asserts that pictures appeal to a primitive mode of reading, one based on immediately perceived analogies of form, analogies which enable an ideologically treacherous, denotative mode of signifying.

That Ruskin and Leroux should write about texts, while Barthes writes about pictures, should not be surprising. Ekphrastic texts have existed since Homer and Philostratus, but it is only with the advent of the museum in the early nineteenth century and the display of art to the general public in "Salons" and expositions, that the description of works of art could become more widespread than an esoteric practice. Thus, while Barthes writes in "Rhétorique de l'image" of mid-twentieth-century advertising, he employs a discourse developed at the same moment as Hugo's new style was improvised; my argument is that both discourses are tainted by their appeal to an impossible mode of signifying, one so appealing, however, that it is very difficult to do without.

This can be called a shortcut to reading; many other terms are possible however: "speed," "deadly poison," "denotation," and "message without a code" are names already seen; "thinking less," "naming with its name," and "the near side of signs" are phrases that will come later. But whatever the name, it designates an impossibility. In this book, two arguments come forward, arguments that converge into one: first, that the shortcut to signification described by Leroux and Ruskin in Hugo's poetry and novels exploits the same error as Barthes's assumption that pictures can be understood without reading. Second, that Hugo's use of this shortcut served as a model for a century of artwriting[5] that followed him. With this aim, I will read different texts of

Hugo's, showing how a reliance on shortcuts to meaning permeates his writings, and how, at the same time, as someone whose understanding of signs is second to none, he always recognized the need to relate signs not simply to meanings, but to other signs as well. This argument is not chronological: the temptation to use shortcuts exists at all times and in all places; I will try instead to examine Hugo's most denotative texts first, and his most readerly texts last. As it happens, this places *Notre-Dame de Paris*, the text one could call the first piece of artwriting intended for general consumption, at the end of my examination of Hugo.

In the second part, I will show how this model of reading or signifying has operated in texts of art criticism, where, because of pictorial subject matter, it seems almost inevitable. The authors I choose might be considered the "school" of an author who had none: Hugo. While Baudelaire has been placed at the center of a Parnassian movement, and Mallarmé and Verlaine, in different ways, at the center of Symbolist movements, attempts to place Hugo at the center of any movement had failed even before his exile. Perhaps he lived too long: if crowds dancing in the streets during the nation's funeral for him in 1885 mean anything, it is perhaps that his presence was oppressive for younger poets. But all the writers discussed, and first among them, Baudelaire (who, of course, resented Hugo while sending him poems), owe a debt to Hugo. Even Sartre's dismissal of Hugo in *Qu'est-ce que la littérature* is tinged with envy, and the portrait he paints of his grandfather in *Les Mots* resembles that of the *père Noël de la poésie* (Gaudon 1969). Hugo's postulate of direct signification appears in most of his texts and in most of his texts is rejected as illusory. But many are the authors who followed him, looking for a "magic word" that would reveal all.

1
Simple Signs in Hugo: Dates, Words, Names, and Facts

Hugo's Dates: The Functions of Chronology

ONE OF LANGUAGE'S PRINCIPAL SEDUCTIONS IS ITS APPARENT ABILity to designate things simply, a simplicity that quickly breaks down on closer inspection. Charles Sanders Pierce (and following him, Jacques Lacan) argued that signs signify not by pointing at things, or even, as Ferdinand de Saussure would have it, at signifieds, but at other signs. Meaning becomes apparent not through the memorization of discrete definitions, but through the interconnectedness of signs, and texts, not dictionaries, are the basis of signification. In this respect, one could say that reference is indeed the foundation of meaning, but one would need to stipulate quickly that by "reference" is understood not a designation of "real" things by signs, but also references by words to other words, like the markers left by scholars in texts, markers that lead to other markers, which in turn . . . and so on.

It is because of such ambiguities in the word "reference" that a bookish, even scholarly tic of Hugo's takes on significance: his inclusion of dates in many of his works. At first glance, these are welcomed by literary critics, for they (one hopes) will allow one to sidestep entire fields of research by telling when texts were written, thus placing them firmly in a real context. Like proper nouns, dates seem to be unequivocal: they designate simply, unlike images and figures, and require no interpretation.

Indeed, few writers have been as calendar-conscious as Hugo was: virtually all of his poems from before the exile are dated, and many from the later period are too.[1] Prefaces, articles, and letters carry indications of day and place of composition. Further, he made sure that his numerous topical pronouncements—speeches before the Assemblée Législative, comments as member of committees, as well as "correspondence" such as *Le Rhin*—were published and dated. Beyond works whose composition or delivery could be dated, Hugo exploited the suggestions of four-digit numbers by using them as titles of poems, chapters, and even a novel.[2] In *Cromwell* (Hugo 1985, 8:5), he used a date as a verse— "Demain vingt-cinq juin mil six cent cinquante-sept" ["To-morrow—'twill be June the twenty-fifth" (Hugo 1909, 3:59)]—and in his comic preface to *Le Dernier Jour d'un condamne,* "Une Comédie à propos d'une tragédie," he belabored the originality of this innovation (Hugo 1985, 1:422). He also ritualistically observed certain anniversaries—those of his first night with Juliette and of the death of Léopoldine come to mind—and used them to suggest the depth of his love or the extent of his grief.

A great variety of forms becomes apparent upon looking at the dates Hugo appended to his works. The early poems end with dates conventionally indicating day, month, and year; sometimes, only a month and year appear, suggesting protracted composition. With *Les Contemplations*, however, few poems dated so precisely can be found, and for the entirety of Book II[3] dates indicate only month and century; never day or year, even if a place-name clarifies things somewhat further. In *Le Rhin*, by contrast, dates at the beginning of each letter indicate month and place, as though day and year were out of keeping with a work whose purpose is to determine, once and for all, the character of the German people. The very structure of *L'Année terrible* is derived from the calendar, for despite the fact that no poem is dated, each chapter is named after a month of the "year" running from August 1870 to June 1871.

While it might seem at first glance that dates provide only the most elementary of meanings in the simplest of ways— designating the position of a work or event along a time-line—it is evident that there is more to Hugo's use of dates than that, for they fall into patterns, and the system of which they are part is not public chronology but a more private one. In *Les Contemplations*, for instance, the dates following individual poems suggest the evolution Hugo called "les mémoires d'une âme" [the memoirs of a soul]; further, even if Book II's poems are deprived of indications of day and year, seven of Book IV's seventeen poems refer to a very specific date, the fourth of September, 1843, the day his daughter drowned.

These patterns are not fortuitous:[4] the dates attached to the poems comprising *Les Contemplations* have been altered to correspond to the *autrefois/aujourd'hui* polarity that structures the collection, and which assigns to lighter, optimistic poems a place in the first part while the darker, apocalyptic works are relegated to the second. Suzanne Nash has argued that this redating has an allegorical function: "By altering the dates, Hugo could organize his work around a specific biographical event and then fill it with providential significance" (Nash 1976, 15). Just as significantly, poems such as "Demain, dès l'aube, à l'heure où blanchit la campagne" are given dates different from the date of composition: when the poem is assigned the date "3 September 1847," "demain" becomes the third anniversary of Léopoldine's death. Nor was such use of dates reserved to *Les Contemplations*: Hugo attributed fictitious dates to many of *Les Châtiments*' poems, perhaps with a view to creating the illusion that the *coup d'état* was more central to his thinking.[5]

It might even be true that Hugo redated his first night with Juliette Drouet: starting in 1835, he kept a *Livre de l'anniversaire* where until 1882 he celebrated each year the renewal of his love for her, referring invariably to the night of 16–17 February, 1833. In the entry for l841, for example, he describes how in 1833, the two were invited to a Mardi Gras ball but found better things to do: "Oui, tu devais aller au bal, et tu n'y allas pas, et tu m'attendis. . . . Cette nuit-là j'ai passé huit heures près de toi" (Gaudon 1964, 206) [Yes, you were going to go to the ball, and you didn't go, and you waited for me. . . . That night, I spent eight hours close to you]. Juliette kept the invitation to the ball they never attended, but it occurred, it would seem, on the night of February 19, 1833 (Huas 1985, 83). Whatever the date of that first date, February 16 took on immense significance for Hugo: it was used to date several poems to Juliette and even the chapter of *Les Misérables* where Marius and Cosette are married: "Le 16 février 1833."

Between these patterns, falsifications, and slippages, a problem emerges: what do these dates mean? Do they designate a day or a year, or do they do something else? This can be asked with some insistence, for among the works that Hugo dated are a dozen poems whose very subjects are dates: thus, "Écrit en 1846" (which wasn't); "Écrit en 1855" (which was); and "15 février 1843." It would seem that in some cases, dates are redundant with title or subject and hence are not significant; this is true for several poems where the date repeats or echoes the poem's title. In several other cases, however, there is a discrepancy between title and date. "Le sept août mil huit cent vingt neuf" is dated "juin 1839," implying a distance between the poem's writing and its subject: the poet possesses hindsight and his ability to consider an earlier event in retrospect ironizes his presentation. In addition thus to the well-known inconsistencies between the dates of Hugo's manuscripts and those of the published poems, there are also divergences between a poem's date and its subject's date. On the one hand, Hugo's dates are independent of his biography; on the other, they do more than echo his titles, and it would follow that such dates possess a meaning of their own.

Three dimensions of each date can be manipulated: its form, its relation to the text to which it is juxtaposed, and its referent. By form are understood the permutations of a conventional date, which nominally includes a place name, a day, a month, and a year. Such a convention can be altered by deleting one or more of its elements, or, perhaps, by developing an element beyond what convention demands. In Book I of *Les Contemplations*, for example, days are ordinarily left out, resulting in dates such as "Paris, octobre 1842" (I, 1), and "Les Roches, juillet 1830" (I, 5). In Book II, the ellipsis is more comprehensive: both decade and year also disappear, leaving dates like "Fontainebleau, juin 18 . . ." (II, 16), and, when the place name also falls, "Mai 1 S . . ." (II, 4). Each omission of this kind removes information, makes the date less precise, renders it more abstract. Dates such as "Août 18 . . ." (III, 25) indicate a season, but no moment in history or biography; "11 décembre" (V, 19) indicates a recurring day, an anniversary perhaps.

At the other extreme one finds dates that contain superfluous information: further specification of the day, as in "Guernesey, 2 novembre 1855, jour des morts" ("À celle qui est restée en France"); of the place, as in "Jersey, Marine-Terrace, 4 septembre 1852" (IV, 4); of circumstance, as in "11 juillet 1846, en revenant du cimetière" (IV, 11). There is a degree of redundancy in such dates, and thus, a degree of insistence.

The opposition of insufficient vs. superfluous information, of ellipsis vs. redundancy, can be exploited, and Hugo did so: the dates of poems from collections published before the exile varied little from the day/month/year formula; with *Les Contemplations*, however, the formal varieties noted were all used. Significantly, the collection's first part "Autrefois," includes dates characterized as insufficiently informative, while the second part, "Aujourd'hui," employs many references to places and conveys much redundant information. The redundancy communicated in these dates seems to correspond to the theme of grief and suffering so prominent in the second part, as though the poet, traumatized, registered incidental information more readily.[6]

Turning to the relation dates can have with the text they locate, one notes that a wide variety exists: a date can explain, justify, amplify, or echo its text, and these relations can be classified with the two catch-all categories: metaphor and metonymy. A metonymic relation of date to a text would explain or motivate it. The date "3 septembre 1847" at the end of "Demain, dès l'aube" implies what "Demain" is, and suggests why that day is significant. Likewise, "11 juillet 1846, en revenant du cimetière" assigned to "On vit, on parle" implies that the occasion for the poem was the final burial of Claire Pradier, Juliette's daughter. A cause-and-effect relation exists between these dates and their poems, the latter being understood as this motivation is grasped.

Two things should be noted here: first, a knowledge of Hugo's life or even French history is presupposed by such relations, for without some external account the date central to *Les Contemplations*—4 septembre 1843—and which falls between poems 2 and 3 of Book IV, would be conspicuous but unintelligible: it might refer to a catastrophe, a scandal, or a conversion, but only biography explains it. The implication here is troubling, to say the least: for such a date to have meaning, knowledge of the private life of the author is presupposed, and while authors hardly flee fame, few take it so much for granted that their biographies form part of the competence required of contemporary readers. Second, these dates signify by restricting the meaning of the works they explain: "On vit, on parle" could easily refer to Léopoldine's death or to a more general fear of aging; the date selects one referent and brings that one to the attention of the reader.

The other relation possible between text and date is metaphoric: these dates already possess meanings analogous to that of their text and, when juxtaposed to the latter, echo and amplify them. Three poems from *Les Contemplations* are dated "jour des morts" (IV, 5; VI, 22; "À celle . . ."). Each one discusses death, whether it be that of the poet's daughter or Death as an abstraction, and that theme is reinforced by the date attributed to it.

Other examples would be "1er mai" for V, 1, which thematizes the spring's renewal of life and love, or "1er janvier" for poems of resolution and confidence (*Chants du crépuscule*, XXVI; *Toute la lyre*, VI, 3, both of which are dated "1er janvier 1835" and were sent to Juliette Drouet). While metonymic dates explain what could be misunderstood without them, metaphoric dates confirm a meaning already understood.

Here it is important to note that metaphoric dates must signify independently of the text they date, for otherwise it would be impossible to establish an analogy between the two, and if so, it follows that such dates must be public. Dates meaningful only to one person cannot be used to "confirm" the meaning of poems; a convention must exist granting them this independent meaning. Thus a third dimension of text-dates—their referents—comes to the fore, and using Aristotle's venerable distinction, dates become either poetically or historically significant. National holidays, feast days, January 1, May 1, July 14, and November 2 are celebrated by all and possess a conventional signification that goes beyond whatever event they might commemorate. By contrast September 4, July 11, February 16–17 refer to events, known to Hugo, Hugo's family (in some cases) and to Juliette. The first series implies general, poetic meaning, the second, restricted, historical meaning. It should be noted, finally, that the two tropes can be used in conjunction: one date, for example, can explain a second which in turn resembles a third; this compound trope has been called metalepsis.[7]

Two dates are of some consequence for Hugo's work. At least nine poems gravitate around Léopoldine's death-date, September 4, 1843. Then, in addition to the 56 entries of the *Livre de l'anniversaire*, another four poems employ the date Hugo celebrated, February 16–17, 1833, and it functions as chapter title in *Les Misérables*.

Hugo did not learn of Léopoldine's death immediately, but read, far away and after the fact, that five days previously the daughter he had not seen since he had left France two months earlier had died. Returning from their trip to Spain, Hugo and Juliette stepped out of the stagecoach at Soubise on September 9, where he, picking up a newspaper in the Café de l'Europe read that Léopoldine and Charles Vacquerie had died in a boating accident on September 4, 1843, and had been buried three days later. Hugo was back in Paris on the 12th. Absent, vacationing with a woman neither his wife nor mother to his daughter, only learning about Léopoldine's death well after her burial, Hugo could hardly have been more vulnerable to self-reproach.

It took him three years to address the subject in poetry, longer still to pay his respects to his dead daughter. The dates, however, that Hugo assigns to his poems tend to suggest otherwise. His inscription of Léopoldine's death-date in *Les Contemplations* implies that the date's importance exceeds his ability to register it, that something happened to the poet even if he was not aware of it: in a word, it was traumatic. But by attaching that date to seven poems from Book IV, Hugo publicizes it, creates an enigma that can be solved only by appeals to external evidence, and its sheer repetition transforms the date from one with a private referent to one with systematic significance. Thus, Hugo's antedating poem IV, 8 to September 4, 1845, implies that he was able to articulate his reaction somewhat earlier than he in fact did.

Of the poems referring to the 4th of September, the untitled IV, 14 of *Les Contemplations*, "Demain, dès l'aube . . . ," and whose date of course is 3 Septembre 1847, is of special importance. The lack of a title and the first word present a question: just what is so important about tomorrow? The poem's date and its surrounding myth fill in the answer, but the way in which this is done is unusual: the poem, dated one day, is actually about the morrow, and the significance of the day anticipated is revealed only by a third date it commemorates. Three dates are in question: 4 September, 1843, and 3 and 4 September, 1847; Hugo refers to the second in order to turn to the third which is explained only by the first. The structure by which one reads this date is analogous to that of a future anterior construction, that of a compound tense where a temporal signified is specified by two movements: tomorrow the poet will recall a date four years previous.

This metaleptic movement is characteristic of recurrent dates for Hugo: take, for example, the question of his and Juliette's "anniversary": "Was it," writes Jean Gaudon, "as the *Livre de l'anniversaire* would have it, the night of the 16th to the 17th of February, 1833, Shrove Saturday? Or will we accept instead the evidence of the invitation-ticket to the ball at the Gymnase for the 19th of February, to which the poet and his beautiful actress did not go?" (Gaudon 1964, xi; author's translation). Whatever the case, Hugo attributes two dates to the great event, 16–17 February appended to the "anniversaries," and February 19 implicit in his 1841 recollection (Gaudon 1964, 205). If the dated invitation is to be believed, the "anniversaries" are actually anticipations of anniversaries, dates from which a future moment is envisaged, and from which in its turn, the past can be recalled: in a word, the structure of "Demain, dès l'aube. . . ." Alternatively, if the date of 16 February is correct, Hugo, in 1841, was looking back at a Saturday through a Tuesday: at an event that preceded another event already in the past, a pluperfect construction. In both cases, however, Hugo is at a double remove from his ostensible object. While one cannot by any means say that this compound articulation defines Hugo's use of dates, one can say it enjoys a privileged position: references to the Revolution are particularly significant in this regard.

The date of 1789 never appears to conclude a poem but it does appear within the text of *Notre-Dame de Paris*. In Book X, chapter 5 of the novel, Jacques Coppenole, speaking to Louis XI in the Bastille, reassures the king that the Revolution is still to come: "quand le donjon croulera à grand bruit, quand bourgeois et soldats hurleront et s'entretueront, c'est l'heure qui sonnera" (Hugo 1985, 1:822) ["when the keep tumbles down with a great crash, when citizens and soldiers yell and kill each other, that will be the hour striking" (Hugo 1993, 486)]. Here, of course, the poet turns to the past in order to anticipate a future that has already occurred. These examples could be multiplied and their field of application extended, but that is not the point. What is is the textual feature that Hugo himself designated as important. First, Hugo's dates refer not to what is commonly called history, but to a chronology existing within the works: before or after September 4, 1843, on February 16, in December 1852, 1853, or 1854. They exist within a defined context and take on significance there. Secondly, within the systems Hugo proposes, one date often takes the place of another: July 17, 1846, for September 4, 1843; *mardi gras* for *samedi gras*. Behind one date lies another; one sign refers to another sign. In his preface to *Bajazet*, Racine wrote that events required distance, either historical or temporal, in order to acquire a tragic dimension (Rat 1960, 355).[8] In the case of Hugo, it is not so much absolute distance as the number of steps that allows events to acquire significance. Thus, by considering one moment through another, Hugo produces an effect—literary significance—and not a documented record. This is true whether one is speaking about a lived event (such as his first night with

Juliette) or a fiction, whether he seeks to create a myth or a reality-effect. In the opposition of two dates, one is pushed either into a background or a foreground; these two movements can be interpreted as myth and realism respectively. September 3, 1847, memorializes September 4, 1843, while February 16, 1833, serves to make subsequent anniversaries of that *mardi gras* more present. In the case of Léopoldine's death-date such a creation of a new system of signification is easy to detect; conversely, in "Le sept août mil huit cent vingt huit" the poem's date (June 1839) adds urgency and immediacy to its final lament of the passing of monarchies. Whatever the case, the use of a compound articulation—metalepsis—increases significance, and if this is so, there is a concrete model for Hugo's conception of historical realism. But if metalepsis increases significance, it also decreases reference: Hugo's dating does not appeal to history, but tends rather to subsume it, for when he establishes chronologies, it is at the expense of conventional, public chronology, and this aim goes beyond his dating of his night with Juliette.

Here, Hugo's chronology is part of a general attitude of "belatedness" (Bloom 1973, 56), but where most poets seek to abolish a precursor, Hugo takes on a different adversary: history itself. As early as 1818, he announced his intention to be an earlier poet ("To be Chateaubriand or nothing!"); he later asserted that he was his own century's sibling ("Ce siècle avait deux ans . . ." [Hugo 1985, 4:565]); he dedicated *Les Voix intérieures* to his father while drawing attention to the absence of that name on the Arc de triomphe, thus begetting his father's fame. Hugo's dating is thus indicative of a larger project: to replace official history with his own chronology. But this can only be because dates for Hugo set into play the narrative transformations that are called fiction. Far from being moorings that anchor fictions in history, Hugo endows them with the same instability as that afflicting tropes, and they no more designate a day than a trope designates a person, place, thing, or idea. But as a consequence of this instability, they no longer simply point, inviting reading instead.

Limits of Performative Language in Hugo's Theater

One of the great attractions of theater for poets is its ability to show what they can only describe with words. Characters become visible on the stage; the set possesses features that can be registered and reviewed during the entirety of an act; the writer can dictate characters' movements to produce signs at odds with the words they use. Hugo's descriptions of costumes, sets, and gestures (especially those in *Ruy Blas*, pages long) suggest how much he hoped to achieve through visual means. Another attraction of course is the depiction of action; this is the very definition of *mimesis*, which, Aristotle tells us, is the "imitation of an action." And of the actions represented, perhaps the most appealing to a writer would be performative utterances, which, magically almost, combine features of language and features of action, for alone among utterances performative utterances are actions. Further, it is impossible to distinguish the forms of a performative utterance from its theatrical representation: more true-to-life than any sword-fight or kiss, a quoted performative is identical to its source. The inclusion of performatives in theater thus creates the illusion of hearing or looking at actions themselves, the illusion of a transparent theater, one where the proximity to the action represented is unusually close.

Indeed, in Hugo's plays, characters promise, swear, acknowledge, and declare with almost pathological frequency, and one could say that his theater is in fact one of performative language. To be sure, their use of performatives could be considered character traits of Marie Tudor, Jean d'Aragon, Louis XIII, and others: after all, Hugo's kings, queens, dukes, and officers are persons for whom to speak is to act, and the use of performative utterances exemplifies the power these people possess. Conversely, these performatives identify them, for only some people meet the criteria for the felicitous performance of these actions. There are, however, some unusual aspects to their linguistic acts; on the one hand, for people in power, their acts are extraordinarily personal. It is one thing for a king to command: that's his job; it is another for him to swear, for that reflects not his position, but his character. Oaths, however, abound in Hugo's theater. In *Marie Tudor*, for instance, the Queen of England swears both on her crown and on the gospel, and to a mere worker at that, that she will reinstate Jane Talbot and marry her to Fabiano Fabiani.[1] On the other hand, these performatives are abused almost as frequently as they are performed: pardons are rescinded, promises broken, oaths left unfulfilled. If so many acts of language are without effect, they hardly constitute an attribute of authority and must consequently serve a greater purpose than that of character description.

In 1985, Anne Ubersfeld noticed this use of performatives in Hugo's theater. Leaving aside those acts of language that form part of a character's portrayal—orders, commands, etc.—she found that Hugo's performatives could be categorized in four groups: prophecies, pleas, pacts, and revelations. More significantly, of these only two have any effect: predictions and supplications are to no avail, while contracts and revelations have consequences (Ubersfeld 1985). For example, Marion's plea to Richelieu in the last lines of *Marion de Lorme* is rejected out of hand, just as the usurer's blessing of Fabiano at the beginning of *Marie Tudor* elicits only anger. Conversely, Hernani's pact with Don Gomez is respected to his death, just as Ruy Blas's revelation of his identity has catastrophic effect. Public, contractual performatives work; personal ones do not. Ubersfeld concludes from this that the emotions of Hugo's characters are radically separated from the outer world, and their identity is constituted by this very separation.

There is much to recommend in this argument, and not the least of its virtues is its interest in abuses of acts of language. That acts having to do with emotion should be particularly impotent is also significant. But do their effects actually define performatives? While the breaking of a promise or the refusal of a plea certainly defines character, it has a much smaller bearing on Hugo's conception of the power of language.

It might be useful at this point to return to some of the seminal writings on performative language, notably J. L. Austin's *How to Do Things with Words* and E. Benveniste's "Analytical Philosophy and Language." Austin describes performatives as utterances that do not describe a state of affairs so much as they actually produce it. For this to occur, these utterances must be made under certain conditions, the absence of any one of which would make the performative "infelicitous," i.e., it would not do what it claims to do. Particular procedures are involved; the procedures must be followed exactly and completely; certain persons must be in attendance, and only some are qualified to use this language effectually. Many factors might make a performative "infelicitous"; however, all infelicities can be categorized in two groups: "misfires" and "abuses":

we shall call in general those infelicities . . . which are such that the act for the performing of which, and in the performing of which, the verbal formula in question is designed, is not achieved, by the name MISFIRES: and on the other hand we may christen those infelicities where the act *is* achieved ABUSES (Austin 1960, 16)

Benveniste (who in many instances faults Austin's analysis) agrees that one should set aside consideration of unrealized performatives, that is, abuses: "It is not this empirical result that counts. A performative utterance is not performative in that it can modify the situation of an individual but in that it is *by itself* an act," (Benveniste 1971, 237). It is plain that Ubersfeld's argument deals mainly with "abuses," and indeed, in Hugo's works, an enormous abuse of performative language does take place. Many of his characters use performatives only in order to "abuse" them. In *Lucrèce Borgia*, for example, Don Alphonse even qualifies oaths as "bad reasons" actually to do something: "Ne jurez pas. Les serments, cela est pour le peuple. Ne me donnez pas de ces mauvaises raisons-là" (Hugo 1985, 8:1019) ["Do not swear. Oaths are good for the common people. Do not give me any of those wretched reasons" (Hugo 1909, 1:410)]. And again, in *Angelo Tyran de Padoue*, Angelo scolds Tisbe for having kept her word and allowed a man to escape: "On promet mais on fait arrêter" (Hugo 1985, 8:1238) ["One promises, but one causes the person to be arrested" (Hugo 1909, 2:51)]. The implication is plain: these characters are free to make promises, but are free also to break any word they might give.

Beyond these all-too-obvious abuses, however, there is an extraordinary concentration of "misfires" among Hugo's characters' performative utterances, and these misfires are of great significance. Far more perplexing than whether the speaker is a man (or woman) of his (her) word are cases where the speaker makes a promise or concludes a bargain under circumstances that void the performance itself of meaning. For example, in the first act of *Cromwell* the Protector's son, Richard, unexpectedly arriving in the midst of a group of conspirators, raises his cup to his lips to drink to the health of Charles II: "Je bois à la santé du Roi Charles" (Hugo 1985, 8:55) ["I drink the health of Charles, our lawful King!" (Hugo 1909, 3:107)]. Beyond the mistrust that his presence arouses among the conspirators, their consequent failure to respond to his toast, and his later disavowal of his gesture, the action itself is incomplete: a crier arrives, Richard never drinks, and the toast, as such, never occurs. Thus, when later, Cromwell learns of the "toast," he blames Richard for something that never happened, even if his son's intentions and motivations were indeed less than loyal to his father.

Such misfires are frequent in Hugo's theater, and in many cases, they profoundly change the meaning of the action. In *Marion de Lorme*, for example, in addition to a multitude of oaths, there are a decree, a royal pardon, the subsequent revocation of that pardon, a supplication, and the denial of that supplication. The play revolves then around the possibility of revising performative utterances: whether, once an action has been outlawed, it can be pardoned; whether, once a king has pardoned an offence, the offence can be reinstated, and so forth. What is at stake concretely is the life of Didier, a young man arrested for dueling after the posting of a royal edict outlawing duels. Little matters that his opponent Saverny survives, or that the crime he is at first charged with is murder: for the sake of the royal decree, he must die. His mistress, Marion, intervenes to obtain a pardon from Louis XIII, but this is in turn rescinded by Richelieu, who in the last scene refuses her desperate plea for a second pardon. It would be easy to become outraged, as it seems Martignac, Minister of the Interior was, at this series of royal uses and abuses of power: decree, pardon, revocation, reinstatement.

On closer inspection, however, it is apparent that there is a series of misfires as much as there is any series of abuses. The decree indeed outlaws any duel:

> Ordonnons et mandons, voulons que désormais
> Les duellistes, félons qui de sujets nous privent,
> Qu'il ne survive un seul ou que tous deux survivent,
> Soient, pour être amendés, traduits en haute cour,
> Et, nobles ou vilains, soient pendus haut et court
> (Hugo 1985, 8:715)

> [Command and order that from this time forth
> All duellists, those fellows who despoil
> Us of our subjects, whether one or alone
> Or both survive, shall straightaway be produced
> Before us, at our court, for punishment;
> And be they base-born, or of noble blood,
> Shall then be hanged
> (Hugo 1909, 1:163)]

However, a coda appears, containing a second performative:

> Et, pour rendre à tout point l'édit plus efficace,
> Renonçons pour ce crime à tout droit de grâce.
> (Hugo 1985, 8:715)

> [And that this edict may
> Be made more efficacious in all ways,
> We do renounce our own prerogative
> Of pardon for this crime
> (Hugo 1909, 1:163)]

On the one hand, the king exercises his power; on the other, he renounces any further use of that power on this matter. Nevertheless, when Marion intercedes for her lover, pointing out that no one died in the duel, the king is moved, and finally reverses himself: "je vous fais grâce à tous!" (Hugo 1985, 8:791) ["For you I pardon all!" (Hugo 1909 1:231)]. The problem is that both word and action have been anticipated by the earlier renunciation: what then is the status of this "pardon"? In a word, the question would appear not to be whether the king is abusing his power by reversing himself, but whether he actually has the power to reverse himself.

But it gets worse. Two possibilities arise when one compares his acts: if his first declaration is felicitous (i.e., if he is qualified to renounce his right to review cases), then the king's subsequent reversal must be a misfire: he is no longer a person who can pardon. If, however, he does in fact pardon, then he must be abusing the first performative. Either the king is abusing his power or he has no power to abuse, and it is impossible to tell which is the case.

Or take *Hernani*. As Ubersfeld has pointed out, the contract Hernani makes with Don Gomez, his rival, is central: in order to repair an offense to Don Gomez, Hernani accepts the latter's help when the king unexpectedly arrives, and grants Don Gomez the right to his life. The word he uses is significant: "Ma tête est à toi" (Hugo 1985, 8:605) ["My life to thee is forfeit" (Hugo 1909, 1:66)]. But later, in Aix-la-Chapelle, surrendering to the king (now the emperor), Hernani identifies himself as Jean d'Aragon, and as such demands the privilege of his rank: "Oui, nos têtes, ô roi, / Ont le droit de tomber couvertes devant toi!" (Hugo 1985,

8:640) ["Our heads, oh! King, Have right to fall before thee covered thus" (Hugo 1909, 1:101)].[2] In other words, he puts forward his already promised head to the emperor, who in turn answers with clemency, allowing the conflict to recede and Don Gomez to make his last-minute claim on Hernani's life. The structure is identical to that found in *Marion de Lorme*: if in fact Hernani has promised his head to Don Gomez, the offer he makes of it to the emperor is an empty gesture; but if in fact this offer is real, Hernani can only be reneging on his pact with Don Gomez. Whatever the case (and again there is no way to tell), Hernani's authority to dispose of his life is in question: offering his head to all takers, he offers it in fact to no one.

A final example, from *Marie Tudor*. The queen has given Fabiano Fabiani, her favorite and lover, a *blanc-seing* (signature in blank) allowing pardon for any offense to its bearer. Later, learning that her lover has deceived her, she promises to oblige Fabiano to marry the woman he has seduced. Thus Fabiano will be obliged to marry (itself a performative) in order to repair an offense for which he has already been pardoned. The reversals subsequently become even more numerous: the queen obtains a death-sentence for Fabiano, thus retracting her promise to force his marriage, and then goes on to delay that sentence.[3] As in *Marion de Lorme* and *Hernani*, if her *blanc-seing* is effective, her oath to Gilbert is empty; if her oath to Gilbert is meaningful, it can only be that she has gone back on her written promise to Fabiano.

Powerlessness or abuse of power: the mighty in Hugo's theater tend ritually to put aside their authority and then to exercise that alienated power.[4] These superimposed promises, oaths and declarations might seem trivial in a theater where performative language is so prevalent, but even at the surface, the issues involved are significant. In *Marion de Lorme*, in *Marie Tudor*, in *Lucrèce Borgia* they lead inevitably to a discussion of the nature of power: can it be alienated? If alienated, can it be exercised? If exercised, does this exercise imply impotence or power so great that it cannot be alienated? In a word, this double articulation of performative utterances opens onto the Sublime. In *Hernani* and *Ruy Blas* the question is rather that of the speaker's identity: does a change of rank, name, or place imply that contracts are void? Do such contracts define one's identity (Ubersfeld's argument), or does a change in one's identity abrogate these contracts? Hugo offers no responses to these questions, and they thus remain, troubling, as they have from their writing, notions of identity and authority.

What is certain, however, is that these performatives are intimately related to writing: in *Marion de Lorme*, decree, pardon, and revocation are written; in *Marie Tudor*, the *blanc-seing* is written; Ruy Blas writes his acknowledgment of his identity and his declaration of fealty to his master. Even Hernani's spoken promise is likened to writing: "Voici le doigt fatal qui luit sur la muraille!" (Hugo 1985, 8:658) ["Behold the fatal finger that doth shine/Upon the wall!" (Hugo 1909, 1:117)]. What is important of course is what writing does to performative utterances: Benveniste points out that they must be unique, referring to a specific context, performed by a specific individual at a specified time:

> The performative utterance, being an act, has the property of being *unique*. It cannot be produced except in special circumstances, at one and only one time, at a definite date and place. . . . This is why it is often accompanied by indications of date, of place, of names of people, witnesses, etc. (Benveniste 1971, 236)

Identifiable times, places, and persons are required by performative utterances; alternatively, one could say that performatives at the very least establish the identity of time, place, and person. But, because they are durable and moveable, the here and now of written documents are uncertain, and thus the context, essential to the felicity of any performative, becomes problematic, whence misfires and abuses.[5]

Who, for example, speaks in the decree outlawing duels in *Marion de Lorme*? The first person plural, the royal "we," ubiquitous and omnipotent, might indicate Louis XIII. It might also mean Louis XIII and Richelieu, who, as it happens, also signs. Now if the "we" refers to the king, the edict's second performative "renonçons à notre droit de grâce" precludes any later pardon, and makes of the pardon Louis grants Marion a misfire. However, if it refers to both Louis and Richelieu, it does not preclude the king's pardon, and makes of this a simple abuse.

Or take for example Hernani's promise of his head to Don Gomez, which takes place before portraits of ancestors, whom Don Gomez designates as witnesses: "(Aux portraits) 'Vous tous, soyez témoins'" (Hugo 1985, 8:618) ["*To the portraits* And all of you are witnesses" (Hugo 1909, 1:79)]. At the very least, one wonders whether a portrait can witness an act. The dramatic conceit is that the pact takes place before memory, before one's conscience, before God, but if so, Don Gomez fudges the act's here and now, by invoking the portraits. He assigns to it the durable, transferable status of its witness. More importantly, he makes this pact with a "jeune homme" whom he knows only as "Hernani." Thus, when later, Hernani acknowledges he is Jean d'Aragon, Don Carlos abandons his pursuit: for the emperor, a change in title—his own or his rival's—abrogates the edict of banishment. Now if this is so, what effect does Hernani's acknowledgment of his father's name have on his own promise? Is Jean d'Aragon bound by Hernani's promise? Jean's offer of his head implies that he is not; his later acceptance of obligation towards Don Gomez implies he is. But if he feels bound, there is still no reason to die, for Hernani promised by "la tête de [son] père" (Hugo 1985, 8:618) (who, incidentally, died beheaded), a man whom Hernani—a refugee requesting anonymity—is unable to name. Hernani's change in name significantly alters the stakes and prevents any immediate assessment of his death's meaning. The agent in Hugo's performatives ceases, on occasion, to be identifiable.

A final example, from *Marie Tudor*. The queen, having promised pardon to the bearer of the *blanc-seing*, condemns Fabiano to death, but he subsequently asks her to redeem her written promise. The two promises of course conflict: "Un serment détruit l'autre" (Hugo 1985, 8:1150) ["One oath doth offset the other" (Hugo 1909, 3:495)], she says. What results is a repeated delay in Fabiano's execution:

> *Simon Renard*: Votre majesté avait pourtant arrêté hier que l'exécution aurait lieu aujourd'hui.
> *La Reine*: Comme j'avais arrêté avant-hier que l'exécution aurait lieu hier; comme j'avais arrêté dimanche que l'exécution aurait lieu lundi. (Hugo 1985, 8:1149)

> [*Renard*: But your Majesty decreed yesterday that the execution should take place to-day.
> *The Queen*: As I had decreed the day before yesterday that the execution should take place yesterday. As I had decreed Sunday that the execution should take place Monday. (Hugo 1909, 3:493)]

This repeated delay is emblematic of Hugo's double performatives: the queen's promises cancel and fulfill each other at the same time, solving the problem at hand, but to do so, requiring an unending exercise of power, whence the moment of the performative act becomes blurred.

Hugo's infelicitous performatives are virtually the contrary of ordinary performatives. If the role of performatives is ordinarily to produce a state that prior to the act did not exist—marriage, banishment, obligation—one must accept that they do produce a kind of stability. Conversely, they fail also to establish the identity of their place, time, and participants. In theory, performative utterances are signs of exemplary simplicity and clarity. After a performative one can refer back to it as a point of departure, much as one refers to definitions in a geometric proof. Not simply are circumstances, participants, and actions well defined, but inscription itself is proof of the actions' occurrence. In Hugo's theater this is not the case: oaths, declarations, and contracts do not lead to certainty, and their profusion, if anything, produces uncertainty. At the very least, the authority of those who, like Hernani or Marie Tudor, abuse them or execute misfires, is diminished, as is that of performative utterances generally.

Far from representing actions whose representation is particularly convincing, the profusion of performative utterances characterizing Hugo's theater produces a literary effect. At the level of the characters, there is indecision; at that of plot, action stops; at the level of language, play arises and forces inappropriate questions on the spectator: how many times can a head be offered before it loses its appeal? Which has a longer shelf life: a renunciation or the execution of privilege? Which takes precedence: a written pardon or a verbal arrest? The language of performatives, ostensibly a language of simple, incontrovertible effect, has become literary.

It is here that the spectacular events of Hugo's last acts take on their meaning. On occasion, these effects depend on props; on others, the action produces the greatest impact. But always, Hugo seeks to create an effect of power. In *Marion de Lorme*, an enormous sedan-chair carried by twenty-four men literally bursts through a wall to attend Didier's execution; in *Hernani*, the conspirators surrounding Don Carlos in the tomb of Charlemagne are in turn surrounded by a still larger group of soldiers; in *Marie Tudor*, at the moment of the queen's greatest duplicity, she opens a curtain onto the city of London, a God-like eye that spies her every move; in *Lucrèce Borgia,* the doors of the dining room where the guests are feasting suddenly open onto the funeral chapel where they all will die. These largely visual effects create sensations that cannot be denied, sensations that are also fairly commonplace.

However, conjoined with Hugo's self-defeating performatives, these *coups de théâtre* take on new meaning. In *Marion de Lorme* one understands immediately, when Richelieu's sedan-chair bursts through the wall, who, in this play about the limits of authority, has the authority to tear down walls, to refuse pardon, to speak from behind a veil. When the queen opens the curtain onto the city, and then, almost immediately, closes it saying "cette affreuse ville nous voit et nous entend" (Hugo 1985, 8:1175) ["that horrible city sees us and hears us" (Hugo 1909, 3:518)], one understands, in this play about power, that true power lies beyond the window. Or *Lucrèce Borgia*: unable to believe anything the characters might say, one can nevertheless believe in destiny, even if it takes a form as banal as death.

Having eroded the reliability of language through a systematic denial of its performative felicity, Hugo postulates a context that replaces language's powers. Language having failed him, he resorts to another system of signifiers; he goes beyond language to another, ostensibly more powerful form of communication. Here, and not in the pathos of emotional impotence, lies the meaning of Hugo's performative language. The sheer number of performatives makes them impossible to overlook, but their infelicity leaves them perplexing. When that infelicity is analyzed, Hugo's promises, declarations, oaths, etc. are seen to fail, not because of some duplicity or some abuse on the part of the characters, but because these acts occur under circumstances where it is impossible to determine their felicity, and these circumstances, of course, are contrived to that end. The linguistic confusion makes the visuals seem compelling, and the effect they achieve is in direct proportion to the infelicity of the character's promises, declarations, oaths, and decrees. He thus promises these spectacular *coups de théâtre* as an antidote to the mess that language can produce; needless to say, this promise goes unfulfilled. Such efforts to produce certainty through other means indicate language's inadequacy for simple signification and subordinate it to the rule of reading.

PEOPLE, PLACES, AND APOSTROPHE IN "TRISTESSE D'OLYMPIO"

Ever since its publication, Hugo's "Tristesse d'Olympio" has attracted attention as strongly as would a map to the fountain of youth: Pierre Albouy's *Pléiade* edition points to works by Maurice Levaillant and Paul Souchon, who designate other biographers. Ultimately, however, all indicate Hugo himself, who for his part initiated this trajectory with the dedication he appended to a manuscript given to Juliette Drouet: "—pour ma juliette (sic)— écrit après avoir visité la vallée de Bièvre en octobre 1837" [—for my juliette—written after visiting the valley of Bièvre in October, 1837] (all translations of "Tristesse d'Olympio are by the author).[1] The poem was supposedly prompted by a visit, which in turn recalled the memory of two summers spent in the vallée de Bièvre in the outskirts of Paris in 1834 and 1835, Hugo with his family at the Château des Roches, the invited guests of Louis-François Bertin, Juliette a lodger in a cottage in les Metz, 4 kilometers away.[2]

The poem is thus frequently taken as autobiographical, recollecting in some way the experiences of the poet himself. Since the poem speaks of "ils" and "elle," it is also taken as biographical, or, at least, an autobiography that conveys information about others. "Olympio" is thus a reference to Hugo, and so much so that it stands, in André Maurois's famous biography, as an alternate name for him (Maurois 1954). Conversely, "elle" must refer to Juliette: who else could have elicited such expressions of love (and loss)? But can lived experiences, even when they are verifiable, control the reading of a text?

If the poem was meant to evoke the summers of 1834 and 1835, standing in for them when Juliette asked (as she frequently did) to return to Bièvre, it is easy to see how it might have failed. Words are a poor substitute for actions, even when they are "given." Finally, perhaps Hugo's happiest experiences of those summers were not with Juliette at all (despite his claims to the contrary), but with his wife and family: years later, the words "douce fée" [gentle fairy], "son pied charmant" [her charming foot], and "folâtre" [wild], used here to describe the other person included in the pronoun "nous" served to describe Léopoldine Hugo.

It would be a fool's errand to follow this line of inquiry much further: the certainty of duplicity between Victor, Adèle, and Juliette allows a single poem to be "given" to several different people, each one receiving the assurance that it "really" was about him or her. The most outlandish of these hypotheses would not involve Juliette at all: why couldn't the poem be Victor's gift to "Olympio" or vice-versa, the one assuring the other of the immortality of memory and the possibility of inscribing such memories on the human soul? If Olympio is the name of the figure designated by "il" throughout the poem, Hugo's gift of the poem to him would be a man's attempt to calm the apprehensions of his immortal soul; if, conversely, Olympio were to give it to Hugo, the poem could be read as the straightforward consolation of a confused and doubting man by the thought of his future greatness.

Similarly, the poem's reference to les Roches or Bièvre cannot be proved, no matter how many other poems by Hugo are dated from the two places. Indeed, Hugo does include an unusual number of spatial deictics, as if to point to a particular place: three "ici" and two "là" beg interpretation, but more significant are the eleven instances of the relative pronoun "où" and the many uses of definite articles with nouns of place: all these markers demand an answer; all insistently ask "Where?" and critics have dutifully responded "Bièvre." Juliette seems to have glimpsed the possibility that memories of Bièvre, if indeed it makes sense to speak of places and lived experiences, would entail at least as many associations with Adèle and Victor's family as they do with her: when Hugo offered her the manuscript, she discounted the value of the poem supposedly commemorating their trysts, as if to say, "No, that's not the place."

What is less doubtful is that the poem is about loss. From indications that nature now "belongs" to others (and is thus unfaithful), to the perfect tense of certain verbs ("avons-nous eu notre heure?" [have we had our hour?]), to indications in the pathetic mode that what once was has now changed, the poem unequivocally states that a happy time is gone. So much is this the case that, when asked to perform the exercise of comparing the poem to Lamartine's "Le Lac," students often declare with every justification that just like Lamartine's poet, Olympio[3] has lost his lover to death: the use of the pluperfect to describe the happy time, the designation of that time as "[les] jours qui ne sont plus" [days which no longer are], intimations of the poet's coming death ("Lorsque nous dormirons tous deux dans l'attitude/Que donne aux morts pensifs la forme du tombeau" [When we both will lie in the pose/Given to the pensive dead by the tomb]), and finally, the contemplation of the unchanging sky in the fluctuating surface of the lake ("Admirant tour à tour le ciel, face divine,/ Le lac, divin miroir!" [Admiring now the divine face of the sky/ Now the divine mirror of the lake!]) all suggest that death has separated the poet from his beloved.

But then the poet voices imprecations against nature, insults one would not find in Lamartine: chief among them is of course the language of jealousy used in the description of nature and the corresponding implication that Nature is an unfaithful lover, who has expressed her sexual pleasure to a third party: "Est-ce que vous ferez pour d'autres vos murmures?/Est-ce que vous direz à d'autres vos chansons?" [Will you make your murmurs for others/Will you make your songs for others?]. Now if Nature is a metonymy for Olympio's lover, the poem is just as plausibly about jealousy as it is about death, jealousy about Juliette's past, perhaps,[4] or maybe about Adèle's visits to see Sainte-Beuve. In either case, the poem is about lost love, more akin to Musset's "Souvenir" than to "Le Lac."

Such loss is figured with far more than metaphors of jealousy and death. From expressions like "il revit ces lieux où par tant de blessures/Son cœur s'est répandu!" [he saw the places where his heart had bled by so many wounds!], "Il voyait à chaque arbre, hélas! se dresser l'ombre/Des jours qui ne sont plus!" [He saw beneath each tree, alas! rise up the shadow/Of days that no longer are!], and "Nos chambres de feuillage en halliers sont changées" [Our leafy bedrooms have turned into hedges!], one would think that the poet is suffering from a loss of desire, a consciousness of mortality, or a fear of inconstancy respectively, symptoms now associated with a major depressive episode and a prescription for Prozac.[5] Even here, images figure loss: "j'ai voulu . . . savoir si l'urne encor conservait la liqueur" [I wanted . . . to know whether there was any more ambrosia in the urn], or "L'arbre où fut notre chiffre est mort ou renversé" [The tree where our initials were carved had died or been uprooted], and "Un mur clôt la fontaine où . . . Elle prenait de l'eau dans sa main" [A wall blocks off the fountain where . . . She used to take water in her hand]. Stranger, perhaps, are other images associated with the poet's melancholy, but whose figures are not of loss: "On a pavé la route âpre et mal aplanie" [The rough and ungraded road has been paved over], "La forêt ici manque et là s'est agrandie" [The forest has been cut here, and there it has grown up]. It would be of course possible to reinscribe such images as images of loss: the surface of the path on which they walk has lost its capacity to show their footprints; the growth of the forest means that the forest such as it once was no longer exists. For the moment however it suffices to say that the sense of loss expands as one reads and re-reads the poem, much as the depth of contemplation increases without limit in "La Pente de la rêverie":[6] jealousy becomes death becomes fear of time and fear of any loss at all. Correspondingly, as Juliette knew so well, the "subject" of the poem becomes less and less possible to define, and less and less can the poem be said either to be "hers" or to be about Bièvre.

Each of these figural currents can be designated the subject of the poem, and as trope for the sense of loss pervading it, each is quite adequate. Each also however fails to explain the poem in its totality, for it leaves out elements better explained by other figures, and thus each explanation also leaves one with a sense of inadequacy, of loss, a loss which of course only heightens the pleasure of reading "Tristesse d'Olympio."

Although this feature will no doubt support yet another inadequate totalizing reading of the poem, like *Les Contemplations* two decades later, the poem articulates a "then" and a "now"; that "now" is in an immediate past, in which Olympio returns to a privileged site, where he once loved a woman, and where he evokes a "then," before the "now" of writing, a sort of pluperfect when the two moments are compared. "Then" is characterized by moments of pleasure, sensuality, togetherness, generosity, and happiness; "now" by meditation, austerity, solitude, refusal, and sadness. An ample supply of citations in this poem supports each of these characterizations and many others besides. More to the point, though, "now" is characterized by an invocation attributed to Olympio and in which he expresses his lament; by contrast, language is absent (to the extent that language can be absent from a poem) from "then": "then" is a place, a house, a tree, a flower, a stream. "Now" is a twenty-nine stanza lament of how things have changed. If there was language then, it was nature that "spoke," not man: "Est-ce que vous direz à d'autres vos chansons?" [Will you make your songs for others?], "Tous nos échos s'ouvraient si bien à votre voix!/Et nous prêtions si bien, sans troubler vos mystères,/L'oreille aux mots profonds que vous dites parfois" [All of our echoes were repeated so well by your voice!/And we so easily, without troubling your mysteries/Lent our ear to the deep words you sometimes speak]. And what attempts Olympio and his lover made "then" to communicate with language were ineffectual: "L'arbre où fut notre chiffre est mort ou renversé" [The tree where our initials were carved has died or been uprooted]. Thus the love that characterized Olympio's happiness was doubled by harmony with nature, an immediacy that allowed man and nature to be one, to share the same thoughts, to echo each other, without having to pass through language. Now if Olympio can or must express himself through language, it is at the price of loss: he distrusts nature and the love he once felt for his lover in no way guarantees present communication: "C'est vainement que nous nous aimâmes" [It was in vain that we loved each other]. Olympio's invocation could simply be the expression of a preexistent sadness, or, perhaps, his sadness could be the result of his articulation, but whether language caused this loss or is one of its effects is not at issue: what is at issue is that language is implicated in this generalized unhappiness.

Most insistent among these linguistic aspects is the tense structure of the verbs, a structure that must be qualified as essentially linguistic:[7] while no tense is reserved to either "now" or "then," verbs are often used in opposition to others, and in those oppositions, the more remote of the two verbs indicates "then": "voulut" vs. "avait vidé" and "avaient tout oublié"; "j'ai voulu voir" and "savoir" vs. "ce qu'avait fait [cette vallée] de [tout ce que] j'avais laissé; "un mur clôt la fontaine" vs. "où elle buvait." "Then" is distinguished from "now" because of these distinctions, and "now" is unhappy because what has cut it off from "then" is language: what language tells can never be as full, as happy, as close as the remembered experience.

Here, Hugo begins to resemble a stereotypical image of Rousseau, someone who distrusts language, especially written language, and prefers to it and its implications metaphors of immediacy: presence, warmth, intimacy, spontaneity, and so forth. And the poem justifies a reading that searches for this theme: "then" is more loving, more spontaneous, more sensual than "now," which can, in the last analysis, be reduced to a long lamentation, the poem itself. This reading is no more successful at explaining the poem in its totality than the others considered: the lovers' intimacy with nature is indicated by their ability to understand the trees' "voices," but one of the activities of the happy time was the inscription of the lovers' "chiffre" on a tree, which of course has since been uprooted. Language might not have been the lovers' most important attribute, but it was definitely present; now, it is all the poet has.

Or perhaps, language is all that Olympio is. The words "Victor Hugo," of course, refer to a man who lived, wrote, loved, and died; "Olympio" is by all accounts a different matter. Even more famous, perhaps, than the "decomposition of the self" that was mentioned earlier, is the 1840–45 fragment of a preface for an as-yet-to-be-completed collection of poems: "Les Contemplations d'Olympio. Préface. . . . il vient une certaine heure dans la vie où, l'horizon s'agrandissant sans cesse, un homme se sent trop petit pour continuer de parler en son nom. Il se crée alors, poète, philosophe ou penseur, une figure dans laquelle il se personnifie et s'incarne. C'est encore l'homme, mais ce n'est plus le moi" (Albouy 1964, 2:1524) [The Contemplations of Olympio. Preface. . . . there comes a certain moment in life when, as the horizon widens endlessly, a man feels too small to continue speaking in his own name. He then creates a poet, a philosopher, a thinker with his self, a figure in which he personifies himself and incarnates himself. He is still a man, but he is no longer a self (author's translation)]. Olympio is thus "just" a figure of speech, a figure of personification. But if Olympio is the personification of Victor Hugo, Hugo must not be a person, for he can be personified, incarnated, as though he were something less than flesh and blood. Olympio is a creature of language. Reading the poem closely, one can identify without fail "il" as "language" and "elle" and "nature" as "the world," where what is said about love or loss always allegorizes a feature of language. The repetition of "tout" throughout the first part of the poem ("Il voulut tout revoir" [He wanted to see every thing once more], "Il voyait à chaque arbre" [He saw beneath each tree], "Tout le jour il erra" [All day long he wandered], "Il erra tout le jour" [He wandered all day]) underscores the poet's will to capture experience with language, and thus the predicament the poem allegorizes is the failure of language to account for the world. Language cannot account for time (tense structures of language are inadequate); it cannot hypostasize the "manifold of sensations"; it cannot capture emotion. Instead, it offers homologues for real experiences: tenses for time; figures for emotion; direct objects for interaction; copulas for copulation; sheets of paper for leaves. Hugo's reaction to this failure is to resort to personification: Olympio is born here, as a personification of the poet (who must, by implication, not be a person).

If "Olympio" is language's admission that it cannot express the poet's feelings, then the many apostrophes of "Tristesse d'Olympio" are an effort by the poem to reinstate the poet in dialogue. When Olympio cries "Oh! Dites-moi, ravins, frais ruisseaux, treilles mûres,/Rameaux chargés de nids, grottes, forêts, buissons" [Oh !, Tell me, ravines, cool streams, ripe trellises /Branches loaded with nests, grottoes, forests, bushes] and "Eh bien! Oubliez-nous, maison, jardin, ombrages!/Herbe, use notre seuil! Ronce, cache nos pas!/ Chantez, oiseaux! Ruisseaux, coulez, croissez, feuillages!" [Well! Forget us, house, garden, shade!/Grass, overgrow our threshold! Weeds, hide our footprints!/Sing, birds! Flow, streams! Grow, leaves!], he effectively populates the poem with listeners, thus confirming his own status as poet. This argument has been made with respect to the figure of apostrophe in general by Jonathan Culler, in great detail and at considerable length, and certainly, his conclusions are entirely apposite in this case:[8] the figures of loss and the figures of apostrophe imply each other. One aspect of apostrophe however dominates here and is explained better by Pierre Fontanier than by Culler: according to Fontanier, apostrophe consists not, as Culler argues, in the invocation of an inanimate as though it were animate; it consists instead in turning one's attention from one object to another as one performs that invocation.[9] For Fontanier, the shift from one object to another indicates an incapacity to focus, due necessarily to distraction, and apostrophe is thus a figure of madness.[10] In Hugo's poem, the accumulations of apostrophe can certainly indicate emotion or even madness, but in either case, there is a persistent tendency to leave the present and shift attention elsewhere. In this sense, "Tristesse d'Olympio" prefigures such poems as "Demain, dès l'aube . . .," where the poet's feeling is translated by his inability to perceive the outside world, and his irreversible withdrawal into an inner rêverie.

The presence of prosopopeia in Hugo's works, and indeed its centrality to that corpus, has been noted by Paul de Man.[11] This figure, and its central place in Hugo's work, offers a solution to the problem that has been slowly appearing over the horizon: why should Hugo's efforts at simple statement produce such convoluted texts? If Leroux's argument that Hugo used symbol to produce a more direct and immediate language is to be accepted, de Man's comment about prosopopeia explains how such an abbreviated discourse might work. Prosopopeia, like apostrophe, is a form of address, one where the presence of absent persons is invoked: the face, the figure of the person named becomes present and lends authority (or some other inflection) to the arguments put forward. For de Man, Hugo's works are predicated on the ubiquitous presence of these faces or masks: Hugo's world is hallucinatory. But such a figure explains how the symbols Leroux noted could be understood in the absence of their code: no learning is needed to recognize a face; two spots of equal size strike us as eyes. In those instances where all that is necessary in order to understand an image is the ability to recognize a person, the work is done for us. But it takes a person to see a person, and as a result, Hugo's apostrophes and prosopopeia are often accompanied by references to the poet himself.

Certainly accumulations, amplifications, and expansions are typical of Hugo, but just as typical is his will to interrupt, to start over, like waves that forever allow one to press new footprints in the sand. Certainly, such a gesture is required for the dialogues, personae, and lyrics that arise from Culler's concept of apostrophe. But revealingly, this happens in the only other vocative of the poem, "O Douleur . . .," which like the apostrophes uses "O" and like them uses the exclamatory mode, but which does not actually speak to any one, or render an absent person present. One could compare this figure to asyndeton or anacoluthon, used at the level of a fiction: an interruption, a failure to follow through on an earlier theme or plot, along with a concomitant introduction of a new train of thought.

Such a trope allows Hugo to become Olympio, someone who does not share the same obligations or responsibilities as Hugo; it allows an apparently referential poem to indulge in referential agrammaticalities; it allows Hugo to imagine a pathetic situation that is not his. But it also allows other dimensions: Hugo turns away from the second Empire to write *Les Misérables*, he turns away from the natural world in "Demain, dès l'aube . . .," he turns away from mortality in "À celle qui est restée en France." This capacity to forget context is essential to his poetics. It allows him to imagine a world where the absence of a loved one will turn him into another man, one who will bemoan his lover's infidelity, his president's perfidy, or his daughter's death.

It should be plain that "Tristesse d'Olympio" is an ancestor of the cycle of poems concerning Léopoldine Hugo: in other words, Hugo's poems concerning his daughter's death, however pathetic they may be, were not a reaction to her death, but the redirection of a current already extant in his poetry to accommodate a historical and biographical event. In 1837, it was Olympio who bemoaned the loss of a loved one; a decade and a half later, Hugo could do so in his own name. "Tristesse" shares with the other poems the apostrophic structure, a theme of loss, an argument of recuperation, and an imagery of darkness that makes it quite comparable. Léopoldine's death is thus inscribed in an ongoing project. The fact that Hugo could write a poem on the occasion of the death of Juliette's daughter suggests that an elegiac voice, independent of deaths and losses, exists in Hugo's poetry, ready to be used in a variety of circumstances. While the death of Léopoldine furnishes by far the greatest occasion for the expression of this voice—the fourth book of *Les Contemplations*—poems like "Tristesse d'Olympio" announce it, and others like "Claire" prolong it.

The autonomy of this voice brings up another problem. That Hugo should have written an apostrophic, elegiac poem is not surprising, even if the form is a somewhat antiquated one to find in the strongest French romantic poet. But that he should have thought to "give" the poem to Juliette Drouet, as if the intended of the poem and his lover were the same, is curious: it is as if what Hugo has to say cannot be said and can only be approximated with this form. Here, the fragmentary nature of any text that uses apostrophe (as defined by Fontanier) becomes apparent: the changes of direction effectively endow the text with new context with each apostrophe. When, as Hugo does, the text invokes Nature, streams, a lover, and memory, this fragmentation becomes extreme, and the poem acquires a modern aspect, much like that of cubist painting, where different patches of the painting's surface imply different points of view or perspectival contexts. In the poem's apostrophes, instead of the creaking of classical forms, it would be better to hear the heralding of a new poetics.

What is achieved by using apostrophes that are apostrophes in name only? Culler argues that apostrophe defines a lyrical mode, in opposition to a narrative mode which would be founded on another figure. "Tristesse d'Olympio" is just such a poem, where the apostrophic dimension is at odds with its narrative impulse, an impulse which, since its first writing, has tried to rewrite it as a fragment of a referential love story, the first chapter of an autobiography, as an intermediate chapter in the marriage of Victor and Adèle Hugo. Hugo, it seems, understood that the poem and the story were different, and, by isolating it, tried to enhance its apostrophic status at the expense of its narrative. This was not to be. In the apostrophic poem, one expects an exclamatory style, largely reliant on noun phrases, linked not by verbs but by apposition, a poem Hugo simply could not write, and which he left to another. These are precisely the devices of Baudelaire's "À une passante," the prototypical modern poem, whose every aspect is inhabited by apostrophe.

QUATREVINGT-TREIZE: REVOLUTION AND ÆSTHETICS

Since Aristotle, if not before, history has been distinguished from poetry, and while the field of poetics has grown to encompass various manifestations of history, one cannot help but feel that the venerable dichotomy is still at work. In the famous paragraph of the *Poetics*, Aristotle attributed to history a circumscribed truth, a truth that fails to imply general laws, while to poetry on the other hand he reserved notions of probability and verisimilitude (Hardison 1981, 17). Although never universally accepted, this distinction met with what was probably its greatest trial in the nineteenth century with the advent of the historical novel. However one wishes to define it, the historical novel's fictitious characters and actions exist in a state of tension with its references to real persons, places, and events, and not the least stimulating of problems confronting the reader of such works is the possibility of confusing elements from one register with those of the other.

This dichotomy has not gone unchallenged, and accordingly a certain number of theories have been put forward to account for the presence of historical details within fictitious frames. Of equal importance are two quite different questions: 1) Is poetic truth indebted to history? 2) What does historical truth contribute to poetry? The first of these questions has received extensive discussion, no doubt because a negative answer would enable one to consider fictions closed works, registers of specifically literary effects, explicable by referring to a certain, limited encyclopedia.

By contrast, the second question implies the dependence of poetry (and literature generally) on a discourse of history, and while in some respects such an assertion is undeniable, it has not received the discussion that the first question has.

The concentration of recent interest on the first question would be satisfactory if one did not occasionally hear insistent calls that works of fiction transmit historical truth. If so, history has a specific function within fiction and cannot be dismissed as an effect like irony or pathos. Among those writers who make such calls, one cannot ignore Victor Hugo, who used history, taken both as the great movements of civilization and as personal biography, as an essential device in his narrative constructions.

A look at *Quatrevingt-treize*, the work in which the questions of the theory of history are most explicitly put, should go far to assess the status of historical assertions within Hugo's thought. The novel of course recounts episodes of the Vendée rebellion during the year 1793; like any other example of the historical novel, it includes references to actual people, places, and events but does so with an insistence that has aroused critical attention. Guy Rosa, for example, has shown how complete Hugo's research for this work was: "the novel employs a great number of historical underpinnings that touch on all aspects of the history of 1793, from the frontier-war to daily life, passing by institutions and political life" (Rosa 1975, 330; author's translation). In addition to its historical aspect, the work's allegorical dimension has also been analyzed (Rosa, Brombert, Petrey), but this dimension actually reinforces the novel's historical claim, for Hugo compares the events he describes to another moment: the Commune.[1] Such use of allegory is characteristic of Hugo's novels, and often the Revolution echoes in them.[2] But however characteristic such categories might be, and however accurate the historical references may be, *Quatrevingt-treize* elicits discomfort in its critics, on the subject, precisely, of its historical content. In his *Victor Hugo and the Visionary Novel*, Victor Brombert puts the question thus:

> It is as though Hugo could not come to terms with the mystery of a historical event that was to usher in a redemptive era of indefinite progress, but that instead, by some inexplicable irony, led to the farcical relapses of Louis Bonaparte's tyranny, then to the horrors of the Commune and its repression. . . . This disturbing tension between progress and recurrence, between concepts of linear and cyclical his-

tory, is manifestly at the center of Hugo's great novel on the Revolution, *Quatrevingt-treize*; (Brombert 1984, 207)

Hugo would like to conceive of history as progress, and wars and revolutions as the necessary painful steps along the way to a brighter future, but the allegories he draws between different events (1630, 1789, 1871) suggest that history is a pointless repetition of horrors. Thus, the novel's long gestation and the numerous hesitations that Hugo experienced as he wrote it. Rosa argues further that the novel is split into two parts: history and fiction. The first, copiously researched, is static, a description of situations prevailing in 1793. The second, consisting of the interplay of its characters, is actually a-historical and does not require the novel's historical basis for its unfolding. In the seemingly unnecessary distribution of labor between Halmalo and Lantenac, for example, Rosa sees an emblem of this "broken convergence": Halmalo is charged with historical, verifiable errands, while Lantenac evolves on an epic plane. Finally, each main character betrays his origins and thus exemplifies a double allegiance, to the historical concept of class, on the one hand, and to the narrative concept of destiny on the other.

Stressing this last distinction, Sandy Petrey has applied to *Quatrevingt-treize* the tools of semiotics and has detected traces of conflict beneath the narrative and thematic levels, at the level of the text's rhetoric. Dividing the text's lexicon into historical and a-historical components, Petrey confirms Rosa's thesis, and shows how far this analysis goes: the very genre of the novel—historical or pastoral—is uncertain.

These analyses are far richer than these suggestions; their shared preoccupation is what is pertinent to this reading; all see *Quatrevingt-treize* as somehow split into historical and fictitious elements, and all see a problem in the integration of history into narrative. A question is asked: What is the status of history in *Quatrevingt-treize*? and all answer that history is at odds with the story's movement. Inasmuch as historical elements are sometimes considered "real," a certain number of false problems surround this question, and among them that of the reliability of the history Hugo presents. Such a question is a dead-end; what is of significance instead is the use to which Hugo puts history; this is what Brombert, Rosa, and Petrey have examined.

At the level of historical detail, important conclusions about

Hugo's æsthetics can also be reached. Furthermore, detail (or trivia if one wishes) is important to consider. Often, it is trivia—dates, names, places—that provide the concrete link to a particular moment of history, the larger movements of history—causes, effects, significance, meaning—functioning more like texts than like referents. Even if trivia do not constitute history, they are a feature of historical discourse that might prove susceptible to analysis.

Sandy Petrey begins his account with a discussion of the *effet de réel*, the logical point of departure. The term, coined by Roland Barthes in 1966, has been analyzed with great success by Michael Riffaterre.[3] While tracing the *effet de réel* to different mechanisms, both Barthes and Riffaterre consider "realism" to be an effect, i.e., an illusion produced by specific textual features, like pathos, humor, and irony. In Riffaterre's analysis, the *effet* results from textual overdetermination: the more an element of the text is "motivated" (by, for example, phonic, metaphoric, thematic, or narrative considerations), the more perceptible will its necessity for the text be, and this textual necessity is decoded by the reader as "realistic." It is thus the consistency of a term within certain codes, rather than any "accuracy" of reference, that produces its realism.

Petrey, however, asks a pertinent question: what if the terms chosen are formally consistent, but historically inaccurate? What effect results then? He exemplifies his misgiving by using a device borrowed from Riffaterre himself (Riffaterre 1979, 26): substituting different proper nouns and dates for a phrase already conceived of as literary, he rewrites the first sentence of *Quatrevingt-treize*:

> Dans les derniers jours de mai 1793, un des bataillons parisiens amenés en Bretagne par Santerre fouillait le redoutable bois de la Saudraie en Astilé. (Hugo 1985, 3:789)
>
> [In the last of May, 1793, one of the Parisian battalions led into Brittany by Santerre was scouring the terrible woods of a Saudraie in Astillé. (Hugo 1900, 7)]

becomes:

> In the last days of May, 763, one of the Aixois battalions brought into Québec by Pétain was searching the awesome Bois de Boulogne in Martinique. (Petrey 1980, 38)

While the syntax of the sentence remains constant, and each proper noun respects the category of its model, the sentence is plainly nonsense: Why? Petrey responds: "Referential ignorance of the hostility between Paris and Brittany is as great an impediment to understanding Hugo's introductory sentence as semantic ignorance of the antonymic relationship between light and shadow is to understanding his conclusion" (Petrey 1980, 38). It is not sufficient to know grammar; one must also know history. Riffaterre could respond to this objection, for the competence he presupposes in his reader is not merely formal or grammatical but includes also a collection of received ideas as large perhaps as that contained by the *Larousse du XIXème siècle*.[4] The juxtaposition of "Bois de Boulogne" and "Martinique" would cancel the "Québec" descriptive system, the juxtaposition of "Pétain" and "763" would cancel the chronological markers, and as such, Petrey's rewritten sentence could be dismissed even in the absence of knowledge of the French Revolution. Conversely, an illusion of historical veracity can be conveyed in the absence of historical knowledge.

While such a response would support Riffaterre's analysis of the *effet de réel*, it leaves an important question unanswered: if overdetermination is sufficient to produce the *effet de réel*, why do writers use verifiable references in some texts? What point is there to including such "facts" if veracity has no bearing on the narrative illusion? Jean Gaudon provides a suggestive answer to this question in his "Vicissitudes du savoir," where he analyzes the purpose and effect of displays of erudition characteristic of all of Hugo's novels. Implying that Hugo's research was nowhere near as thorough as his admirers claimed, Gaudon asks why the novelist so frequently attracted attention to this weakness by making so many verifiable assertions. These gratuitous statements, Gaudon argues, are analogous to the "gratuitous details" that vehicle the *effet de réel*; in many cases in fact such "facts" simply heighten the narrative illusion. In other instances, however, the erudition displayed has no purpose whatever, neither narrative function nor realistic justification. Such for example is the sentence from *L'Homme qui rit* where Hugo explains how Dirry-Moore received his title: "d'une seigneurie que sa mère, qui venait de mourir, lui avait léguée dans cette grand forêt d'Ecosse où l'on trouve l'oiseau Krag, lequel creuse son nid avec son bec dans le tronc des chênes" (Hugo 1985, 3:481) [from an estate which his mother, who had just died, had left him, in that great forest of Scotland, where is found the krag, a bird which scoops out a nest with its beak in the trunk of an oak"(Hugo 1900, 176]). Gaudon comments thus:

> it seems however that in Hugo's case the "small true detail" possesses another function, both closer to and further afield than that of the pure "reality-effect." The "knowledge-effect" occurs when the referent too is beyond the reader's ken, thanks to a manipulation of historical facts that deprives them not simply of a signified, but of an identifiable referent. (Gaudon 1985, 30; author's translation)

Beyond intimidation and information, such Rabelaisian displays of knowledge have a comic motivation: "The way in which Hugo gleefully tramples what one thinks to be his idols is here the source of a fundamental ambiguity. As always, these excesses of expression are compulsory, and it is the cult and illusions of knowledge that pay for them." (Gaudon 1985, 34; author's translation).

Erudition certainly is used to comic effect in Hugo's works, and especially in *L'Homme qui rit*, the *effet de réel* and the *effet de savoir* just as certainly do not exhaust the effects of historically accurate detail in works of fiction. Many instances can be found where the *effet de réel* could be maintained by purely formal means, and where references to historical trivia produce no comic effect. In *Quatrevingt-treize*, the enumeration in "9 = 380" of the *croisière française* confronting the Claymore as dawn appears on the horizon elicits just this question. The ships are named *Côte d'or*, *Expirimentée*, *Dryade*, *Résolue*, *Richemont*, *Athée*, *Calypso*, and *Preneuse*. At least some of these names refer to ships that actually existed: the *Résolue*, for example, was launched in Saint-Malo in 1778 and indeed carried 32 cannon (Boudriot 1975, 3:262); the *Côte d'or* had in fact been christened the *États de Bourgogne*; ironically, after the Jacobin ascension to power of June 1793, it was to be renamed the *Montagne*, to become the *Peuple* a few months later, and finally to become the *Océan* (Jenkins 1973, 211n.).

Of course, it could be objected that the competent reader knows the names of French warships, and such information forms part of her decoding abilities, and if this is true, the use of such detail never produces anything more than an *effet de réel*. But if such details are indeed trivial, their use is very strange indeed, for their inclusion never seems to take the reader beyond the point of pure information. If they are known, their use is redundant, but if they are not, they are useless. Rosa phrases the paradox thus: "they are given as though known, recalled or pointed out, rather than reported, without the explanations that, in the absence of a solid historical framework, would allow one simply to understand them" (331; author's translation).

Two things should be noted to start: this information is not easy to come by, and there is no reason to doubt the implication of Hugo's footnote (Hugo 1985, 3:819) that the names were only discovered by consulting the *Archives de la marine*. But such knowledge is not necessary to be a competent reader; what is is a second fact to note. The lexicon from which the names of French warships are taken is tightly controlled and thus easily manipulated: feminine figures of Latin mythology (*Junon*, *Vénus*), noun-forms of feminine adjectives denoting moral qualities (*Indiscrète*, *Sérieuse*), and the names of regions of France comprise a large fraction of these names.

These two premises granted, the question arises: if it is so difficult to verify his research, and yet so easy to fake it, why did Hugo in a work of fiction use obscure historical information? The theoretical question can be phrased with greater generality: if, as Riffaterre has demonstrated, following formal codes suffices to produce the reality-effect, what other purpose is served by using references that do not form part of the reader's competence?

To recall the different positions on this point: Riffaterre defines the *effet de réel* as a response on the part of the reader to formal overdetermination. Petrey argues that for there to be an *effet de réel*, more than formal competence is necessary on the part of the reader: she must possess historical knowledge of the topic discussed. To such objections Riffaterre responds that much "history" is nothing more than received ideas and hence enters into the reader's formal competence. Gaudon here argues that historical details produce an effect distinct from the *effet de réel*, the *effet de savoir*, where the author informs, intimidates, or amuses the reader. But even so, a question remains: Is this the only function of the historical trivia with which Hugo's works—novels, poems, travel accounts—abound?

If Hugo and others refer, even when it is not evident that they are doing so, to really-existing persons, places, things, or events, it is because the real existence of those persons, places, things, or events is somehow of importance. This evident statement implies nonetheless a substantial departure from the æsthetics of Kant, which, through Victor Cousin's offices, were those of nineteenth-century France. It has been shown elsewhere[5] how this theory was disseminated and distorted by its French importers; in the present case Kant's initial statement and Cousin's version of that statement require reading.

In the first moment of the "Analytic of the Beautiful," Kant distinguished the pleasure of beauty from that produced by the satisfaction of a need: one does not declare an object beautiful solely because it offers some satisfaction; on the contrary, beauty is discerned even where no need is met, and æsthetic judgment is thus disinterested. In this respect, the Beautiful is distinct from the Agreeable and the Good, both of which imply interest on the part of the judge. Such interest is not characteristic of the Beautiful, and one can say that to the extent an object responds to an interest, to the same extent does any judgment of that object fall short of being æsthetic.

An important question of course remained: how does one know whether an æsthetic judgment is truly disinterested? To this Kant offered a novel response, one that recalls the question at hand, the status of historical reference in works of fiction. When one asks whether an object is beautiful, Kant wrote, "One must not be in the least prepossessed in favour of the real existence of the thing, but must preserve complete indifference in this respect, in order to play the part of judge in matters of taste" (Kant 1952, 48). Further, concern with an object's real existence implies desire: if it is important that it exist really, it is an object of desire: "Both the Agreeable and the Good involve a reference to the faculty of desire. . . . It is not merely the object, but also its real existence, that pleases" (Kant 1952, 48). In other words, concern with an object's real existence implies interest and desire, and thus precludes an æsthetic attitude.

Victor Cousin's formulation, which Hugo might have known, is quite similar:

> (. . . the sentiment of the Beautiful is wholly disinterested; . . . far from its occasioning the least desire in us to possess, to enjoy the object, to make it our own altogether, our sentiment, so to speak, is poised upon itself, and spreads around a kind of veneration that holds the me with the me.) (Cousin 1849, 72).

If beauty does not depend on the real existence of its object, a fiction can be beautiful, and any real object is only beautiful as if it were a fiction. Here Cousin's formulations are entirely canonical; in his examples, however, he addresses a problem which Kant did not, the æsthetic status of historical realism. Realism is not of itself beautiful; such works are beautiful only in spite of their realism:

> were you to show me Brutus, in his very robe; were you to bring back the very dagger, the instrument of his vengeance; unless the character of Brutus is *naturally* Beautiful, it will never be Beautiful on the stage. Illusion then, is not the sentiment of the Beautiful. . . . I do not say that illusion cannot accompany the sentiment of the Beautiful, but I maintain that it does not constitute it. (Cousin 1849, 80–81)

Contradicting Aristotle, who in the fourth book of the *Poetics* argues that representation can make what in real life is ugly, beautiful,[6] Cousin asserts that the representational illusion has of itself no æsthetic value.

In two respects then, historical realism is antithetical to academic æsthetics: on the one hand, the model of beauty is fiction, for fictions alone imply a disinterested judgment; on the other, when reality is imitated, the accuracy or artistry (the "realism") of the imitation is of no importance to its æsthetic value. But it is precisely reality and realism that Hugo invokes in his æsthetics.

Almost constantly, it would seem, *Quatrevingt-treize* is punctuated by reversions from obvious fiction to verifiable fact. The first chapter of Part 11, "À Paris," furnishes a case in point. Rosa has attested to the accuracy of Hugo's use of detail (329–30); this detail, however, is interspersed with anecdote, producing, at the level of reference, a tension analogous to that noted by Rosa between fiction and history, and by Petrey, between proper and common nouns. Thus Hugo dramatizes revolutionary inflation through the use of prosopopoeia:

> Le louis d'or valait trois mille neuf cent cinquante francs. Une course en fiacre coûtait six cents francs. Après une journée en fiacre on entendait ce dialogue:—Cocher, combien vous dois-je? Six mille livres. Une marchande d'herbe vendait pour vingt mille francs par jour. Un mendiant disait: *Par charité secourez-moi! il me manque deux cent trente livres pour payer mes souliers*. (Hugo 1985, 3:862)

[A Louis d'or was worth three thousand, nine hundred and fifty francs. A ride in a hackney-coach cost six hundred francs. After using a hackney-coach for a day this conversation was overheard:—
 "Coachman, how much do I owe you?"
 "Six thousand francs."
 A greengrocer woman made twenty thousand francs a day. A beggar said: "For the sake of charity, assist me! I need two hundred and thirty livres to pay for my shoes. (Hugo 1900, 98)].

It is as though fact were insufficient without dramatic representation, and dialogue meaningless without concrete references.

Further, such references serve to buttress the anecdotes or fictions that adjoin them. The description of Cimourdain, whose presence literally squares the triangle of Danton, Robespierre, and Marat (Hugo 1985, 3:871) is one such example. Associated with the great moments of the Revolution (Hugo 1985, 3:864), he is to a certain extent both its principle and one of its principals: "En révolution rien de redoutable comme la ligne droite. Cimourdain allait devant lui, fatal. . . . il dépassait la Convention, il dépassait la Commune; il était de l'Évêché" (Hugo 1985, 3:866) ["In a revolution, nothing is more terrible than a straight line. Cimourdain went straight ahead, as sure as fate. . . . He went beyond the Convention; he went beyond the Commune; he belonged to the Évêché" (Hugo 1900, 104)]. His portrayal, however, remains stereotypical, for he personifies the antithesis of the political priest and his portrait is comprised largely of oxymorons: "l'effrayant homme juste . . . virginité sinistre," and "il fallut qu'il fût infâme ou sublime" (Hugo 1985, 3:867) ["frightfully just man . . . forbidding virginity . . . he must be infamous or sublime" (Hugo 1900, 106–7)]. What is necessary then is to particularize him, but, instead of using description with its accompanying *effets de réel*, Hugo chooses to use an *effet de savoir*. "Tel était Cimourdain. Personne aujourd'hui ne sait son nom. L'histoire a de ces inconnus terribles" (Hugo 1985, 3:867) ["Such was Cimourdain. No one to-day knows his name. History has more than one such terrible Unknown" (Hugo 1900, 107)]. It is of course true that no one knows Cimourdain's name, true too that history has its "terrible Unknowns," but Hugo uses ignorance itself as proof of Cimourdain's existence, and this existence as the particularizing attribute of a character he has just qualified as having "l'apparence d'un homme ordinaire" (Hugo 1985, 3:867) ["the appearance of an ordinary man" (Hugo 1900, 107)]. In other words, existence (and fallaciously derived existence at that) is in and of itself a particularizing attribute of fiction.

In *Quatrevingt-treize*, Hugo associates historical reference with this device. In Book II, the passenger carried by the Claymore is pointedly left unnamed, his disguise is obvious (Hugo 1985, 3:801); those who know his identity refer to him as "général" or "cousin" (Hugo 1985, 3:800). Hugo nevertheless refers to him as "le paysan," "l'homme" or "le vieillard."[7] A mystery ensues which Hugo conspicuously maintains. The passenger refuses to reveal his identity to Halmalo, preferring instead to give him a symbol of his authority, and thus attaches considerable suspense to his identification. It is only in Book III that he is identified, and then, by the beggar Tellmarch, as the marquis de Lantenac. But in the same short chapter, the edict outlawing Lantenac and putting a price on his head is signed "Prieur de la Marne" (Hugo 1985, 3:841). Two recognitions are thus assimilated: the reader recognizes "Lantenac" as the solution to a mystery while Prieur de la Marne recognizes him as an adversary. That a really existing person should recognize Lantenac implies the reality of the latter, and this "real existence" is designed to increase the effect of surprise as the reader understands who the passenger is. Here, historical detail serves an æsthetic purpose: to augment the terror and pity resulting from recognition.

Hugo thus uses history to amplify fiction's effects: history is fiction's supplement, both as the addition that makes up for fiction's lacks, and as fiction's unneeded aide. The use of historical references in "9 = 380" accentuates the pathos of the David-and-Goliath struggle; the reference to Prieur de la Marne increases one's awe on recognizing Lantenac. This device is a constant feature of Hugo's works. The grim tongue-in-cheek title for chapter III, iii, 1, "Le Massacre de Saint Barthélemy," neither explains nor allegorizes the events of the chapter, in which Michelle Fléchard's children destroy the pseudo-gospel according to Saint Bartholemew; rather, it associates that destruction to the historical massacre and thus assimilates 1793 to the wars of religion. It thus functions like a sounding-board, resonating to a meaning without interpreting or duplicating it.

Several conclusions can be drawn from this analysis. First, and most obviously, Hugo's use of historical references constitutes one of several features that distinguish his æsthetics from the

Kantian æsthetics prevailing in France at mid-century. These references imply that their real existence is significant, and such an implication is inadmissible in canonical definitions of beauty. As a result of such references, Hugo's fictions become interesting, in the strong sense of the word: they respond to and feed a desire for knowledge, thus deflecting any pure æsthetic appreciation towards a quest for information. Curiosity replaces the willing suspension of disbelief. When Hugo uses such references, he creates a sub-species of the *effet de réel*, i.e., the *effet de savoir*, where gratuitous and circular displays of knowledge create an effect different from verisimilitude. The *effet de savoir* can intimidate or amuse, but more importantly, it endows ordinary narrative devices with greater meaning: recognitions are more significant; obstacles more imposing, ellipsis more weighty. What is known to be fiction is affected by what is known to be fact, and if so, historical references function in their context like symbols, for they promise and deliver a deeper meaning, while irradiating that meaning to their context. One could say that Hugo uses historical fact as fiction's supplement: these gratuitous allusions indicate the closure of the text, its self-sufficiency, while at the same time betraying an absence it can only designate but never fill: that of reference.

It might seem that this argument denies any place for history in the text; that is not its aim. What is is how apparently historical markers produce an effect subordinate to formal considerations. History is not to be found in such deictics as proper nouns or dates, but somewhere else, and I would suggest the famous image of the loose cannon to explain the relation of text, reference, and history. It is not, Hugo points out, the cannon's movement that causes destruction, but that of the ship, which is in turn moved by the sea, and the sea, by the wind (Hugo 1985, 3:808): the inertia of the cannon relative to these forces causes catastrophe. The status of reference is analogous: by their relative fixity, proper nouns, dates, and so on, form stationary points around which the text moves, and as it moves, produces its effects. It is not historical references in the text, but the forces beyond it, and moving it in relation to them, that must be called history, and it is thus the resistance of these references to purely formal analysis that indicates history's presence.

2
Hugo's Textual Systems: Antithesis, Inscription, Ekphrasis
Politics and Æsthetics of Race in *Bug-Jargal*

IN MARCH OF 1818, VICTOR HUGO PUBLISHED THE FIRST INSTALLMENT of a short story in his *Conservateur Littéraire*; this story was taken up again and greatly amplified seven years later, republished anonymously as the novel *Bug-Jargal*. In 1831, on the occasion of yet another edition, this one signed, Hugo explained that the first version had been written to win a bet, while the later novel was being republished in order to inform readers of what the author's early interests had been, "comme ces voyageurs qui se retournent au milieu de leur chemin et cherchent à découvrir encore dans les plis brumeux de l'horizon le lieu d'où ils sont partis" (Hugo 1985, 1:278) ["like those travelers who turn about when their journey is half done to discover amid the mists the horizon, the place whence they came" (Hugo 1894, v)]. Hugo at thirty years of age thus presented the novel as a curiosity, interesting if not in itself at least for the light it might shed on its now famous author. Further, he implied that the views of potential interest were those of the novel, not those of the story, and it is thus the circumstances of the story's composition, not its content, that he explains.[1]

Yet what the novel is about is paramount: its references to places and events define its import, and it begs consideration as a historical document, but whether of France's or Hugo's history remains a question. Set during the revolt in Santo Domingo of August, 1791,[2] the novel sits uneasily with 21st-century racial sensibilities: it recounts the progress whereby a young white colonialist comes to recognize a black leader of the rebellion, Bug-Jargal. What is at stake in this recognition is Bug-Jargal's identity (as the son of an African king), his courage, his strength, and, most importantly, his moral worth. But all is measured by the hero's own standard: it is not a question of whether Bug-Jargal is strong, good, or brave, but whether he is *as* strong, *as* good, or *as* brave as his white adversaries. The hero's sidekick, Thadée, even comes to say of Bug-Jargal: "c'était le premier brave de la terre, après vous . . . mon capitaine" (Hugo 1985, 1:904) ["the bravest man in the world,—except you, Captain, if you please" (Hugo 1894, 155)]. Despite these tips of the hat in the direction of racial equality, the phrase "pour un nègre," as in "comme sa figure était belle pour un nègre" (Hugo 1985, 1:884) [his face was handsome, for a Negro], returns frequently enough to make modern readers prefer to take *Bug-Jargal* as Hugo himself suggested in 1832, as a curiosity rather than as an exposition of his views on race.

Nevertheless, one must give Hugo credit: other public stands on issues of race should suffice to indicate commitment to a cause of racial equality, and these of course refer to persons, places, and events. In 1859, for example, he wrote a letter on the trial of John Brown protesting the institution of slavery: "Il y a des esclaves dans les états du Sud, ce qui indigne, comme le plus monstrueux des contre-sens, les états du Nord" (Hugo 1985, 10:513) [There are slaves in the southern states, the most monstrous of contradictions, something that makes the northern states indignant]. And after Brown's hanging, writing to the editor of the Haitian journal *Le Progrès*, he wrote:

> Puis qu'il n'y a qu'un père, nous sommes tous frères . . . Poursuivez votre œuvre, vous et vos dignes concitoyens. Haïti est maintenant une lumière. Il est beau que parmi les flambeaux du progrès, éclairant la route des hommes, on en voie un tenu par la main d'un nègre. (Hugo 1985, 10:526)

> [Since there is only one father, we are all brothers. . . . Pursue your works, you and your worthy fellow-citizens. Haiti is now a light. It is beautiful that among the torches of progress illuminating man's way, we should see one held in the hand of a Negro.]

Of course, these are relatively safe positions to occupy: a self-exiled Frenchman, and a world famous one at that, Hugo could easily afford to criticize slavery and he did so. His statements prove that he was aware both of race and racism; further, that he should have included questions of race in his works is only logical, both for their ethical aspect and for the formal antitheses that they inevitably bring up. But why was he so ashamed of Bug-Jargal that he presented it as a curiosity rather than as a work of which to be proud? Its content can hardly be reproached; its exploitation of race in the service of the ethical argument is likewise admirable. Despite these strengths, Hugo did modify it substantially, rewriting it as a book in 1825–26. The modifications that Hugo performed made it into a novel, Georges Piroué and Kathryn Grossman have argued, and transform it from a novel into a Hugolian novel. At the same time, however, those changes represent a retreat from the political engagement of the first Bug-Jargal, and made of it a more æsthetic work. Nevertheless, the revised version is something for which Hugo expresses shame six years later. Why? *Bug-Jargal*'s evolution allows one to glimpse Hugo's thought in the process of formulation, before it is cast in the forms that define Hugolian discourse. In a word, *Bug-Jargal* represents the two poles of a fundamental choice made by Hugo in the late twenties, between politics and æsthetics. This choice defined his later æsthetics and rendered some of his later political positions ambiguous.

The story from 1818 runs thus: The hero, Delmar, is asked to explain how he came to own the dog Rask, so beloved of him and his men that one of the latter, Thadée, risks his life to save him. Rask was first owned by Pierrot, a slave on Santo Domingo, where Delmar was growing up. What follows is therefore Delmar's account of Rask, and, of course, of Pierrot.

Pierrot, admired by all the slaves for his self-sacrifice and his majesty, is condemned to death by the hero's uncle for having raised his hand against him to protect a fellow-slave. At once befriended by Delmar, he escapes from prison, and shortly afterwards there is a slave rebellion which the white colonialists unite to put down. In battle, Delmar is captured by one of the black leaders, Biassou, while the whites capture a black leader, the mysterious Bug-Jargal. Biassou frees Delmar on his word as a Frenchman that he will return for his execution; during this period of liberty, Delmar finds Pierrot, who, it turns out, is none other than Bug-Jargal, the rival leader of the black slaves. He in turn has been freed by his French captors, leaving ten hostages in his place, in order to enable him to save Delmar; Bug-Jargal explains that even if the French colonialists have lost much in this rebellion, their loss is nothing compared to that of the slaves:

he, for example, is the son of an African king, he was sold into slavery, his wife was killed, and his children also died. Bug-Jargal orders the execution party to spare Delmar, but the treacherous Biassou nonetheless waves the black flag that signifies that Delmar has been put to death. Thus when Bug-Jargal returns to his French captors to take the place of the hostages, he is summarily executed by Thadée before Delmar can return.

The 1826 edition includes changes that could be called variants, but differs from its predecessor mainly by its additions: it is more than twice as long as the first version. The smaller changes include a name-change for the hero, from Delmar to D'Auverney, and changes in the names of the secondary characters. But it is the insertion of two new characters and one group of characters that changes the story most: the hero acquires a love-interest, Marie, who serves as a point of opposition between D'Auverney and Bug-Jargal, rivals for her affections. At the same time, another slave leader is added, Habibrah, who serves before the revolt as the tyrannical supervisor of his brothers, and afterwards, as the *obi*, or witch-doctor of the ex-slaves. And the colonialists as a group are fleshed out by the addition of several individuals, who first discuss gruesome means of putting down the revolt, and then, having been captured, display a cowardice matched only by their earlier brutality, begging for a mercy that is then denied to them. Finally, the novel has an epilog that indicates the fate of its protagonist.

For Georges Piroué, it is the addition of Marie that is most significant, for the love rivalry opposing D'Auverney and Bug-Jargal separates and binds the two men: from a simple story of military values, *Bug-Jargal* becomes far more complex through the addition of Marie: "an element that could be taken as conventional and unimportant, as an ornament added to please and to move, changes everything from the top to the bottom. A woman has entered the arena. Woman in *Bug-Jargal* opens up a world of shadows Hugo's exploration of which will henceforth be endless" (Piroué 1970, iv–v; author's translation).

Indeed, Bug-Jargal must overcome his resentment of D'Auverney and surrender to his rival the woman he loves; D'Auverney must acknowledge the bravery, etc., of a man he can only call his rival. And certainly, the presence of Marie changes the static opposition of the two male characters and makes it dialectic, as it were, anticipating the antithetical constructions of *Ruy Blas* or

Les Misérables.³ For Grossman, though, the changes go further: if Marie is a typical, virginal Hugolian heroine, she is herself opposed to the new character of Habibrah, who is a typical Hugolian villain, related to Han, to Claude Frollo, and to Hardquanonne.⁴ A pairing of angel and devil results, like those of Claude and Esmeralda, Marie and Salluste, Josiane and Gwynplaine.⁵ As Grossman has convincingly shown, this construction exemplifies the pairing of grotesque and sublime first advocated in the "Préface" of *Cromwell* (Grossman 1986, 59). Since, however, Bug-Jargal's love is unrequited, since there is never any question that Marie reciprocate his love, since, in a word, Bug-Jargal loves from a safe distance, through song rather than through dialog, one should qualify this love more as an æsthetic attribute of his character than as a real plot possibility. Indeed, other than declaring his love, Bug-Jargal does nothing with it or for it: it has no future. One could say that he is destined to fail in love, just as Hernani is destined to die, Ruy Blas destined to fail, Jean Valjean destined to be persecuted. Such a concept of destiny is antithetical to the freedom of choice implicit in political engagement.

While Marie's presence makes the story more engaging, the same cannot be said of the addition of Habibrah, the supervisor/witch-doctor, whose primary purpose seems to be to exercise cruelty and strike terror on blacks and whites alike. It is this use of stereotype in the second version that attracts Christopher Miller's attention: "The story juxtaposes a stereotype of the 'good Negro,' *le nègre généreux et révolté*, named Bug-Jargal, to that of the 'bad Negro,' the 'Bizarre' obi" (Miller 1985, 109). Certainly Habibrah goes beyond the requirements of his office, meting out more severe punishments than D'Auverney's cruel uncle ever demanded. And as *obi*, he carries out a sacrilegious black mass parodying the Catholic mass; at his death, literally struggling to take D'Auverney into the abyss with him, and that, after having been spared by the hero, he incarnates treachery and blind vengeance, willing to die if he can thereby cause the death of his enemy. As a negative version of white values, he simply reinforces stereotypes of Africa and Africans.⁶

But beyond the issue of stereotype another question comes to the surface in Miller's reading: that of opposition. Good and bad blacks are opposed, and this antithesis is part of a more general tendency in western writing from Herodotus onwards to deny representation to Africa: such self-canceling formulations leave Africa a blank.

> Consciousness is 'utterly' denied to these specific groups [the Garamantes and Atalantes reported by Pliny]; for them a complete nullity is reserved, and they represent a complete refutation of the notion of civilization as based on consciousness and inter-subjectivity. . . . Africanist discourse in the West is one in which the head, the voice—the logos if you will—is missing. (Miller 1985, 27)

Hugo's *Bug-Jargal*, especially the second version, is part of just such a project, but the novel also has a specifically political dimension, for its self-canceling racial oppositions betray a political stance, if only the refusal of politics.

The group of colonialists is another matter, and its presence significantly modifies the story: first, it must be noted that its members are revolutionary stereotypes. There are, for example, an economist, a *négrophile* and a *philanthrope* among them. Their presence draws *Bug-Jargal* into relation with contemporary events in France, and makes of its slave revolt a commentary on the Revolution. Representing an insurrection of slaves, Bug-Jargal offers a reversed image of the French Revolution: slaves revolting against their masters, but those masters are "enlightened;" a king dying, but that king is king of slaves; mass decapitation, but of the insurgents, not of the masters. Irony pervades this representation of revolt: in order to intimidate the rebellious slaves, one colonialist (the *philanthrope* at that!) generously offers to behead five hundred of his slaves and to display their severed heads before the fort. At this point, it should be noted that the novel ends with D'Auverney's condemnation to death by the Convention for having recounted the anti-revolutionary story just read; by contrast, the story has no such ending, and indeed, is supposed to have been recounted fully fifteen years after the events it relates, that is, in 1806 or 1807. As for the colonialists, while punctuating their speeches with revolutionary rhetoric—the adjective "ci-devant" comes back frequently, even to modify the word "noirs"—their speech lacks any revolutionary ideal. Slave-owners, they hardly believe in *liberté* or *égalité*, and they certainly deny *fraternité* to the slaves, who frequently use the word *frère*.

The royally subsidized Victor Hugo, who eight months previously had attended the coronation of Charles X and had written a poem celebrating the event, could not have said anything plainer: the revolution was an exercise in hypocrisy. Its leaders did not believe in equality or brotherhood; the use of terror was at odds with humanitarian ideals; its control of speech denied it the right to claim liberty as one of its aims. Finally, the coda appended to the story also attacks the revolution: D'Auverney is killed following the telling of Bug-Jargal's story, and the news of his death in battle arrives at the same time as a decree from the Convention that he is to be put to death for having told it. The government he defends decides to take his life, and not only that, does so at the very moment he gives his life for that government. The irony of this decision can only leave one speechless. There is no recognition, no gratitude, no understanding, not even tragedy here: an inhuman, inflexible power simply refuses to acknowledge its adversaries: Bug-Jargal, D'Auverney, or others. Here is a structure that will be re-employed in *Le Dernier Jour d'un condamné*, *Hernani*, *L'Homme qui rit*, and other works, and that Hugo will sometimes call destiny.

The difference in the ends of the two stories echoes the more general differences. In the first version, the black man dies, the white man lives; in the second, both die. The first construction is about as simple an indicator of injustice as one can find in a narrative; the second inevitably attenuates that judgment. While it could certainly be argued successfully that the story is improved by the additions, the difference between the two versions points out a feature of the first that was abandoned in the second: a desire to denounce injustice clearly and unequivocally.

More generally, a story of racial inequality and oppression in the first version becomes in the second a more personal story where a struggle of egos displaces the struggle of equals. As it becomes more personal, its political message becomes confused, for the struggle for equality implied by the opposition of D'Auverney and Bug-Jargal is neutralized by comments on how unjust egalitarian government is. The story also becomes more abstract and extreme: from a study in black and white, the story becomes a study in good and evil too. At that point, *Bug-Jargal* becomes more racist, because in order to produce absolute oppositions, it must resort to stereotypes of the kind exemplified by Habibrah; in order to produce antitheses, it must abandon the ideological thrust of the first version; in order to imply destiny, it must forsake freedom.

What must be pointed out here is just how big these changes are, and just how Hugolian they are too. If the first version was a story of honor, valor, and belated recognition of those qualities, the second is quite different. If one accepts conventions that reduce soldiers to embodiments of strength and weakness, courage and cowardice, honor and treachery, it must follow that there is a very egalitarian thrust to the first version of *Bug-Jargal*. If the whites are brave, their black enemies are just as brave; if the blacks are cruel, their cruelty is more than matched by that of the whites; if whites suffer in the rebellion, that suffering is not to be compared with that of their black slaves. And it is thus not by accident that the story is punctuated, as Piroué has noted, by Bug-Jargal's recurrent vocatives: *frère*. By contrast, the second version loses this thrust and acquires a different dimension: one stops, amazed. Amazed by Bug-Jargal's generosity, by the *obi*'s treachery, by Biassou's cruelty, by the colonialists' cowardice, not encouraged to act, or even to speak on behalf of the oppressed slaves. One is dumbfounded, speechless before this compound of betrayals, and even if one could name it, with which treason would one start? In a word, the second version is sublime: the pairing of extremes of virtue and evil in the opposition of Marie and Habibrah, the postulation of a blind, relentless, overpowering, and inhuman force called the revolution, the terror practiced by whites and blacks alike are characteristics of that æsthetic. Indeed, the very notion of terror, whether that practiced by the *Comité de Salut Public* or that practiced in *Bug-Jargal*, is sublime. Kant indicated that in some cases, fear was an attribute of an æsthetic reaction: even a fearful object, if contemplated from a safe distance, can inspire awe and be sublime.

> Bold, overhanging, and, as it were, threatening rocks, thunderclouds piled up the vault of heaven, borne along with flashes and peals, volcanoes in all their violence of destruction . . . make our power of resistance of trifling moment in comparison with their might. But, provided our own position is secure, their aspect is all the more attractive for its fearfulness; and we readily call these objects sublime. (Kant 1952, 110)

At another point, Kant calls war "sublime," and clearly, the bravery of the blacks, the cowardice of the whites, the cruelty shared by both races, are fearful, but sublime when contemplated from a safe distance. If an ideological message requires some course of action, before the sublime, one simply stops in awe and amazement, unwilling to relinquish the safe position one occupies. In other words, the first version of *Bug-Jargal* was, at some level, an exhortation to action, while the second leaves its reader in an attitude of contemplative passivity.[7]

Here, confirming Piroué's and Grossman's theses—that the second version of *Bug-Jargal* must be recognized as first step towards a definitive Hugolian æsthetic—are the contrasts, antitheses, and paradoxes that Baudelaire so disliked[8] but that do characterize his dramatic and novelistic forms. Here also is the attitude that will characterize his lyrical poetry and that is absent from his political poetry: ideological theses are incompatible with contemplation, just as Hugo had to finish *Les Châtiments* in order to write *Les Contemplations*.

One could even say that this attitude of "contemplation" informs and deforms all of Hugo's considerations of race: if the first version of *Bug-Jargal* was a cry against real racial injustice, Hugo's subsequent writings on race made race a marker of an æsthetic, not a political, orientation. History recedes in favor of poetry. There are in fact very few texts about race in the rest of Hugo's works, as if this question were no longer appropriate material for his new æsthetics: an allusion to race in *Ruy Blas*, the letters on the trial and execution of John Brown that have already been mentioned, an address to women exiled from Cuba in 1870.

The passages from *Ruy Blas* are perhaps exemplary of Hugo's definitive attitude: in the fourth act of the play, Don César returns to Seville, only to land in Don Salluste's hideaway, where, entirely by accident, he must play the role of the man who is playing the role of César. By a series of extraordinary coincidences, he first undoes Salluste's wicked machinations, and then, just as accidentally, allows Salluste to reconstruct them. In the midst of this comic interlude, two black pages wait on César:

>*(Il agite la sonnette. Entre un des noirs.)*
> Tu sais écrire?

>   *(Le noir fait un signe de tête affirmatif. Étonnement de don César.)*
>   *(A part.)*
>   Un signe!
>   *(Haut.)*
>   Es-tu muet, mon drôle?
>   *(Le noir fait un nouveau signe d'affirmation. Nouvelle stupéfaction de don César.)*
>   *(A part.)*
>   Fort bien! continuez! des muets à present!
>   *(Au muet, en lui montrant la lettre, que la vieille tient appliquée sur la table.)*
>   —Écrivez-moi là: Venez.
> *(Le muet écrit. Don César fait signe à la duegne de reprendre la lettre, et au muet de sortir. Le muet sort.)*
>   *(A part.)*
>   Il est obéissant!
> (Hugo 1985, 8:113)
> [*He rings the little bell. One of the Negroes enters.*
>   Do you know how to write?
>   *The Negro nods affirmatively. Don Caesar is astonished.*
>   *Aside*
>   A sign!
>   *Aloud*
>   Are you dumb, you rascal?
>   *Again the Negro makes the sign of affirmation. Fresh stupefaction of Don Caesar*
>   *Aside*
>   Well! Continue! Mutes appear to be the latest thing!
>   *To the Negro, showing him the letter which the old woman holds on the table.*
>   Write "Come" there.
> *The Negro writes. Don Caesar signals to the Duenna to take back the letter, and the Negro to go. Exit the Negro.*
>   He is obedient!
> (Hugo 1995, 313–14)].

Although the scene is comic its circumstances are quite serious: César's blind actions affect the life and happiness of the play's protagonists; more generally, set in the decadence of seventeenth-century Spain, the play unfolds against a backdrop of the colonial exploitation of the New World, which has corrupted the Spanish nobility; Salluste, for example, has sold César as a slave; Ruy Blas, the hero, represents the oppressed classes who see none of the wealth that the conquest of the New World has brought to the aristocracy. And while the blacks are not Salluste's slaves as such, they might as well be: mute, obedient, the pure executors of orders coming from elsewhere, they are nothing but the instruments of another's will. Indeed, their comic function is to provide incongruous obedience to their new, illegitimate master. In sum, while there is an ample context for an ethical discussion of the politics of race, Hugo envisages only the comic effects race might contribute to a discussion of the unauthorized exercise of power: the political has become æsthetic.

The passages from *Ruy Blas* are however parts of a work of fiction and might thus be ambiguous indicators of Hugo's attitudes on race; let's look at something that is less equivocal. In 1859, on the occasion of John Brown's failed raid on Harper's Ferry, Hugo wrote twice about the problem of slavery in the United States. First came an open letter to the United States of America, published in several European newspapers, and then a letter to the editor of the Haitien *Le Progrès*. In the open letter, he protests both the institution of slavery and the miscarriage of justice that John Brown's trial exemplified, the first with relation to the notion of freedom that America is supposed to incarnate, and the second by depicting the appalling circumstances of Brown's trial, which are of course opposed to the noble intentions the failure of which made the trial take place. Along the way however, the rhetoric of Hugo's letter gains the upper hand: blacks are opposed to whites, slaves to free men, North to South, light to darkness. The passage ends: "Oui, que l'Amérique le sache et y songe, il y a quelque chose de plus effrayant que Caïn tuant Abel, c'est Washington tuant Spartacus" (Hugo 1985, 10:514) [Yes, let America know it and think about it, there is something more frightening still than Cain killing Abel, it is Washington killing Spartacus (author's translation]. As the antitheses are multiplied, the probability of Brown's death becomes more and more certain: the comparisons with Abel and Spartacus promise as much. It is as if, even as he argues that Brown should be spared, Hugo was constructing an argument that would glorify him in death; it is as if even as he pleads for Brown's life, he is starting to build his tomb. It would be difficult to conceive of a better image of destiny. In his subsequent letter to Heurtelou, editor of *Le Progrès*, when he argues that race is of no consequence, he comes out with this startling statement: "Il n'y a sur la terre ni blancs ni noirs, il y a des esprits; vous en êtes un. Devant Dieu, toutes les âmes sont blanches" (Hugo 1985, 10:525) [There are neither whites or blacks on earth, there are spirits, and you are one of them. Before God, all souls are white (author's translation)]. The æsthetic value of whiteness is so compelling that, in addition to assuming that "white" is a complimentary adjective, for its sake Hugo sacrifices the political argument that the difference between white and black is of no consequence.

In 1870, while France was preoccupied with the question of the succession to the Spanish throne, a revolt in Cuba was harshly repressed by Spain. Three hundred Cuban women who had fled to New York asked Hugo for his support, and he responded with a letter and a declaration of the rights of Cubans. In the letter, he condemned the Spanish repression of the insurrection, qualifying it as the suppression of liberty and of self-determination, as racism, as colonialism:

> Aucune nation n'a le droit de poser son ongle sur l'autre, pas plus l'Espagne sur Cuba que l'Angleterre sur Gibraltar. Un peuple ne possède pas plus un autre peuple qu'un homme ne possède un autre homme. Le crime est plus odieux encore sur une nation que sur un individu: voilà tout. Agrandir le format de l'esclavage, c'est en accroître l'indignité. Un peuple tyran d'un autre peuple, une race soutirant la vie à une autre race, c'est la succion monstrueuse de la pieuvre, et cette superposition épouvantable est un des faits terribles du dix-neuvième siècle. (Hugo 1985, 10:639–40)

> [No nation has the right to hold another under its thumb, no more can Spain hold Cuba down than England can hold Gibraltar down. One people can no more possess another people than one man can possess another man. The crime is just more odious when committed against a nation than committed against an individual. That's all. To increase the scope of slavery is to increase its infamy. One people tyrannizing another people, one race squeezing the life out of another, is the monstrous sucking of an octopus, and this horrifying superimposition is one of the terrible facts of the nineteenth century. (author's translation)]

The clarity of this declaration is admirable, as is Hugo's uncompromising political stand. As the declaration develops, however, Hugo multiplies the analogies and antitheses typical of his æsthetics, producing such statements as "Eh bien, si la France avait encore Haïti, de même que je dis à l'Espagne: Rendez Cuba! je dirais à la France: Rends Haïti!" (Hugo 1985, 10:640) [Well, if France still held Haiti, just as I say to Spain, Give back Cuba! I'd say to France, Give Haiti back!] To obtain the parallelism Hugo invokes an unreal condition, immediately associating his statements regarding Cuba with hypothetical statements regarding Haiti, and distancing himself from the cause of the Cuban women as he does so. And thus in his declaration of the rights of Cuba he comes to an apparent compromise regarding Spain's colonial conquests: "Il (the Spanish people) a colonisé; mais comme le Nil déborde; en fécondant" (Hugo 1985, 10:642) [They colonized, but as the Nile overflows: fertilizing as it does so]. What was an incitement to action has become an invitation to appreciation.

It is tempting, given Hugo's fascination with progress, that slow but steady evolution of things towards the Good, to think that the same principle is true of Hugo's life. This is not the case. If anything, the second version of *Bug-Jargal* shows a young man who has hardened his position against the revolution and employs simplification and stereotype to belittle and ridicule it. What is also true is that Hugo was to abandon this position entirely a few years later. But what should be stressed is that this change is not evolutionary, but revolutionary. Like Hernani, like the poet of *Les Contemplations*, like Jean Valjean, like Javert, Hugo underwent a conversion in about 1830, a conversion made all the more dramatic by his earlier anti-revolutionary rhetoric.

For Hugo, ideology and æsthetics are opposed, and not simply in the conventional sense that politics don't make good subjects of novels, the famous *coup de pistolet* (pistol shot) that Stendhal scorned. Rather, the æsthetic attitude he seeks requires an entirely passive view of opposed forces, where their symmetry and balance can be appreciated without for a moment requiring or even implying the choice of one side or the other, for to do so would be to leave the position of safety that allows contemplation. One doesn't simply avoid politics in good books; it must be neutralized, neutralized by carefully balancing opposed positions, and even if that neutralization can only imply a different politics and a different ideology, that of contemplation. For the function of that æsthetic is to neutralize politics.

The Discipline of Letters: *Le Dernier Jour d'un condamné*

The death penalty, never far from the American consciousness, has elicited renewed debate in recent years, and Victor Hugo's novel on the subject—*Le Dernier Jour d'un condamné*—has appeared frequently in critical studies. France abandoned decapitation after the execution of Hamida Djandoubi on September 10, 1977, but the novel has lost little of its appositeness, perhaps because of the pains the author took not to discuss the *condamné*'s life and or the circumstances of his crime. One can reasonably assume that the fears and hopes expressed in the novel are just as plausible today in Huntsville and Terre Haute as they were in 1830 Paris.

That the novel is "about" the death penalty has not been debated since its first anonymous publication; its initial success was such that in subsequent editions, beyond adding his name and a preface, Hugo provided a short polemic dialogue to the novel, bringing into sharp focus its plea to abandon execution. What is at issue, Hugo argues in the preface, is the suffering that inevitably occurs whenever the death penalty is applied, whether the criminal deserves harsh punishment or not. Hugo enumerates a gruesome list of botched executions, where the words "cruel and unusual," were they ever to figure in the French *Code Pénal*, would have to apply. Dull blades, resistant sinews, murderers begging to die are described. The penalty is all-too-often a torturous procedure, despite the fact that Guillotin's purpose in proposing the regular use of decapitation was to eliminate the exorbitant displays of cruelty meted out to ordinary criminals.[1] But Hugo's argument implicitly goes further. Since he provides no account of the *condamné*'s execution, one can only surmise that it proceeds without a hitch, and if so, the argument is more radical still: even when properly applied and correctly executed, the penalty causes terrible, unacknowledged suffering.

These concerns are presented ironically in the "Comédie à propos d'une tragédie," the mock discussion of the novel that Hugo placed before the work from the third edition on. There, different types—a *gros monsieur*, a *poète*, a *chevalier*, among others—all condemn the story, claiming to have "suffered" because of its graphic description of the subject.[2] The oxymoronic title suggests a grotesque comparison: that æsthetic considerations should be equated to moral argument and that the suffering of salon-bound literati can be likened to that of a man put to death. Such invidious comparisons imply that France should continue to kill its criminals, but refrain from discussing or depicting executions. Hugo's evident sarcasm here argues compellingly against anyone who would criticize the work for æsthetic reasons and thus forces his readers to consider its ethical dimension alone: a stunning argument.

Indeed, it is hard to read the novel without experiencing a deep feeling of revulsion at the *condamné*'s predicament, for it is the act of reading itself that propels the *condamné* towards his death. Its words are the hero's life, and as each one is read he has less time to live. There is an awkward plot-turn whereby the condemned prisoner, writing away in his cell, is interrupted by his jailer to learn that he will die within twelve hours. Further, images of execution are written into the text at every turn, as though echoing the thought that causes the criminal to suffer. His life is thus "cut" into two parts, before and after his sentencing; images of decapitation also pervade his thoughts awake and asleep; his thoughts are fixed on the "head" of state, who alone has the power to pardon him; the text is inconclusive, cut off, as it were by the words "quatre heures," the time at which he was to be taken to the scaffold; the story of his life is missing from the text. It is quite tempting indeed to sum up the novel with the narrator's own words:

> Ils disent que ce n'est rien, qu'on ne souffre pas, que c'est une fin douce, que la mort de cette façon est bien simplifiée.
> Eh ! qu'est-ce donc que cette agonie de six semaines et ce râle de tout un jour ? Qu'est-ce que les angoisses de cette journée irréparable qui s'écoule si lentement et si vite ? Qu'est-ce que cette échelle de torture qui aboutit à l'échafaud ? (Hugo 1985, 1:473)

> [They say that it is nothing, and that one does not suffer; that it is a painless end, and that death has been much simplified by this invention.
> What about this six weeks of agony, and this death-rattle which lasts a whole day ? What about the indescribable agony of this day, which passes so slowly and yet so quickly ? What about this long ladder of tortures which leads up to the scaffold? (Hugo 1894, 444)]

But is it decapitation that causes this revulsion? After all, this is a first-person narrative, and the conventions of this form stipulate that the writer be alive at the moment of writing. Yet the revulsion is there, due to the expression by the narrator of his terror at anticipating death and to a *propter hoc ergo post hoc* conclusion that he has died. But there is more to the novel than an obsession with the guillotine: reflections on incarceration, prison's effects on prisoners, jailers, and wardens, the effects of punishment on those not punished, and so forth.

It might be useful at this point to mention a text to which *Le Dernier Jour d'un condamné* may be compared, the 1821 *Soirées de Saint-Pétersbourg* of Joseph de Maistre. As much in favor of the death penalty as Hugo was opposed to it, de Maistre conceived of punishment as the essential guarantee of law and the executioner as the necessary agent of such punishment. Laws are not obeyed out of respect for the good they can do or the order they impose but for fear of the punishment inflicted when they are broken; the chief role of the sovereign is that of judge. Referring to a Hindu text arguing that punishment alone governs humanity, de Maistre states: "je ne crois pas qu'il soit possible d'exprimer avec plus de noblesse et d'énergie cette divine et terrible prérogative des souverains: La punition des coupables" (de Maistre 1980, 1:31) [I do not think it possible to express with greater nobility and energy the terrible prerogative of sovereigns: the punishment of the guilty (author's translation)]. Such emphasis on penalties implies an agent to execute them, to punish, torment, and kill criminals: "De [là] . . . résulte l'existence nécessaire d'un homme destiné à infliger aux crimes les châtiments décernés par la justice" (de Maistre 1980, 1:32) [Whence the necessary existence of a man destined to inflict on crimes the punishments imposed by justice]. De Maistre thus portrays sovereignty as expressed completely by a man who is nonetheless excluded from all intercourse with society, a pariah and scapegoat:

> il naît comme nous; mais c'est un être extraordinaire, et pour qu'il existe dans la famille humaine, il faut un décret particulier, un fiat de la puissance créatrice. Il est créé comme un monde. . . . À peine l'autorité a-t-elle désigné sa demeure, à peine en a-t-il pris possession, que les autres habitations reculent jusqu'à ce qu'elles ne voient plus la sienne. C'est au milieu de cette solitude et de cette espèce de vide formé autour de lui qu'il vit seul avec sa femelle et ses petits, qui lui

font connaître la voix de l'homme; sans eux il n'en connaîtrait que les gémissements (de Maistre 1980, 1:32–33)

[he is born as we are, but he is an extraordinary being, and in order that he may exist within the human family, a particular decree, a fiat of creative power, is necessary. He is created like a world. . . . Scarcely have the authorities designated his dwelling-place, scarcely has he taken possession of it, than other homes withdraw until they do not see his place. It is in the middle of this solitude and this sort of vacuum formed about him that he lives with his female and his young, who recall the human voice to him; without them all he would know would be moans (author's translation)]

This exclusion of the executioner from society is central to de Maistre's argument. To justify the sovereign's violence, de Maistre separates him (and his agent, the executioner) from society, which is universally afflicted by Original Sin: corrupt and deserving of punishment. On the one hand, the sovereign and his agent, performing a violence criminal at anyone else's hands; on the other, a population deserving of punishment whether criminal or not. Insisting on the essential justice of punishment, de Maistre voices the rarely-heard argument that it would be better to err on the side of a too frequent use of the death penalty than to fail to punish malefactors:

Comme il est très possible que nous soyons dans l'erreur quand nous accusons la justice d'épargner un coupable, parce que celui que nous regardons comme tel ne l'est réellement pas; il est, d'un autre côté, également possible qu'un homme envoyé au supplice pour un crime qu'il n'a pas commis, l'ait réellement mérité par un autre crime absolument inconnu. (de Maistre 1980, 1:35)

[Just as it is entirely possible that we are in error when we accuse justice of sparing a guilty criminal, because the man we are considering is not; so also is it, on the other hand, equally possible that a man sent to the scaffold for a crime that he has not committed merits that fate for another, entirely unknown crime. (author's translation)]

It would be hard to imagine a theory of law more opposed to Hugo's, which presupposes the essential good of man, the possibility of redemption, and the need for education to nurture the former and enable the latter. It would be hard too to imagine an argument more different from Hugo's, which at every turn insists on the similarity of the executioner and his victim. First and foremost, the sovereign and the *condamné* are bound with a curious bond: Bicêtre possesses "un air de château de roi" (Hugo 1985, 1:436) ["the air of a royal chateau" (Hugo 1894, 360); when he witnesses the chaining of the convicts, the jailer tells the *condamné* that from his vantage point he will be "comme le roi" (Hugo 1985, 1:443) ("like the king" (Hugo 1894, 379). The king's agents are not extraordinary, but excessively ordinary: far from exhibiting some divine exemption, they are the products of their surroundings, to the point where they resemble their jails and dungeons. Their minds are not different from those of others, but fundamentally like them. The "justice" that sends men to the scaffold is not a reflection of divine providence, but the result of a procedure so human that even prisoners can plausibly mete it out.[3] The echoes and reversals that punctuate Hugo's texts on punishment, and their logic, imply a clear meaning: if the judge cannot be distinguished from the accused, if the jailer cannot be told from the jail, if the executioner is a man like the condemned, it can hardly follow that justice is anything but human and thus subject to all of men's failings. The expansive tendency of Hugo's argument, while typical of his style, also serves an argumentative purpose by undermining the fundamental presuppositions of death-penalty advocates such as de Maistre.

As a result of this conflation of prisoner and jailer, jailer and jail, executioner and victim, Hugo's argument, as much as it might be intended to combat the death penalty, becomes a comment on the penal system. This is of course a plot necessity deriving from Hugo's choice of first-person narrative—the condamné cannot be dead, and the book must take place somewhere. It is however also a result of the fundamental similarity between the death penalty and the effects of incarceration. If Hugo is to oppose the death penalty, he must somehow favor incarceration: there is no other option in this woeful debate. But a force is present in *Le Dernier Jour* that assimilates incarceration and decapitation, effectively undermining the essential argument, the argument that is so important that Hugo saw fit to underline it twice, by his additions of introduction and preface. To say that the penal system puts prisoners to some sort of legal or social death is to make the death penalty a death along a continuum of deaths and thus not extraordinary at all.

This tendency in Hugo's text has been noted by several authors, and probably first of all by the author himself. Thus, in a book emphatically not about the death penalty, but rather about an alternative to it, *Le Dernier Jour* serves as an illustration not of execution but of incarceration. (Foucault 1974, 300). Foucault's *Surveiller et punir* begins with an extended account of the extravagant suffering visited upon criminals under the *ancien régime*. Not simply were they executed with a cruelty whose inventiveness was matched only by its violence, but they were made to endure, before dying, injuries whose sole purpose was to recall the harm they did with their crimes. By comparison, the sheer uniformity of capital punishment by means of the guillotine appears banal, even merciful. Foucault is hardly interested, however, in this evolution in the death penalty. His attention goes instead to the subsequent choice of incarceration, and the development of a penal system one of whose avowed aims is to improve the criminals it shuts in, but whose acknowledged effect is to produce an entire class of delinquents. What Foucault argues is that the penal system that arose to implement judicial sentencing has usurped much of the power of the courts. Further, this system is structurally identical to that used in other institutional settings, where the control of large numbers of people is an aim: schools, hospitals, offices, and factories.

A work of architecture is what Foucault chooses to exemplify the system's workings: the 1791 Panopticon, a model prison designed by Jeremy Bentham.[4] In the Panopticon, cells are arranged in a circle around a central observation-post, their inner wall barred and exposed to the view of the observer, who is sheltered from the view of the prisoners. The prisoners, always on view; the guard, always able to view whichever prisoner he chooses while remaining invisible to them. This is the model of surveillance, generating its own structures of power, which Foucault then exposes: in prisons, the classification of prisoners according to the severity of their crime; the authority, wielded by the guards, to move prisoners into and out of solitary confinement; the authority to release (or to recommend release) of prisoners "for good behavior." Such a system of observation, rewards, and punishments amounts to a para-judicial network that duplicates the judicial system, but unlike its model, answers only to itself.

The prison system has used its "educational" or "reformist" mandate to create structures of power which operate without respite on their prisoner objects and which fail to realize their stated ambition. Instead, they have created petty differences: privileges and punishments imposed by prison professionals, whose aims are different from those of the judges serving in the courts. The prison system functions by classifying, locating, scheduling, and disciplining the population it houses and by monitoring the comings and goings of those it has released. As it exercises those prerogatives, it mixes convicts and ex-convicts, first-time prisoners and recidivists, and effectively educates them to become repeat offenders or perpetual delinquents. Most disturbingly, this system is invisible to the judicial system that uses it, as well as to those it employs.

The prison system is a modern invention. Foucault frequently employs a binary historical opposition that opposes "now" to "before," where "before" is the *ancien régime* and "now" refers to the modern period. In other parts, where a more striking antithetical contrast is sought, Foucault opposes the modern period to antiquity, as in this passage concerning the revolution brought about by the Panopticon:

> Notre société n'est pas celle du spectacle, mais de la surveillance; sous la surface des images, on investit les corps en profondeur; derrière la grande abstraction de l'échange, se poursuit le dressage minutieux et concret des forces utiles; les circuits de la communication sont les supports d'un cumul et d'une centralisation du savoir; le jeu des signes définit les ancrages du pouvoir; la belle totalité de l'individu n'est pas amputée, réprimée, altérée par notre ordre social, mais l'individu y est soigneusement fabriqué, selon une tactique des forces et du corps. (Foucault 1974, 252–53)

> [Our society is not one of spectacle, but of surveillance; under the surface of images, one invests bodies in depth; behind the great abstraction of exchange, there continues the meticulous, concrete training of useful forces; the circuits of communication are the supports of an accumulation and a centralization of knowledge; the play of signs defines the anchorages of power; it is not that the beautiful totality of the individual is amputated, repressed, altered by our social order, it is rather that the individual is carefully fabricated in it, according to a whole technique of forces and bodies. (Foucault 1977, 217)]

The opposition is too simple to employ chronologically, and Foucault goes to great pains to show how this evolution cannot be reduced to a punctual revolution. He points out, for example, that "discipline" existed under the *ancien régime*, where, for example, during times of the plague, the social equivalent of a lock-down was used to prevent further spreading of disease; by contrast, even as society seeks more and more to use the penal system to render "justice," the displays associated with ancien régime torture live on: Foucault cites "le grand spectacle de la chaîne" (Foucault 1974, 305) ["the great spectacle of the chain-gang" (Foucault 1977, 262)] of July-Monarchy France, as if to prove that the institution of the prison changed nothing.

Aware that it is futile to categorize punishment according to chronological criteria, Foucault cites structural criteria with somewhat clearer results: what distinguishes the two systems are different structures of observation, differences between who does the observing, and how many are observed:

> L'Antiquité avait été une civilisation du spectacle. « Rendre accessible à une multitude d'hommes l'inspection d'un petit nombre d'objets » : à ce problème répondait l'architecture des temples, des-théâtres et des cirques. . . . L'âge moderne pose le problème inverse : « Procurer à un petit nombre ou même à un seul la vue instantanée d'une grande multitude. » (Foucault 1974, 252)

> [Antiquity had been a civilization of spectacle. "to render accessible to a multitude of men the inspection of a small number of objects": this was the problem to which the architecture of temples, theatres, and circuses responded. . . . The modern age poses the opposite problem: "To procure for a small number, or even for a single individual, the instantaneous view of a great multitude." (Foucault 1977, 216)]

Foucault thus discerns a fundamental difference between modern times and earlier times in the treatment society reserves for those whom it would punish, and overlays this difference with a structural model where the observer is opposed to the observed. Both the opposition of subject and object and the distinction of present and past are essential elements of Hugo's account of the condemned man's last day and are fundamental to Hugo's poetics. This is so much the case that it is legitimate to ask whether Hugo chose the topic of his novel because it illustrated these concepts so well, or whether he prolonged and developed these concepts because they were so productive in *Le Dernier Jour*. When comparing Hugo's novel to Foucault's work, another aporia comes to the fore: given the resemblance between the novel and the essay, and the concomitant fact that they nominally treat different subjects, can one say that one subject is subordinate to the other? That the modern death penalty is merely an individual manifestation of the penal system? Or, on the other hand, that the regimentation and the discipline of the penal system are simply minor manifestations of the power displayed at full strength in the death penalty? Arguments could easily be made in both senses, showing the cruelty of prisons, hospitals, and even schools, or showing, on the other hand, that execution is simply the extreme point of a logic that sorts, labels, encloses, and trains.

"Autrefois" and "maintenant" are the words the *condamné* uses to order his life: before sentencing, there was freedom, movement, and pleasure, and that, even if he was a convict facing life imprisonment, since his sentencing, he has been unable to move, feel, or think: his life has been turned inside-out, even if its events and circumstances remain identical to those that immediately preceded his last day in court. The opposition, both antithetical and chronological, is extraordinarily rich for Hugo. It structures his poetic masterpiece, *Les Contemplations*, which it divides into two parts. It structures the poem "Ô strophe du poëte, autrefois, dans les fleurs . . ." (Hugo 1985, 5:455–56). It underlies the temporality of *Notre-Dame de Paris*, where gothic exuberance is compared favorably to modern parsimony. What Hugo does with the opposition, however, is more important than its ubiquity: in every case, freedom, sensuality, and pleasure characterize the world of "before"; constraint, enclosure, imprisonment, and economy characterize the world of "after." It is not much of a step to see in the former an illustration of the æsthetic attitude, which is characterized by freedom and pleasure,[5] and in the latter an exemplification of cognition. Since Kant's third *Critique*, æsthetic pleasure has been considered as distinct from cognition or understanding, and often, the replacement of the former by the latter has been depicted as a loss. Hugo certainly adheres to this view: when poetry ceased being pastoral or lyric and became philosophical or contemplative, he writes, something was lost, but something too was gained. Certainty replaces pleasure; knowledge has a value comparable to that of delight.[6]

It is common for Hugo to depict understanding with images of enclosure or imprisonment: understanding is achieved only by using systems of thought, systems that do not allow the free play characteristic of æsthetic pleasure. Whether figured as the grid pattern of modern streets, as in *Notre-Dame de Paris*, or the use of logic and criteria, as in "Ô strophe du poëte . . .," rational thought is presented as confining, and images of prisons, wards, and tombs come to mind. At the same time, such thought is presented as powerful, possessing the ability to coerce agreement, an ability never ascribed to æsthetic thought, which, as Kant so succinctly put it, "has often enough to put up with a rude dismissal of its claims to universal validity" (Kant 1952, 54). The ability to extract agreement from a resisting interlocutor through logical argument is a form of power, a power circumscribed by the limitations of systematic thought. Hugo represents this limited thought with the figure of an imprisoned monarch: in "Ô strophe du poëte . . .," contemplative poetry presides as the queen of the underworld, possessing power but only in the dark dominions of Hades. In *Ruy Blas*, Marie de Neubourg has the power to do anything she wishes, the ability to exile and to promote, provided only that she remain within the tight bounds of court protocol.

If the same constellation of ideas is viewed from Foucault's perspective, a comparable linkage between external, concrete events or sensations and internal modes of thought becomes visible. To take the nominal subject of *Surveiller et punir*: the prison system that arose to take the place of corporeal punishment has, over the decades, become internalized. The physical punishments of yesterday were replaced with the petty vengeances of bureaucrats now; the chains of prisoners have been replaced with expectations and anticipated sanctions; their cells are replaced with lines on tables and spaces on forms. The wrath that used to be exercised on their bodies is now registered in their bodies, their "corps dociles."

At the same time, the penal system has become increasingly rational: it gives itself a rationale—to "correct" deviant behavior—and it implements that program with various plans. Prisoners (but also patients, students, and others) are labeled, classified, and distributed; minor judgments are exercised at all points of their programmed existence; conformity to a rational model is both expected and enforced. The amount of record keeping required is prodigious, for each of these steps is a step in a bureaucracy that must justify its existence. This inscription is so important that one could consider it the real force behind the penal/medical/scholastic institution: as one enters into the institution, one enters into a world of records, records of judgments written as much on paper as they are on men's souls. In such a system, each observer keeps a record of the observed and expects too to be observed and recorded in his or her turn, which implies the extension of the system well beyond its initial bounds, to any area touched by its particular bureaucracy.

For Hugo, it is this writing that is the center of the system: no one can write without subjecting oneself to the laws of writing, which ultimately record oneself. This is scarcely visible in *Le Dernier Jour*, where the *condamné* alone seems subject to the weight of the judgment imposed on him. Even other prisoners are happy and carefree by comparison with him. However, his inscription in the system (where, of course, he leaves a written record of his existence, just as the previous occupants of his cell did before him) comes to imply others: his warden, for instance, is obsequious before him as he leaves for the scaffold. "Le directeur . . . a exprimé le désir que je n'eusse pas à me plaindre de lui ou de ses subordonnés" (Hugo 1985, 1:453) ["The Warden . . . expressed a hope that I had no complaint to make of him or his subordinates" (Hugo 1894, 398)]. Evidently, someone to whom he answers supervises his work, to fault him when complaints are made. One wonders, however, where the suggestion-box would be located. The prison thus affects not simply those who are being punished (or corrected), but anyone who comes into contact with it, so much so that, like Foucault's *corps dociles*, bodies are molded by the penal system to the point where the prison is inside them. Hugo's jailers are also prisons: "Ce bon geôlier, avec son sourire bénin, ses paroles caressantes, son œil qui flatte et qui espionne, ses grosses et larges mains, c'est la prison incarnée, c'est Bicêtre qui s'est fait homme" (Hugo 1985, 1:453) ["The good jailer, with his benign smile, his honied words, his eye which fawns upon you and watches you at the same moment, and his great, coarse hands, is the incarnation of the prison,—he is Bicêtre made man" (Hugo 1894, 399)].

Here is the moment where the *condamné* most resembles the writer. In the final line of "Ô strophe du poëte . . .," for example, Hugo writes that with poetry's adoption of the contemplative mode, now queen of the underworld, she sits on her throne "feuillette[r] le registre" of passions. Poetry: passive, judging, supervisory; the passions: objects of her judgment. One detects a comparable closing-in and darkening of vision in "On vit, on parle . . ." as the career of writer becomes clearer and more restrictive.[7]

It is not the hygiene of letters, though, that constitutes its prison-like structure, however Hugo might have lived it. It is writing itself, the fact that writing lives on as the trace of thought, that makes it dreadful. Take the fall of Ruy Blas: he is done in by his former master Don Salluste, but only because his signature and the title of lackey mean something. Another man might simply have repudiated his master and denied the authenticity of his sworn statements: that Ruy Blas believes he is bound by them, regardless of his worth or the viciousness of Don Salluste's machinations, means that for him, writing is a prison. Hernani's promise to Dom Gomez is in the same category, as is Monsieur Madeleine's rising to identify himself as Jean Valjean when another man is accused of being that ex-convict. These performatives that bring an indicting past are certainly figures of writing, but so are other figures. Olympio's descent on the circular stairway of memory figures the introspective turns of writing, writing that only allows one to go "deeper" because with each turn of the screw, it generates a record of the current state of reflection. The disappearance of the sensory world before the eyes of the thinker in "La Pente de la rêverie" depicts writing, as do most figures of contemplation: the loss of sense-certainty accompanies the growing conviction that metaphors and tropes have meaning. In the same way, the increasing importance of phantoms and spirits, especially visible in *Les Contemplations* is a correlate of Hugo's commitment to writing: when, for example, he asks the spirit in "À celle qui est restée en France" (Hugo 1985, 5:553) to sit up and hold the book, one must assume that it is the tangibility of the words in the book, and the fact that the words in the book are the words one is reading, that permits the perception of the invisible, the phantom of his dead daughter. She, of course, is buried in France, forever imprisoned in a coffin there, unlike her living father.

This is not just Hugo's problem either. Fredric Jameson, quoting Nietzsche, speaks of the "prison-house of language" (Jameson 1975), the effect that results when language's limitations on consciousness are perceived. And Foucault, in his analysis of the "système carcéral," as it has come to be known over the past two centuries, describes a system that distinguishes one population (criminals) from another, that weaves a "tissue" [*tissu*] of relations between different instances of power, and that endures and expands because of the power relations it creates for its employees to use. It is as if writing were a prison, and prison were a form of writing: the two institutions imply each other.

Foucault's analysis can hardly be improved on. But what does such an identification do for readers of literature in general, and readers of Hugo in particular? The implication is that writing is confining, that each word written entails a loss of freedom. Each sentence is a commitment or engagement restricting possible later choices and so much so that a poem, story, or play resembles nothing so much as a journey through a building where doors lock automatically behind one. The reader, whose options for interpretation decline in number as she progresses in the text, senses an entirely comparable loss of freedom. Hugo's text thus allegorizes writing and reading, and these ready echoes inevitably produce pathos and empathy for the convict.

What Hugo and Foucault agree on is that the prison defines a set of social expectations and a corresponding set of behaviors. Incarceration, whether physical or imagined, produced a space of confinement, a space defined by social systems and reflecting those systems. Physically, this space is the penal system; psychologically, this space is literacy. If prisoners become numbers, poets become words, but both experience these transformations as losses, as deprivations. Inevitably, it seems, these facts—sources of pathos when one reads for the sociological content of the novel—become images of writing itself. And while there is no great surprise in learning that prisoners do not appreciate physical confinement, it might be news that literacy could be experienced as something other than liberation. In the case of Hugo, where he stages writing as the product of confinement and coextensive with confinement, there can be no doubt.

Certainly writing is implicated in "Une Comédie à propos d'une tragédie," where the "Chevalier" remarks ruefully "depuis la prise de la Bastille on peut tout écrire" (Hugo 1985, 1:428) ["since the Bastille fell anyone can write anything" (Hugo 1894, 345)]. To this the "Monsieur Maigre" obliviously replies "Le moyen qu'un juré condamne après l'avoir lu!" (Hugo 1985, 1:428) ["How can any jury convict after reading it?" (Hugo 1894, 345)]. When these characters condemn the book they are of course killing the messenger, but, as a matter of fact, in Hugo's thought writing has many points in common with death.

The novel is so constructed that its very publication constitutes another sign that the convict has been put to death, and his last two words—QUATRE HEURES—join the names and dates scribbled on the walls of his cell to sum up the abbreviated lives of the people they designate. But the most pathetic of these allusions to writing is without doubt the scene where the convict sees his daughter once again, and where she demonstrates to him her progress in learning to read: what she reads is what she has in her hand, the flyer sold outside on the place where the scaffold is set up, and which announces his execution: "—A, R, *ar*, R, Ê, T, *rêt*, ARRÊT . . . Je lui ai arraché cela des mains. C'est ma sentence de mort qu'elle me lisait" (Hugo 1985, 1:478) ("S, e, n, *sen*, t, e, n, c, e, *tence*, SENTENCE—" I snatched it out of her hand. It was my own death-sentence she was reading me!" (Hugo 1894, 354–55)]. Like his text, this one is truncated, incomplete. This one announces his death, but even if it did not it would suggest it, for what writing announces (because its function is to survive) is death, and by this very capacity writing recalls death to us.

The extravagant display of sovereignty characteristic of earlier forms of punishment is not entirely gone: the inscription of crimes on the bodies of criminals is still performed, albeit metaphorically. As they enter the penal system, they are reduced to words, numbers, or units in a space divided into cells. This rigorous subordination to a rational system must entail some loss on the prisoner's part, if only of freedom, but probably of much more. Through conditions of incarceration and parole, through stigma attached to prisoners on release, the penal system writes the prisoner's crime deeply into his body in a torturous procedure that can only recall the gruesome practices of the pre penal era. This reflects of course a world unchanged by the penal institution, but also the nature of writing, which no penal system will ever change. And if writing is a prison, one cannot help but try to escape.

READING AND REFERENCE IN *NOTRE-DAME DE PARIS*

> . . . plastic forms were texts entrusted to stone, to lines or to colors; to analyze a capital or an illumination was to make manifest "what it meant": to restore language where, to speak more directly, it had been divested of its words.
> —Foucault (author's translation)

"Ceci tuera cela" (Hugo 1985, 1:617) [This will kill that (Hugo 1993, 190)]. Claude Frollo's famous reference to gothic architecture and printed books respectively has been easily accepted, too easily perhaps if one also accepts that books are not supposed to kill, and great works of art are not supposed to die. It is tempting, however, to see what has led to the present state of things as inevitable and thus as logical. There are more books now and fewer gothic cathedrals—revolutions helping here—and saying that the former caused the latter enables the sleep of reason to continue undisturbed. But as a member of the *Comité pour la préservation des monuments historiques*, Victor Hugo could hardly have believed that the disappearance of gothic architecture was inevitable, nor could he have believed that books such as *Notre-Dame de Paris* would spell the end of buildings such as Notre Dame de Paris. Implicit in the question of superiority is that of comparability: that plastic works should be compared to books is only logical, but to dismiss further consideration of that resemblance by saying that one will "kill" the other begs the question: are they fundamentally different?

The benign, consecrated explanation of the apparent contradiction appeals to an inflated sense of self and to a desire on the author's part to consider his works as equivalent or superior to the constructions of the past. However, when a reader learns of the book's ostensible superiority in a book of the same name as its doomed rival, when "ceci" refers to books in general, but also to the book she holds in her hand, when, by acceding to the author's assertion the reader only proves the merit of reading itself, it seems that this conclusion has been foreordained, and that Hugo is asking his reader to accept the "logic" of the statement in order to discourage her from reading any further.

Frollo's assertion stands thus as a sort of sibylline monument and even if it insinuates one interpretation by flattering one's knowledge of "history," its meaning remains obscure. Hugo himself said that the birth of printing caused the intensely variegated forms of gothic architecture to disappear, to be replaced by far less idiosyncratic forms. With the advent of literacy, there no longer was a need for plastic representations of religious beliefs, and indeed a century later an iconoclastic movement found itself at war with the church. Later, at the dawn of the "information age," Marshall McLuhan proposed a history which to all intents and purposes reads like another gloss on Frollo's:[1] print would bring about changes far from texts and scriptoria, affecting areas such as speech, national identity, and dress (McLuhan 1964). All these consequences are fascinating, but are they, even when they come from Hugo himself, readings of Frollo's phrase? What indeed is the force of the verb "tuer" here? Wouldn't "remplacer" or "supplanter" (considerations of prosody aside) have sufficed? Why the violence, or does in fact the passage from architecture to printed page involve a violence unpleasant to think about?

The inclination to follow the well-worn path of the history of ideas, which understands Hugo's aphorism as if it were a three-word abridgement of Hegel's *Æsthetik*, is all too great, and instead of looking for glosses for Frollo's phrase, it might be more illuminating to consider the context provided by the novel itself. "Ceci tuera cela" is uttered by Claude Frollo, as he languishes in his cell, a deacon hopelessly in love with the gypsy Esmeralda. He is no more capable of not loving the girl than he is of changing base metals into gold, or of reversing the course of history, represented to him by the printed book lying on his table. Thus when he scratches the word "'ΑΝΆΓΚΗ"[2] (Hugo 1985, 1:687) with his compass on the cell's wall, its meaning is overdetermined: it designates his fate to love, his fate to fail in his alchemical experiments, the cathedral's fated disappearance. Moreover, the first fate dictates the second, and the second echoes the third. This inscription moreover is itself doomed: centuries later, or so Hugo's note runs, the narrator himself finds the word "'ΑΝΆΓΚΗ" scratched on the cell-wall, and this word, the residue, as it were, of Claude Frollo's miserable existence, inspires the novel:

> Ces majuscules grecques, noires de vétusté et assez profondément entaillées dans la pierre, je ne sais quels signes propres à la calligraphie gothique empreints dans leurs formes et dans leurs attitudes, comme pour révéler que c'était une main du moyen-âge qui les avait écrites là, surtout le sens lugubre et fatal qu'elles renferment, frappèrent l'auteur . . .
> C'est sur ce mot qu'on a fait ce livre. (Hugo 1985, 1:491)

> [These Greek capitals, black with age and quite deeply incised into the stone, certain characteristics of Gothic calligraphy somehow stamped on their form and attitude, as if to reveal that it was a medieval hand that had written them, above all the dismal sense of inevitability conveyed by them, made a deep impression on the author . . .
> This book was written about that word.]
> (Hugo 1993, 7)

In a twist anticipating Marcel Proust's *À la recherche du temps perdu*, Hugo makes the story's product its origin, the concrete sign motivating the fiction that produces it, enabling it to be written in its turn. Thus, if the word cannot be found, there is no evidence for the story, while, conversely, its presence "proves" the story's veracity. The game delights and seduces, as it convinces the reader that if the sign existed, its referent must have too, and thus a real Frollo and a real Quasimodo lurk behind the cathedral's graffiti.

And there is more: "Depuis, on a badigeonné ou gratté (je ne sais plus lequel) le mur, et l'inscription a disparu" (Hugo 1985, 1:491) ["Since then the wall has been distempered or scraped [I forget now which] and the inscription has disappeared" (Hugo 1993, 7)]. "'ANÁΓKH" is written on the wall of the cathedral, and its longevity is limited only by that of the surface on which it is inscribed. But since the cathedral is doomed, it follows that "'ANÁΓKH" also is doomed. Having once advanced the Greek word as proof of his novel's truth, the narrator thus withdraws it and that proof becomes as evanescent as the fiction it motivates. Was the word ever there? Was it ever written? Did its writer exist? And more crucially, is the word not disappearing like the very cathedral on which it was supposedly written? Or even worse, doesn't the disappearance of the word now prove Frollo's assertion, "Ceci tuera cela"? For if the word disappears, it must be because its material substrate has been worn away or covered over with whitewash. At the same time, the disappearance of the word implies the disappearance of the novel, for without it, how could the novel have been written? The implications are maddening, and far from calming any anxiety surrounding the production of the novel, "'ANÁΓKH" exacerbates it.

Further illustration of this anxiety occurs later in the novel, when Jehan, Claude Frollo's younger brother, comes to visit him in the cell where the deacon has scratched his mark. As if to restore the reader's confidence in the novel's verisimilitude, Hugo writes: "Les personnes qui seraient curieuses aujourd'hui de visiter cette porte la reconnaîtront à cette inscription, gravée en lettres blanches dans la muraille noire: J'ADORE CORALIE. 1823, SIGNÉ UGÈNE. *Signé* est dans le texte" (Hugo 1985, 1:683) ["Anyone today curious to visit this door will recognize it from the following inscription, carved in white letters on the black wall: 'I ADORE CORALIE 1823. SIGNED UGÈNE.' The word 'signed' is in the text" (Hugo

1993, 284)]. If Hugo displays an almost obsessive need to point out the cell's location, these markers also share a common impermanence. The image of a palimpsest springs to mind, where one incised marker—"'ΑΝΆΓΚΗ"—is scratched out only to be replaced by another—J'ADORE CORALIE. 1823, SIGNÉ UGÈNE. On the one hand, Frollo's inscription might still be there, overwritten by many others: after all, there are so many words written in the stairs of cathedral towers: hasn't just one been written by someone other than a tourist? But on the other, the substitution of Frollo's *idée fixe* with UGÈNE's declaration reveals a very troubling possibility: now not only the presence of the sign, but its absence too serve as references for the story.

UGÈNE's graffito is troubling in another sense: the fact that the name is that of Victor's brother Eugène, who, in love with Adèle Foucher, went mad on the night of Hugo's marriage to her, has been commented (Robb 1997, 97–98). Beyond its circumstances, its content too is bizarre: that instead of "just" signing "UGÈNE," UGÈNE should also write that he is signing "UGÈNE" suggests vertiginous possibilities of using performative utterances to cast prior performatives as constatives. First, UGÈNE signs; then, UGÈNE writes that he signed ("SIGNÉ UGÈNE"). At this point, there is nothing to prevent him from saying that he wrote that he signed, or that he wrote that he said that he wrote that he signed, and so forth.

Thoughts of Marx and tragedy's replacement by farce are not entirely out of place here, for after all, Marx was talking about revolution and violence, and revolutionary violence—which defaced the cathedral—is one source of Hugo's anxiety. Nor is the palimpsest out of place, for what arouses Hugo's fears is the predicament of all writing, any inscription: its propensity to be erased, especially by another text.

Tellingly, the very passage where UGÈNE's graffito supplants Claude's contains a reference to the plastic arts. Hugo compares Claude's cell to one depicted by Rembrandt in his famous engraving of "Faust": "il y a en particulier une eau-forte qui représente, à ce qu'on suppose, le docteur Faust, et qu'il est impossible de contempler sans éblouissement" (Hugo 1985, 1:683) ["there is one etching in particular representing, so it is supposed, Doctor Faustus, which any viewer must find quite dazzling" (Hugo 1993, 284; figure 1)]. Although this cell is comparable to Frollo's ("Quelque chose d'assez semblable à la cellule de Faust s'offrit à

Figure 1. *Faust in His Study*, Rembrandt Harmensz van Rijn

la vue de Jehan") (Hugo 1985, 1:684) ["Something rather similar to Faust's cell presented itself to Jehan's eyes") (Hugo 1993, 284)], Faust's vision represents a success, the very success Frollo seeks in vain: the engraving depicts the moment when Faust looks up to see the secret of the kabbala revealed in his cell. For Frollo, by contrast, the only object available to fascinate him is "une ronde toile d'araignée" (Hugo 1985, 1:684) ["a circular spider's web" (Hugo 1993, 285)]. And if Frollo's search is for the secret word of wisdom—"il ne s'agit que de retrouver le mot magique" (Hugo 1985, 1:686) ["all that is needed is to find the magic word") (Hugo 1993, 288)]—the only word he can utter is "Esmeral," a mere fragment signifying the priest's loss of faith, his loss of alchemical abilities, his fall. On the one hand, the work of the visual artist depicts a moment of seeing, of understanding: Faust sees something; what he sees is a vision; what the vision reveals is a long-sought secret. On the other, what Frollo sees is only too common; his sight of the spider-web prevents him from learning the secret he so desperately seeks; the word he utters is the wrong word. Writing conceals vision.

One scratched word replaces another; one word is spoken where another is needed; but the engraving, by contrast, betrays no such fear. Writing only offers obstacles to pictures' tantalizing promises. What Hugo discovers and dreads is the endless substitution of one sign by another, a perspective that reduces all artistic effort to insignificance or madness: "SIGNÉ UGÈNE". Nor is this problem solved in any way by the printing-press, a conclusion that might be suggested by the fact that Rembrandt's work is engraved. If anyone knew just how ephemeral or incomplete a printed work could be it was Hugo, whose volume edition of *Bug-Jargal* entirely eclipsed its first publication in the *Conservateur Littéraire*, and whose "definitive" edition of *Notre-Dame de Paris*, ostensibly the eighth,[3] was only the first to include "Ceci tuera cela," either as a phrase or as a chapter.

The difficulty of the book's killing of the edifice has hardly been commented; Hugo invites his readers to think that reading is easy, and that there is no mystery to printing's sudden defeat of architecture. That texts require decoding is brushed away by Hugo's bland assurance:

> Qu'on ne s'y trompe pas, l'architecture est morte, morte sans retour, tuée par le livre imprimé, tuée parce qu'elle dure moins, tuée parce qu'elle coûte plus cher. Toute cathédrale est un milliard. Qu'on se représente maintenant quelle mise de fonds il faudrait pour récrire le livre architectural . . .
> Un livre est si tôt fait, coûte si peu, et peut aller si loin. Comment s'étonner que toute la pensée humaine s'écoule par cette pente? (Hugo 1985, 1:626)

[Make no mistake about it, architecture is dead, dead beyond recall, killed by the printed book, killed because it is less durable, killed because it costs more. Every cathedral is a thousand million francs. Now try to imagine what capital outlay would be needed to rewrite the book of architecture . . .
A book is soon finished, costs so little and can go so far! Why be surprised that all human thought should flow down that slope? (Hugo 1993, 204)]

The carving of an alphabet in millions of consciousnesses costs "si peu"; by contrast, a work in stone is expensive! Ernst Gombrich is of course correct to underline the extent of decoding involved in the reading of visual images (Gombrich 1969, 39). However deep this encoding may be, it is nowhere near as deep as that of texts and numbers, for which there exist institutions whose sole goal is to inculcate literacy and numeracy. While artists are indeed trained, the reading of their works is not taught by a corresponding institution, and no term—say, "iconacy"—exists comparable to "literacy." Nevertheless, Hugo presents printed works as "easier" than sculpture or architecture.

One reader who has responded to Hugo's insistent interrogation of writing's powers is Marcel Proust, but his debt to Hugo is hardly evident. The edition of À la recherche du temps perdu overseen by Jean-Yves Tadié counts only a handful of references to Hugo, and even these are strikingly ambiguous: at the salon of Mme de Villeparisis, Hugo's name, like that of Lamartine or Balzac, is a just synonym for "literature," while at Mme de Guermantes's, "Hugo" serves as a litmus-test for mastery of the canon. But even if it seems that any author's name would have sufficed in these passages, and that the generality of "literature" indicates no engagement of these texts by Proust, it is nonetheless a telling compliment: what is true of the poet will be true of all writing, and even Victor Hugo's stature can be increased by this assimilation. One might even hear an anxiety of influence when Proust dismisses Hugo in favor of Ruskin: "Le porche d'Amiens n'est pas seulement, dans le sens vague où l'aurait pris Victor Hugo, un livre de pierre, une Bible de pierre: c'est 'La Bible' en pierre" (Proust 1971, 88–89) ["This porch of Amiens is not merely a stone book, a stone Bible, in the vague sense in which Victor Hugo would have understood it: it is 'the Bible' in stone" (Proust 1987, 19)]. So, when Proust speaks of gothic cathedrals, as he often does, one should listen for echoes of *Notre-Dame de Paris*, just as Marcel searches Oriane de Guermantes's conversation for allusions to Hugo's poetry: his works, as part of the canon, are presupposed.

There are other reasons to invoke Proust: like Hugo, he was deeply interested in the relation of the plastic arts to literature, and like Hugo, Proust attempted to rally opposition to the destruction of cathedrals, albeit through laws concerning the status of religion under the Third Republic.[4] One of the more peculiar aspects of the resemblance Proust bears to Hugo is the conjunction of medieval sculpture and concern about the impact of art, a concern betraying a fear of violence: will gothic cathedrals' stone sculptures survive the tests of time? Certainly both writers could have chosen more recent works to elicit the question of art's longevity: sculptures that have been around for a thousand years tend to prove the permanence of art rather than its fragility. Proust's and Hugo's concern for art's durability arises then not so much from a desire for immortality, but from something else, and that of both of them is unwarranted by the actual state of the sculptures in question.

Proust's refutation of Hugo occurs indirectly, in his preface to (his translation of) Ruskin's *Bible d'Amiens*. Within this discussion of Ruskin's work, Proust alludes to a page of the very early *Seven Lamps of Architecture*[5] where a description not of Amiens but of Rouen cathedral is to be found. What is in question is initially the description and discovery, and later, the appreciation of a small sculpted figure of the "Portail des Libraires," that is, the north transept façade (figure 2). In this account, which Proust casts as a quest, he, accompanied by a friend, searches for a sculpture mentioned by Ruskin in *The Seven Lamps*, and having found it, goes on to assess the relation between criticism and works of art. Proust offers what appears to be a point-by-point rebuttal of Hugo: where Frollo's quest fails, Proust's succeeds, and he finds what he is looking for; where Frollo pronounces the wrong word, Proust's Ruskin names correctly; where Hugo sees a radical difference between the visual arts and writing, Proust only sees continuity: a sculpture is drawn, the drawing is described, the description is read, and through all these different media, a single message is transmitted.

The passage is conceived in terms that endow the critic with Christ-like attributes[6] and resonates with allusions to the liturgy,

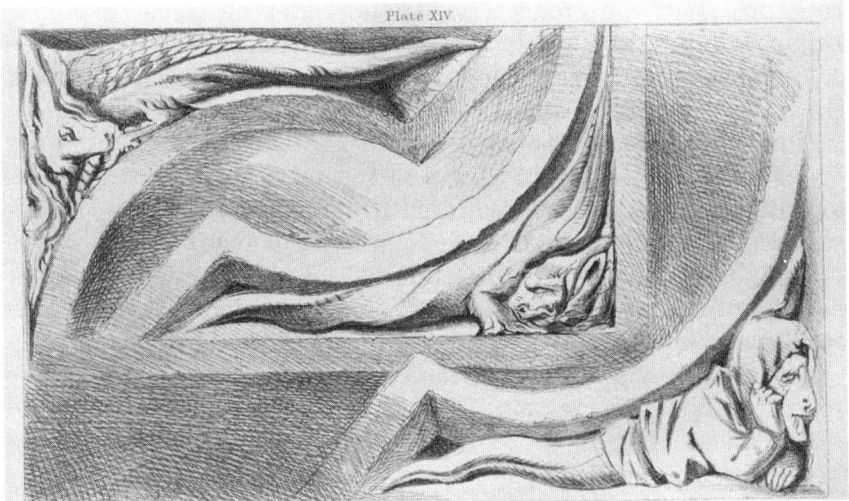

Figure 2. *Little Figure* of Rouen Cathedral, John Ruskin

a pervasive feature of Ruskin's prose but unusual in the case of Proust.[7] Here is the conclusion of Proust's commentary on Ruskin:

> Il l'a dessinée, il en a parlé. Et la petite figure inoffensive et monstrueuse aura ressuscité, contre toute espérance, de cette mort qui semble plus totale que les autres, qui est la disparition au sein de l'infini du nombre et sous le nivellement des ressemblances, mais d'où le génie a tôt fait de nous tirer aussi. En la retrouvant là, on ne peut s'empêcher d'être touché. Elle semble vivre et regarder, ou plutôt avoir été prise par la mort dans son regard même, comme les Pompéiens dont le geste demeure interrompu. Et c'est une pensée du sculpteur, en effet, qui a été saisie ici dans son geste par l'immobilité de la pierre. (Proust 1971, 125–26)

> [He made a drawing of it; he spoke of it. And the harmless and monstrous little figurine will have come back to life, against all hope, from that death which seems more total than the others, which is the disappearance into the midst of infinite numbers and the leveling down of similarities, but from which genius rescues us. Finding the figurine there again, one cannot help but be touched. It seems to live and to gaze, or rather to have been caught by death at the very moment of its gaze, like the Pompeians whose movements remain suspended. It is a single thought of the sculptor, in fact, that has been arrested here in its movement by the immobility of the stone. (Proust 1987, 46)]

Ruskin doesn't believe in death; Ruskin himself won't die; Ruskin, by finding, naming, describing, and drawing the "little figure" brings it back to life, abolishing death itself as he does so: "rien ne meurt donc de ce qui a vécu, pas plus la pensée du sculpteur que la pensée de Ruskin" (Proust 1971, 126) ["nothing therefore dies that has survived, no more the sculptor's thought than Ruskin's thought" (Proust 1987, 46)]. It would be hard to imagine a more seductive paraphrase of the Christian resurrection narrative; indeed, Proust himself establishes the analogy between the two stories with his reference to a Last Judgment sculpture on the tympanum of the central portal, and by naming Ruskin himself a Judge: "Tel qu'au jour du Jugement qui non loin de là est figuré ". . . le Juge a dit: 'Tu as vécu, tu vivras'" (Proust 1971, 126) ["As on the Day of Judgment, which is represented near by . . . he says 'Those who have lived will live'" (Proust 1987, 46)]. Ruskin rescues the little figure from a death caused by wear and erosion, but also from the death of going unrecognized, unappreciated, lost among thousands of other, similar sculptures. Writing does not "kill" sculpture, but brings it back to life. Further, even if Ruskin does describe the figure ("les nommant de leur nom" ["naming them by their names"]), Proust says that his procedures are also plastic: "Il l'a dessinée, il en a parlé" [He made a drawing of it; he spoke of it]. And it is these gestures—naming, drawing, speaking—that bring the sculpture back to life from the near-death where it lingered for so long: "Et la petite figure inoffensive et monstrueuse aura ressuscité, contre toute espérance, de cette mort qui semble plus totale que les autres" (Proust 1971, 126) ["And the harmless and monstrous little figurine will have come back to life, against all hope, from that death which seems more total than the others" (Proust 1987, 46)]. These endearing characterizations also promise that works of art will never die, provided that they are the subjects of criticism. If it suffices to point, to name, to draw, to judge, to describe—the gestures ascribed to Ruskin in Proust's story—in order to recall dying works from the dead, it follows that virtually any discussion of a text, a sculpture, a painting, or a building will endow its subject with immortality. This is a heady claim. And it becomes all the more so by virtue of the fact that it does what it describes, according to the conventions of performative language: by naming Ruskin a judge, Proust ascribes to him the power to name the figure, and his "correct" naming legitimates Proust's own naming of Ruskin as judge. But the gaze that Ruskin detects, the power that Proust finds in Ruskin's prose, might be there, and then again, they might not. Certainly, the insertion of these details within the context of a discovery narrative goes very far in suggesting their presence. What does happen however is that Ruskin attributes a gaze to the sculpture, and Proust attributes power to Ruskin, and such attributions require only reading to be felicitous. Moreover, since one's vanity as reader-who-would-be-writer is in play, it is impossible not to accept this invitation.[8]

For Proust, writing's promise is thus infinite. On the one hand, it distinguishes the sculpture from thousands of others, halting the erosion that destroys identity. Presumably, this function is accomplished by the name, endowed by the critic as though by the Good Sheperd: "les nommant de leur nom." But the sculpture also recovers its gaze, its "regard," and thereby communicates the sculptor's thought. Here, it is not simply protected against time but acquires thought and a soul. "Resurrection" is thus not simply a guarantee of endurance, but a metaphor for life. Being the subject of Ruskin's description does not simply restore the sculpture to its initial state but in fact endows it with a soul or spirit, something it had never had: "Tu as eu raison de rester là, inregardé, t'effritant. Tu ne pouvais rien attendre de la matière où tu n'étais que du néant" (Proust 1971, 127) ["You were right to remain there, unlooked at, crumbling. You could not expect anything from matter, where you were but nothingness") (Proust 1987, 48)]. A product of thought, stone sculptures attract thought: "ce qui est sorti d'une pensée peut seul fixer un jour une autre pensée qui à son tour a fasciné la nôtre" (Proust 1971, 127) ("what emerged from one man's thought can alone one day capture another thought, which in turn has fascinated ours") (Proust 1987, 47–48). But these works go further: they select the critic who will describe them: "quelquefois l'Esprit visite la terre; sur son passage les morts se lèvent, et les petites figures oubliées retrouvent le regard et fixent celui des vivants qui, pour elles, délaissent les vivants qui ne vivent pas et vont chercher de la vie seulement où l'Esprit leur en a montré, dans des pierres qui sont déjà de la poussière et qui sont encore de la pensée" (Proust 1971, 127–28) ("sometimes the Spirit visits the earth; at his passage, the dead arise, the forgotten figurines reawaken and capture the attention of the living who, for them, forsake the living who are not alive and go seeking life only where the Spirit has revealed it to them, in stones that are already dust and yet still intellect" (Proust 1987, 48)]. The words "gaze" and "spirit" might suggest here that the critic is a creator, endowing inanimate objects with life, but in fact the relation is far more complicated: if they take their life from the critic, they also sometimes reduce him to the state of inanimate object. Like vampires or the undead, works of art take the life of those they touch. Thus, a "spirit," visiting the earth, enables a sculpture to respond to the reader's gaze, but also, and just as importantly, it enables the reader to discover the sculpture. It is not just Ruskin who resurrects the sculpture, or Proust who resurrects Ruskin, or the reader who resurrects Proust: it is also Ruskin who is resurrected in his reading of the sculpture, Proust who is resurrected in his reading of Ruskin, and the reader who is resurrected by reading Proust. Only print can produce this resurrection: the multiplication of readers occasioned by publication, together with the durability of stone, permits the chance encounter of a reader and a text. Many stones go unread; many would-be readers find no texts; on occasion, however, a text finds a reader and both come to life.[9]

Much more could be said about Proust's discussion of Ruskin's writing; for the present purposes, however, it suffices to consider Rouen a cathedral and Ruskin a writer, much like Notre-Dame de Paris and Hugo.[10] From this perspective, Proust's text responds to Hugo's claim that the book spells the end of sculpture and architecture: indeed, printed texts can remedy the deficiencies of unique works by offering the kind of immortality otherwise denied them. To "Ceci tuera cela," Proust responds "Tu as vécu, tu vivras" ["Those who have lived will live" (Proust 1987, 46)]. [11] This refutation of Hugo and its concomitant promise of renewed life are very gratifying, especially if one is a critic. It depends however on persistent slippages characteristic of Proust's æsthetics and writing. Ruskin names the figures on the church, but he names them "with their name"; he endows them with life, but they were already alive; they risk dying, but they were dead already. Someone rescued the forgotten sculpture, but one can't be sure whether it was Ruskin, Yeatman, or Proust. If it was Ruskin, something he did—but one can't be sure whether it is naming or drawing, describing or judging—brings the sculpture back from the dead. And finally, when the sculpture comes back to life, one isn't sure whether life is best characterized as "regard" or "pensée." Proust does however find life where Hugo found death, and death for Hugo is just as problematic as life is for Proust.

To do so, Proust has had to employ a concept of the sign that is ultimately denotative: when, for example, in his story, he says that Ruskin named the sculptures "with their name," this concept becomes apparent. While one can name as one pleases (and thus, there is no wrong or right name for a child, for instance), not simply does Ruskin here name the sculptures, but the name he uses is true. This implies that there is an immediacy, a presence to the sign that exists only in denotations: "Chaque fois que je crois à la vérité, j'ai besoin de la dénotation" (Barthes 1975, 71) ("... each time I believe in the truth, I have need of denotation" (Barthes 1977, 67)], Barthes said. The signifier is related foremost to its meaning, and secondarily, if at all, to other signifiers. Thus, the "little figure" Proust finds leads back to Ruskin's drawing which in turn goes back to the anonymous sculptor's work. Signs are transparent, uncluttered with reference to other signs, more like Faust's vision than Frollo's magic word.

What is at stake in this forgotten argument—and what elicits its accompanying insistence—is far from evident. It is plain, however, that Proust extends a hope—qualified as redemption or salvation—that he attaches to printed texts and that compensates for the effect of time on matter. What is equally plain is that this hope is not explicit in Hugo's text. And finally, since both texts thematize the relation of print to the plastic arts with such hyperbole—whether the effect is death or eternal salvation is of less importance—it is also evident that this relation is at the source of their anxiety. While it might be difficult to conceive why millennial monuments should arouse the pity of thirty-something writers, it is obvious that the task of transposition should elicit uncertainties about the very possibility of the project. Not surprisingly, these paradoxes of description are related to the ones that were elaborated by Hegel in his *Phenomenology* (Hegel 1977, 58–79); more surprisingly, though, Proust's mentor, Anatole France, returns to the same metaphors and the same story to discredit Hegel's analysis.

France's "Le Langage métaphysique" appeared in the 1892 collection *Le Jardin d'Épicure*. Through the character Polyphile, France argues that philosophical language, as exemplified by Hegel, is characterized by a vocabulary that has undergone such extensive transformations that it no longer claims any sensory reference: it is purely abstract. Like the stones of Paris or Rouen, it has been worn down, he asserts, only to add that it is just such "wear" that has allowed philosophers to assert this language's rigor. Philosophy is thus like old coins prized by collectors: "Ces pièces n'ont rien d'anglais ni d'allemand, ni de français; nous les avons tirés hors du temps et de l'espace; elles ne valent plus cinq francs: elles sont d'un prix inestimable, et leurs cours est étendu infiniment" (France 1921, 197) ["These pieces have nothing either English, German, or French about them; we have freed them from all limits of time and space; they are not worth five shillings anymore; they are of an inestimable value, and their circulation is extended infinitely" (France 1920, 208)]. Polyphile's irony, however, is clear: such wear could never increase a coin's value, and if the words of metaphysical language have lost their features, this loss is as tragic as the death of cathedrals and gothic sculpture:

> tous les mots du langage humain furent frappés à l'origine d'une figure matérielle et que tous représentèrent dans leur nouveauté quelque image sensible. Il n'est point de terme qui primitivement n'ait été le signe d'un objet appartenant à ce monde des formes et des couleurs, des sons et des odeurs, et de toutes les illusions où les sens sont amusés impitoyablement. (France 1921, 205)

> [all the words of human speech were in the first instance struck with a material type and that they all represented in their original freshness some sensible image. There is no term which was not primitively the sign of an object belonging to the common stock of shapes and colours, sounds and scents, and all the illusive phenomena whereby our senses are mercilessly cajoled. (France 1920, 214)]

There are certainly thinkers who could be identified as the target of Polyphile's irony; none is quite as apposite as Ferdinand de Saussure whose work in linguistics overlaps France's both logically and chronologically. Saussure's definition of the sign as part of a system of signifying oppositions (Saussure 1972, 160; Saussure 1959, 116), and comprised of a signifier and a signified, is often considered an expulsion of reference: meaning is generated by a system of oppositions within and among words, independently of any reference to things outside of language (Saussure 1972, 160). This simplification of Saussure's thought is reductive in the extreme, but it does permit the establishment of a link between France's article and Proust's essay: both writers voice a concern that concrete reference may be forgotten. France protests philosophy's claim to pure abstraction; Proust bemoans the loss of specific referents for literature.

Up to this point, the argument could be assimilated to other expressions of nostalgia, whether personal, artistic, etymological, or philosophic, where the compensatory value of novelty is nothing by comparison with what has been lost to the passage of time. Polyphile, however, now makes a startling claim: that old meanings are never lost but live on to inflect the sense of words even when they are taken with new meanings, returning like ghosts to exert an untoward influence on logical arguments, preventing philosophy from ever attaining the precision it seeks, and instead reducing it to superstition and ideology:

> si je connais que c'est avec les restes effacés et dénaturés d'images antiques et d'illusions grossières, qu'on représente l'abstrait, aussitôt l'abstrait cesse de m'être représenté, je ne vois plus que des cendres de concret et, au lieu d'une idée pure, les poussières subtiles des fétiches, des amulettes et des idoles qu'on a broyés. (France 1921, 211)
>
> [if I convince myself that it is with the defaced and disfigured remains of ancient images and gross illusions that philosophers represent the abstract, *ipso facto* the abstract ceases to be represented to my mind; I see nothing but the ashes of the concrete, and instead of a pure, immaterial idea, merely the finely comminuted dust of the fetishes, amulets, and idols that have been destroyed. (France 1920, 218–19)].

Discrediting philosophy's claim to make true statements, Polyphile asserts that metaphorical origins remain, still operative, under the surface of apparently abstract language. The argument appears subversive, but a consoling thought also pierces through: metaphors never die; language, no matter how abstract, always contains references to concrete things and never entirely escapes figurality. Jacques Derrida has summarized France's dialogue as a narration of philosophy's "white mythology": "Mythologie blanche—la métaphysique a effacé en elle-même la scène fabuleuse qui l'a produite et qui reste néanmoins active, remuante, inscrite à l'encre blanche, dessin invisible et recouvert dans le palimpseste" (Derrida 1972, 254) ["What is white mythology? It is metaphysics which has effaced [*sic*: "erased" transmits the sense I am following better] in itself that fabulous scene which brought it into being and which yet remains, active and stirring, inscribed in white ink, an invisible drawing covered over in the palimpsest" (Derrida 1974, 9)]. A primal scene of metaphorical substitutions lurks behind the serene surface of philosophical discourse, and just as one can see ancient etymons in modern words, even if those words are abstractions, so also can one see primitive beliefs in the language of philosophy. Not only does the past live on in current linguistic usage, but a past is privileged: each abstraction has an origin, an etymon possessing authority. Never mind that that origin came from somewhere, that there must be an etymon for the etymon, that the absence of earlier attestations can hardly prove that a root is original: one state of the language is true, and that state endures. Derrida unerringly identifies the logocentrism of this story; what does not retain his attention is what the story does not say: that every etymon has obliterated another one, just as metaphysics erases its own figurality.

Polyphile's claim is damaging: what is found in philosophy's avatars are "fétiches," "idoles," and "amulettes," the accessories of superstition and religion, but also representations or images of the divinities revered, and as such, works of art. Within abstraction, metaphor; at the heart of philosophy, fiction; the claims give ample reason to doubt philosophy's ability to generate true statements, but also imply that literature is the unrecognized origin of philosophy, and that whatever is lost in terms of truth is gained in terms of æsthetic play. Such an investment would explain why Proust elaborates his resurrection narrative, but it hardly explains why Hugo displays a concern and an anxiety out of proportion to the apparently inconsequential subject of his writing: it is not because it cannot preserve that writing does not preserve; it is because writing destroys. One does not forget as much as remember something else; it is not the scraping that renders the text on the parchment illegible as much as the text written over it.

When Proust and France claim that figures—whether stone sculptures or turns of speech—live on, they are making a bundle of claims: if a word's meaning lives on, despite language's efforts to purify itself of concrete reference, and poisons or perverts the "abstractions" derived from it, it is just as clear that no new language will ever be possible: traces of earlier states will forever be visible. And if a stone sculpture can come back to life, so can the past; if a work of art can regain its "gaze," no work of art ever dies; if prose can resurrect stone sculpture, prose can represent plastic form more generally. It is not simply the "life" of the author that is at stake but the possibilities of writing, and for Proust in 1900 such possibilities are clearly limitless.

This is not the case for Hugo. At the most general level, the difference is to be read in the tragic context of Hugo's depiction of the cathedral, a context very different from that produced by the repeated triumphs and revelations that characterize Proust's description of Rouen. More specifically, the treatment of the two engravings by the authors is telling: for Proust, Ruskin's engraving is simply a step in a continuous narrative that runs from search through discovery, drawing, naming, and describing, to resurrection. Plastic representation is entirely comparable to linguistic decoding. For Hugo, on the contrary, Faust's revelation of the mystic circle is absolutely incompatible, both in medium and in outcome, and despite the similarity of its context, with Frollo's frustrated search for a magic word. There is no continuity between Faust and Frollo; neither is there continuity between word and image. At the limit, texts do not transmit meaning as much as they create it, and that creation is always associated with the erasure of prior meaning.

This can only indicate a profound divergence between the authors concerning the effects of written language. For Hugo, a text replaces something else which is lost as the new text comes into being. Writing erases as much as it records, it supplants an earlier state and will be supplanted in its turn. When Hugo writes that "this will kill that," he means just that: writing destroys earlier texts. By contrast, Proust and France contend that language records and preserves: what is present in concrete figures lives on in words, and that presence can be transmitted from one text to another, conferring immortality on the presence, authority on the author. Such a contention should be recognized as a consolation for a loss that neither author cares to admit, and indeed it should be recognized as an entirely successful attempt to overwrite Hugo's text with the palimpsest of critical discourse.

3
Literary Accounts of the Visual Arts: Narrative, Citation, and Attribution
Painting Pictures with Words

CRITICS AGREE THAT *NOTRE-DAME DE PARIS* HAD ITS ORIGINS IN romanticism, but this assertion should not be understood too easily: the Gothic subject matter, the gloomy story, the local color and the hyperbole of the novel make it prototypically romantic, but the contention also addresses a rhetorical concern that preempts other descriptions and establishes strong links to Hugo's other works. This concern is what Pierre Leroux identified as "le style symbolique," and which revolves around a hope that poetic language on occasion points directly at meanings without passing through a decoding process. Leroux claimed that Hugo employed this "style" with a view to achieving greater "speed"; as motivations go, this is acceptable, but speed is not the only feature of this hoped-for language: direct communication, truth, reference, transparency, and many other valued concepts rely on this communicative short-cut, this ellipsis of decoding.

What was not plain to Leroux is that his friend Hugo was well aware of how seductive this language could be and how utopian it is too. Hugo weaves his signifiers into webs of meaning: even when he strives for simplicity, unequivocal meaning, a "mooring" in reality, his words are so embedded in the text that it becomes difficult to tell whether meaning derives from a referent or from reference to other terms. Dates may refer to his life but also to the fiction of Olympio's time-line; names might refer to persons but also to personifications; promises and oaths might divide narratives into moments "before" and moments "after" the linguistic act, but then again, they might not. Textuality always reasserts itself in Hugo's writings.

This is true even of ekphrasis, the word-pictures that describe pictures, monuments, and buildings: *Notre-Dame de Paris* includes many such pictures. Here, descriptions of art recede before Hugo's awareness of language, which is paramount for him. Where Hugo's novel had the greatest effect, however, is in the field of art criticism: Ruskin's outrage at Hugo's "immorality" certainly betrays a fear that Hugo was doing something here that endangered him. This "danger" is mentioned by Hugo himself in the famous phrase comparing sculpture to printed books: "Ceci tuera cela." If books endanger plastic works it is not because they are of a different medium; if anything, they are like architecture, sculpture, and pictures, for all of these media require reading, and reading implies a code. Hugo states as much when he call the cathedral a "vaste livre de pierre."

The danger books pose to architecture, sculpture, and painting is the danger books pose to books: writing tends to overwrite other writing, creating palimpsests where one hopes to find clear inscriptions. Indeed, there never is, nor has there ever been, any word written on a blank page: everyone uses used words, just as everyone drives a used car, and each word carries with it traces of prior use, traces conferring connotations, figural meanings, ambiguities, and other surprises. In this respect, a word is absolutely unlike a picture, which is supposed (but supposed only) to designate its meaning or its referent intuitively. In the myth of Zeuxis, birds—figures of unschooled readers possessed of no codes—recognized the grapes the painter had painted, and pecked at them, proving the excellence of his work (Bryson 1983). But this conception of the picture, and of representational art more generally, is founded on a notion of transparency that is questionable in the case of pictures, utopian in that of words.

This notion has famous defenders, and among them, Marcel Proust, where it appears most conspicuously in his art criticism. Since Proust's concept of the sign is elsewhere far more textual, the question arises: is endorsement of the myth of Zeuxis part of what could be called the discourse of art criticism? When one describes and evaluates representational art, is it somehow necessary to state that images can achieve unmediated significance, and that the only mark of quality in paintings or sculpture is its ability to do so?

In the following chapters, just how literature has taken up the challenge of the plastic image will be discussed: does it acknowledge that pictures can convey meaning directly? Does it claim that privilege for itself? Does it recognize a fundamental similarity between itself and the plastic image? These questions come up insistently in the art criticism of the century following *Notre-Dame de Paris*: this is only logical, for one task set for the art critic, if only as a phatic utterance (to establish what it is that is being discussed), is to describe the work of art. To describe a work of art is in some way to represent it, and if the art is representational, the representation of a representation results: comparisons between the two representations are inevitable, and any consequent author will follow this comparison, one which might very well bring her to reverse herself.

READING AND DENOTATION

Many difficulties face scholars who attempt to study across disciplines, and not the least of these difficulties are the institutional boundaries and methodological presuppositions defining the aims of work in different fields. Art history places tremendous importance on its historical method, for example, and this for many valid reasons. But if a scholar of literature whose training is in interpretation approaches a painting or a sculpture, she might find that the hermeneutic insights she brings are dismissed and her work scrutinized for historical insights that lack entirely. Even when a method is agreed upon, as is the case in some instances of cultural studies, it is rarely subjected to the kinds of rigorous examination that underlie strong claims to re-direct research in the humanities.

Such is the case of semiology, inaugurated a century ago by Ferdinand de Saussure,[1] which received a second wind in the fifties and sixties with the work of Roland Barthes, and which, since the advent of cultural studies, has enjoyed a new life as the model of a cross-disciplinary methodology.[2] The appeal of semiology is undeniable, even for those writers who discard most of the trappings of the field: an overarching discipline based on the linguistic model, it claims to offer a key to the analysis of most cultural offerings, of what Saussure called "les signes au sein de la vie sociale" (Saussure 1972, 33) ["signs within society" (Saussure 1959, 16)]. Not simply does it promise analyses already performed by Barthes—of fashion, of painting, of photography, of popular fiction, and of fads—but it does so by claiming that language (already familiar to any would-be analyst) is the originary interpretive model. Thus Barthes's decoding of Japanese culture rapidly followed his discrete analyses of Erte, Arcimboldo, and *Elle* magazine, and this in turn gave rise to other essays in comparable fields, Jean Baudrillard's *Amérique*, for example, Michel Foucault's famous chapter on *Las Meninas* (Foucault 1966), or even Jacques Lacan's reading of Holbein's *Ambassadors* (Lacan 1973).

Studies like Baudrillard's, Foucault's, or Lacan's provide fascinating insights into both their nominal subjects and their methods, but it appears that their interpretations or conclusions might not be as assured as those derived from texts. A case in point is Barthes's own "Rhétorique de l'image," where, under the guise of decoding a photographic advertisement, he shows how semiology performs the critical reading of a visual image and how this method contributes to understanding the photographic medium more generally.

The article appeared in *Communications* in 1964 (Barthes 1982), when Barthes took as his subject an advertisement by the Panzani corporation for several food products—cheese, tomato sauce, pasta—which were depicted among fresh produce— onions, peppers, tomatoes—spilling out of a *filet* posed on a tabletop. He showed how the overflowing *filet* served as an updated cornucopia, how the proximity of fresh produce implied "freshness" for the manufactured goods, and how the red, white, and green of the tomato, onion, and pepper respectively connoted the "Italianness" of the French company's offerings by invoking the colors of the national flag. Up to this point, Barthes's analysis could be considered little more than a brilliant interpretation of a well-constructed advertisement, replete with its "hidden persuaders" (Packard 1963); what makes his article significant for literary studies is his contention that in the advertisement, as elsewhere, two registers of meaning work against each other. On the one hand, there are "denoted" meanings: round forms of red, green and white represent tomatoes, peppers and onions, for example, in a kind of signifying that is only too familiar and always taken for granted. On the other, abstractions such as "freshness" and "Italianness" spring from definite codes: the cornucopia, a conventional symbol in the visual arts and possessing its own iconography; flags, conferring the status of "national colors" on certain groups of two or three primary colors. While the meanings of the first are evident, "transparent," those of the second are learned though the acquisition of codes; the former are "natural," the latter, "cultural"; the former are analogical, the latter are arbitrary. At this point Barthes introduces his most subversive claim: denotation serves here as everywhere to "naturalize" connoted meanings. Denoted meanings, which appear with the necessity of evidence, confer that necessity and that implication of self-evidence on signs that are neither necessary nor self-evident, the connoted meanings of pictures and texts. To return to the Panzani advertisement, just as one says that the red form can only "be" a tomato, one also says, based on that reading, that Panzani products can only be fresh or Italian. Denotation serves as a Trojan horse to bring all the complexities of coded ideological or commercial messages into any "reading" of what appears to be a simple photograph.

This reading is exemplary because it supplies a model for reading visual images in linguistic terms, because it subsumes the entire field of iconography into available semiotic codes, and because as a result of the foregoing it opens visual images to a wide range of ideological analyses. It relies, however, on the distinction of connoted and denoted meaning that Barthes first put forward in his *Éléments de sémiologie* (Barthes 1965, 163–68): denotation is the paradigmatic sign where a signifier simply signifies its signified. The canonical examples of this concept of the sign come from Saussure who in his *Cours de linguistique générale* exemplified the sign with an ideogram representing the sign split into signified on top, signifier on the bottom, using the word *arbor* for the latter, and an icon of a tree for the former.[3] By contrast, a connotation is a sign in which the signifier is itself a complete sign—signifier and signified—possessing its own signified, which is, needless to say, of considerable abstraction.[4] Thus, if one exemplifies connotation with the word *arbor*, the Latin signifier of course denotes a tree, but the use of this very example produces definite connotations: familiarity with Saussure's text, ironic distancing from that text, and so forth. It was connotation and its characteristics that Barthes championed: its arbitrariness, its multiplicity (that a single sign could have multiple significations in different codes), and its evident ideological content: "dans le système herméneutique, le signifié de connotation occupe une place particulière : il opère une vérité incomplète, insuffisante, impuissante à se faire nommer : il est l'incomplétude, l'insuffisance, l'impuissance de la vérité" (Barthes 1970, 68) ["in the hermeneutic system, the connotative signified occupies a special place: it brings into being an insufficient half truth, powerless to name itself: it is the incompleteness, the insufficiency, the powerlessness of truth" (Barthes 1974, 62)]. By contrast, denotation, which in 1964 "naturalized" connoted meanings, came by 1975 to form part of a repressive "truth" structure. In *Roland Barthes* of that year, he wrote: "La dénotation serait un mythe scientifique: celui d'un état 'vrai' du langage, comme si toute phrase avait en elle un *etymon* (origine et vérité)" (Barthes 1975, 71) ["Denotation would here be a scientific myth: that of a 'true' state of language, as if every sentence had in it an *etymon* [origin and truth]" (Barthes 1977, 67)].

Almost a decade before Barthes wrote his article on the advertisement, Ernst Gombrich gave a series of Mellon lectures at the National Gallery in Washington, later published as *Art and Illusion*. Although the present argument concerns not how images are formed, but how they are described, one of the recurring themes of Gombrich's book and lectures was that the evidentiary aspect of visual images is an illusion. There is nothing simple about the "resemblance" of a two-dimensional image to a three-dimensional form, and both the production and the reading of such images is every bit as informed by codes as that of texts. Viewers are trained to perceive depth in pictures, as they are trained to perceive superposition and roundness. While such training takes the form of repeated exposures to images rather than that of formal schooling, it is presupposed by painting and photography.

One prefers however not to acknowledge it, to claim that one perceives images rather than that one decodes them. This is so much the case that one readily confuses representations for what they represent, as if readings of representations were so obvious that the former could be taken for the latter. Such is the case of Condillac, who wrote that pictures were the "natural" means of representing words or actions, more direct or immediate than "later" written forms: "The most natural means was therefore to draw the pictures of things. To express the idea of a man or a horse the form of one or the other will be represented, and the first attempt at writing was but a simple painting" (Derrida 1982, 312). And yet later, Condillac asserts that painting differs from writing only by a number of degrees of complexity: "This is the general history of writing conveyed by a simple gradation from the state of painting through that of the letter" (Derrida 1982, 313).[5]

Such is the case of Hegel too, who, in the introduction to his *Æsthetics* asks rhetorically what an artist would do if the fish he had drawn were to rise up and speak against him:[6] the fish and its visual image resemble each other so much that the name of one can be used for the other. Or to return to Saussure: when, in his seminal distinction of signifier and signified, he needs an example, he uses an icon to exemplify a signified. While a word—*arbre*, for example—might lead to confusion as to whether its "concept" or "image acoustique" was in question, with a picture there is no such danger. A picture is thus supposed unfailingly and immediately to designate its signified.[7] This hope, optimistic at best, error-inducing at worst, certainly indicates the prestige of the image.

The art historian Janet Wolff points out that this method treats images as though they were signs, and this in two senses (Wolff 1992). Firstly, it is assumed that if they are signs, they are always denotative signs, the simplest kind of sign. Secondly, it is also assumed that they are transparent, that they efface themselves before their signifier. In both cases, there is an aspect of the plastic arts that escapes when the linguistic model is imposed too strongly. This aspect, according to Jean-Paul Sartre, is a quality of "things":

> L'écrivain peut vous guider et s'il vous décrit un taudis, y faire voir le symbole des injustices sociales, provoquer votre indignation. Le peintre est muet: il vous présente *un* taudis, c'est tout: libre à vous d'y voir ce que vous voulez. Cette mansarde ne sera jamais le symbole de la misère; il faudrait pour cela qu'elle fût signe, alors qu'elle est chose. (Sartre 1948, 62)

> [The writer can guide you and, if he describes a hovel, make it seem the symbol of social injustice and provoke your indignation. The painter is mute. He presents you with *a* hovel, that's all. You are free to see in it what you like. That attic window will never be the symbol of misery; for that, it would have to be a sign, whereas it is a thing. (Sartre, 1988, 27)]

While it is not obvious just what constitutes a "thing," it is clear that Sartre seeks to distinguish signs and plastic forms. When used to name things, signs recede and disappear in favor of what they name: "la nomination implique un perpétuel sacrifice du nom à l'objet nommé ou pour parler comme Hegel, le nom s'y révèle l'inessentiel, en face de la chose qui est essentielle" (Sartre 1948, 64) ["naming implies a perpetual sacrifice of the name to the object named, or, as Hegel would say, the name is revealed as the inessential in the face of the thing which is essential" (Sartre 1988, 29)]. If there is something that cannot be analyzed with the tools of semiology, it will not appear in interdisciplinary study.[8] Thus, Wolff quotes an expression of regret at the loss that the "new art history" (that is, interdisciplinary art history) experiences even as it extends into new domains: "When an article analyses the images of women in paintings rather than the quality of the brushwork, or when a gallery lecturer ignores the sheen of the Virgin Mary's robe for the Church's use of religious art in the Counter-Reformation, the new art history is casting its shadow" (Wolff 1992, 708).

To say that something is lost when the model of linguistic analysis is applied to plastic arts is evident; to say that what is lost is significant is not so. In the case of Barthes, however, the loss is perhaps greater than it would first appear. For example, even when it is accepted that he overstates his case when he contrasts denotative and connotative meaning in the Panzani advertisement, one still wonders whether Barthes's claim that visual images smuggle ideological significations into their understanding is not apposite. The argument that he has oversimplified the model of reading images would seem to have little impact on his conclusion. However, if one accepts also that apparently "denoted" meanings are not denoted at all, but are decoded according to strict (albeit habitual) rules, the argument suffers a setback. If denotations are always connotations in disguise, there is precious little "naturalization" they can do. Barthes thus can no longer claim that the first layer of interpretation is "natural" and thus, that images' denotations "naturalize" ideological significations. This "anti-natural" argument is particularly dear to Barthes, and to lose it because his model of denotation cannot be defended is of some consequence.[9]

One can quite easily wonder why Barthes would have overlooked Gombrich's work, or, more generally, an argument as evident as that put forward in *Art and Illusion*. Even if the work was not translated into French until 1971 one would think that

3: LITERARY ACCOUNTS OF THE VISUAL ARTS 113

someone as fascinated by codes and as sensitive to images as Barthes would have hesitated to invoke denotation in their case. Instead, eager to make the case for "plural" signification, Barthes recruits denotation as a bad cop who will become progressively more corrupt over the next dozen years. Barthes admits that denotation is a useful fiction, a sort of constable of the community of letters:

> *Dénotation/connotation*: ce double concept n'a donc de valeur que dans le champ de la vérité. Chaque fois que j'ai besoin d'éprouver un message (de le démystifier), je le soumets à quelque instance extérieure, je le réduis à une sorte de couenne disgracieuse, qui en forme le substrat vrai. L'opposition n'a donc d'usage que dans le cadre d'une opération critique analogue à une expérience d'analyse chimique: chaque fois que je crois à la vérité, j'ai besoin de la dénotation. (Barthes 1975, 71)
>
> [Denotation/connotation: this double concept therefore applies only within the field of truth. Each time I need to test a message (to demystify it), I subject it to some external instance, I reduce it to a kind of uncouth rind, which forms its true substratum. The opposition therefore only functions in the context of a critical operation analogous to an experiment in chemical analysis: each time I believe in the truth, I have need of denotation. (Barthes 1977, 67)]

What the essays that follow ask is whether what occurred to Barthes in this instance is not the fate of all interdisciplinary studies, whether attempts by literature to work outside of the discipline of letters (and certainly, Barthes did write literature) are not destined to retreat into literary formulations when they encounter the otherness of the discipline they encounter. The awkwardness of interdisciplinary studies might be likened to the efforts of blind men to understand a still-glowing meteor that has fallen to earth: each experience of the meteor will be brief and painful and will engender an attempt to account for it in terms whose familiarity belies the fundamental difference of the experience.

An obvious place to consider such questions would be Marcel Proust's "Sur la lecture," originally the preface to John Ruskin's *Sésame et les lys*,[10] an apology for the pleasures and virtues of reading in the increasingly materialistic society of nineteenth-century England. Proust reading Ruskin on reading has obviously to do with reading, but has also to do with another discourse: Ruskin's English, of course, but Ruskin's earnest, messianic and pedantic bent too, considerations far from Proust's acknowledged intent. Proust's essay appears as preface to his translation of *Sesame and Lilies*, where Ruskin pleads with his public to improve their reading: the quantity, the quality, and even the quality of the printing of the books they read. "Do you long for the conversation of the wise? Learn to understand it, and you shall hear it" (Wedderburn 1903–12). It quickly becomes apparent that Proust's conception of reading differs entirely from Ruskin's idea of "conversation." Days spent reading are precious days, he writes, but the pleasure one remembers of them might not be the one that one chose when one withdrew to read. "ce qu'elles [childhood readings] laissent surtout en nous, c'est l'image des lieux et des jours où nous les avons faites" (Proust 1971, 172) ["what it [reading] mostly leaves in us is the image of the places and the days when we did this reading" (Proust 1971, 27)]. Even if one did not "enjoy" the beautiful day and remained indoors to read, one's recollection could very well not be of the book read but of the day forsaken, and so much so that later, when one re-reads the book read long ago it is not to renew acquaintance with its author or its characters, but in order to find the room where one read it, or the day it was opened.

Reading is thus a substitutive process: in order to read, the reader substitutes one world for another; when she re-reads, the reverse substitution takes place. Whenever one reads, one's goal is far away. Further, reading, she reads with a different self than the self of social interactions, and this difference permits reading to be creative, and social interactions to be sterile.

This conception, of course, is not Ruskin's. *Sesame and Lilies* presents reading as a conversation-with-a-great-author,[11] a pleasure to be compared favorably to dining on delicate food or inhabiting a grand house. Proust, by contrast, considers reading an essentially solitary exercise: not simply does one retire from social interactions in order to read, reading is emphatically not structured like a social interaction. Reading produces a dialogue much different from the conversation one could conceivably have with an author, and this has everything to do with the social "strength" of the reader. There are readers, Proust writes, who would waste the conversation that takes place in the flesh, but who would engage in productive dialogue with the author's written text:

> cette impulsion que l'esprit paresseux ne peut trouver en lui-même et qui doit lui venir d'autrui, il est clair qu'il doit la recevoir au sein de la solitude. . . . De la pure solitude, l'esprit paresseux ne pourrait rien tirer, puisqu'il est incapable de mettre de lui-même en branle son activité créatrice. Mais la conversation la plus élevée, les conseils les plus pressants ne lui serviraient non plus à rien. . . . Ce qu'il faut donc, c'est une intervention qui, tout en venant d'un autre, se produise au fond de nous-mêmes, c'est bien l'impulsion d'un autre esprit, mais reçue au sein de la solitude. (Proust 1971, 180)
>
> [it is clear that this impulse which the slothful mind cannot find within itself and which must come to it from others must be received in the midst of solitude. . . . The indolent mind can obtain nothing from pure solitude since it is incapable of setting its creative activity in motion. But the loftiest conversation, the most pressing advice, would be of absolutely no use to it. . . . What is necessary, then, is an intervention which, while coming from another, takes place in our own innermost selves, which is indeed the impetus of another mind, but received in the midst of solitude. (Proust 1971, 41)]

Further, the "dialogue" of reading is essentially discontinuous and asymmetrical: authors might discuss subjects for eminently personal reasons and yet elicit a far more general reaction from their readers.[12] The text is the furthest point of the author's thought, yet it is just the beginning of his reader's; "ce qui est le terme de leur sagesse ne nous apparaît que comme le commencement de la nôtre" (Proust 1971, 177) ["that which is the end of their wisdom appears to us as but the beginning of ours" (Proust 1971, 35)]. A text that satisfies its author may only elicit desire in its reader. Reading is thus a withdrawal into solitude, a solitude where one comes into contact with an author, but this contact is attenuated in the extreme: there is no domination by the author; the reader is free to end the dialogue when she sees fit, with no consequences. Even when she is touched by the author's thought, that contact is oblique: what is an end for one is a beginning for the other; satisfaction for the first only initiates desire for the second. Reading nevertheless implies effort.

With his emphasis on "creation," Proust has defined reading as writing, or, more precisely, as interpretation: reading always implies the generation of a new text, a text tropologically related to the first: not a copy, but a metonymy, a metaphor, or an allegory of the first. Reading is a substitutive activity characterized by effort, endangered by laziness, resembling conversation far less than it does manual labor. Conversely, it would seem that there is no writing (at least for the "esprits paresseux," who seem to be everywhere) that is not at one point reading.

What seems to be the case for reading seems also to be the case for theory: the clarity of theoretical discourse—necessary in order to formulate a poetics—cannot coexist with literature. A text troubled by this oppostion is Paul Verlaine's "Art poétique" of 1882, first published when Saussure was 25 years old. The poem is well-known, but it is unfortunately known mainly by its first verse—"De la musique avant toute chose"—which is read as if its meaning were transparently accessible, and worse, as if that meaning dispensed one from reading the rest of the poem.

Art poétique	**The art of poetry**
De la musique avant toute chose,	Let's hear the music first and foremost,
Et pour cela préfère l'Impair	And that means no more one-two-one-twos . . .
Plus vague et plus soluble dans l'air,	Something more vague instead, something lighter
Sans rien en lui qui pèse ou qui pose.	Dissolving in air, weightless as air.
Il faut aussi que tu n'ailles point	When you choose your words, no need to search
Choisir tes mots sans quelque méprise:	In strict dictionaries for pinpoint
Rien de plus cher que la chanson grise	Definitions. Better the subtle
Où l'Indécis au Précis se joint.	And heady Songs of Imprecision
C'est des beaux yeux derrière des voiles,	Imagine fine eyes behind a veil,
C'est le grand jour tremblant de midi,	Imagine the shimmer of high noon,
C'est, par un ciel d'automne attiédi,	Imagine, in skies cooled for autumn,
Le bleu fouillis des claires étoiles !	Blue entanglements of lucent stars.

Car nous voulons la Nuance encor,	No, what we must have is more Nuance.
Pas la Couleur, rien que la nuance !	Colour's forbidden, only Nuance !
Oh ! la nuance seule fiance	Nuance alone writes the harmonies
Le rêve au rêve et la flûte au cor !	Of dream and dreams, of woodwind and brass.
Fuis du plus loin la Pointe assassine,	Clever-clever phrases are deadly,
L'Esprit cruel et le Rire impur,	So too are rapier Wit and cheap Laughs,
Qui font pleurer les yeux de l'Azur,	Ubiquitous garlic of bad cooks,
Et tout cet ail de basse cuisine !	Only fit to fill blue air with tears.
Prends l'éloquence et tords-lui son cou !	Grip eloquence by the throat and squeeze
Tu feras bien, en train d'énergie,	It to death. And while you're about it
De rendre un peu la Rime assagie.	You might corral that runaway, Rhyme,
Si l'on n'y veille, elle ira jusqu'où?	Or you'll get Rhyme Without End, Amen.
O qui dira les torts de la Rime?	Who will denounce that criminal, Rhyme?
Quel enfant sourd ou quel nègre fou	Tone-deaf children or crazed foreigners [sic]
Nous a forgé ce bijou d'un sou	No doubt fashioned its paste jewellery,
Qui sonne creux et faux sous la lime?	Tinplate on top, hollow underneath.
De la musique encore et toujours!	Music, more music, always music !
Que ton vers soit la chose envolée	Create verse which lifts and flies away,
Qu'on sent qui fuit d'une âme en allée	Verse of a soul that has taken off
Vers d'autres cieux à d'autres amours.	Into other stratospheres of love.

Que ton vers soit la bonne aventure	You must let your poems ride their luck
Eparse au vent crispé du matin	On the touch of the sharp morning air
Qui va fleurant la menthe et le thym...	Touched with the fragrance of mint and thyme...
Et tout le reste est littérature.	And everything else is LIT-RIT-CHER.

(Verlaine 1999, 123–25)

The title of the poem is of course allusive: Horace's *Ars poetica* comes immediately to mind, as does Boileau's "L'Art poétique," and the mere fact that one can't decide which (or is it another still?) of these is alluded to should suggest that the poem's meaning is not easily arrived at. In the wake of these august references, however, the poem is too often considered a prescription of the do's and don'ts of poetry, a prescription—whether it is there or not—which is often taken to spell out the "symbolist" æsthetic of the 1870s and 1880s. The poem is thus read as an "art poétique" of those decades and of that "school," and all-too-conveniently answers the question that was never asked: What is symbolism?[13] The poem is assumed to be a theoretical pronouncement, one with a historical dimension too.

At the same time, however, the poem seems to miss its mark, for if its first line proclaims "music" as its ambition, it is hard indeed to imagine a conception of music that would allow for the commands, warnings, and other stern advice that seem to come more from a dogmatic pedant rather than a helpful fellow-poet.[14]

Since "Art poétique" includes imperative verbs in the familiar "tu" form ("préfère," "fuis," "prends," "tords"), futures with imperative meaning as well as jussive subjunctives ("tu feras bien," "que tu n'ailles point"), it is assumed that it relays advice given to novice poets: use lines of uneven length; be vague, not precise; don't use rhyme; don't use wit or local color. These recommendations have accordingly been assimilated to the "music" promised in the first stanza and recalled in the last, but such a reading hardly does justice to the poem which, on the face of it, includes far more than some naked prescriptions and prohibitions: what need is there to put such words in verse? Verlaine's 1890 statement "Je n'aurai pas fait de théorie" [I will not have written any theory (author's translation)] should warn against such reductive readings.[15]

One crucial problem in "Art poétique" concerns the interpretation of the last line: "Et tout le reste est littérature": the line can be read in conformity with the conventional reading of the poem as a dismissal of all that does not correspond to the prescriptions and prohibitions as "just" literature or "mere" literature: debased verbiage comparable to the "literature" received in a showroom extolling a product one might buy. Such an interpretation is possible at the limit, but one must wonder about a work of literature where "literature" is a pejorative epithet. If, however, one must read "littérature" as pejorative, the reader should consider herself warned: this poem's definition of key terms will be at variance with her expectations.

One such term is "poetry": if this text is a poem, shouldn't it fall under the aegis of an "art poétique"? It seems however that the text considers itself in no way controlled by the propositions it puts forward. For example, if indeed it dissuades poets from using rhyme or from being too precise, why is it so explicit, and why does it obey a conventional rhyme scheme? If rhyme is just the "jewel" of a "nègre fou," does that not imply that the poet is one such "nègre fou"? And since writing is closer to the subject than is race, shouldn't the "secondary" sense of "nègre," that is, someone who writes pieces signed by another, be invoked here? And further, if the poem is thus a "jewel," and the poet, correspondingly a "nègre fou," wouldn't this imply a kind of alienation: the poet as a slave, writing under someone else's dictation: his muse perhaps? And doesn't this begin to recall the words of Verlaine's erstwhile lover Rimbaud: "Je est un autre"? And thus, doesn't the text provide the best possible counter-example of the precepts it argues?

Or the matter of "color": from Sainte-Beuve (certainly a proponent of authoritative poetics)[16] on, the word had come to mean "local color," that is, the use of a descriptive terminology derived from the objects described, not from a pre-existent poetic lexicon. Sainte-Beuve labeled these terms "mots propres,"[17] and the practice of using them is often designated with the terms of "realism" or "reference": Verlaine's "music" is thus anti-realist and anti-referential, hardly a novel conclusion. But one of the objects described here is poetry, and the word used is "art poétique," certainly a "mot propre," and just as certainly a reference, albeit in a textual, not a referential sense, that is, if the two uses can be distinguished. In this case, Verlaine's use of reference enhances its "color" even if the colors chosen are the blacks, whites, and grays of theoretical discourse. Verlaine replaces reference (to things) with reference (to texts) and thus avoids the sobering effects of precision while retaining great precision in his textual references and calling them intoxicating ("grises"): if this sounds like a bad joke, it should, because jokes are what Verlaine wants to avoid ("Fuis du plus loin la Pointe assassine/L'Esprit cruel et le Rire impur"), and if you can't avoid them, at least you can make them bad, which it seems is what Verlaine has done to his reader by initiating this sort of double-think.

The poem's prescriptions and prohibitions contradict its own forms, and its last word is so ambiguous as to constitute the first attested use of "littérature" in a pejorative sense.[18] Perhaps then that line is better read differently, even literally: "everything else is literature," that is, what is not accomplished by following a formal poetics is literature, while that which does follow is not. Certainly a rhymed poem disparaging rhyme invites such an interpretation, as does a precise, enumerative poem advocating imprecision. While such an interpretation cannot be grounded in letters from the author professing an intention, it certainly credits the poem with more possibilities than does the conventional one, and indeed, transforms a poetics into a paradox, or less hyperbolically, into a negative example. Seek music, the poem argues, and do so by writing verses in uneven meter; avoid precision, avoid color, avoid wit, avoid eloquence, and restrain rhyme. If you follow these steps, you will have conformed to a poetics: all else is literature.

Indeed, the series of "thou shalts" and "thou shalt nots" resembles the Ten Commandments more than it does any poem, but while the poem is brandished by teachers like verses from Leviticus, it claims to emulate Psalms, and the tension between this ambition and its practice is productive: should one follow its advice or not? Is it to be obeyed or to be read? And, if one refuses to read, which of its contrary lessons ought one to learn? Rhyme or meter? Color or nuance? Wit or high seriousness? As one hesitates between these principles or procedures, an equilibrium glimmers, perhaps best described as harmony or music, existing not in the poem but in the reader, inviting her to read the poem one more time to see if it can't be grasped more surely. Between the play of lesson and example, one is compelled to engage in a circular reading that attempts to resolve the contradictions that exist between the two levels. Poetry here does not resemble conversation so much as it resembles the work of an artisan.

Certainly there is a lesson for reading Verlaine here: other of his poems respond well to efforts to weigh the complex web of relations that gives words the qualities of things. Sometimes, though, the results are somewhat unexpected. The 1895 "Aegri somnia" is a case in point. From about 1885 onwards Verlaine suffered from ulcers on his left leg and spent several stays in different hospitals as a result. He thus addresses himself, asking whether, for the past ten years, his "membre raide" hasn't been a ball and chain, a divine punishment, or a diabolic attack on his Christian patience. He concludes that this trial will only prove his zeal and bring him up, as if on wings, to God.

Aegri somnia	**Feverish Dreams**
Depuis dix ans, ma jambe gauche,	For ten years now, left leg of mine,
Tu me jouas combien de tours!	You've played your tricks on me.
C'en est lassant, cela me fauche,	It tires me out, it knocks me flat.
Cela va-t-il durer toujours?	Must I endure much more of it?
Si je marche, je me figure	When I walk it feels as if
Que je traîne un boulet, forçat	I'm dragging a ball and chain like a poor
Innocent, mais tu n'en as cure!	Innocent convict, but what do you care?
—Qui donc voulut que tant pesât	Whose idea was it that this stiff
Derrière moi ce membre raide	And painful appendage should drag
Et douleureux? le diable ou Dieu?	So heavy behind me? Satan's
Est-ce à mes péchés le remède,	Or God's? Is this the remedy,
L'expiation? Lors, c'est peu.	The expiation of my sins?
Ou bien Satan, jamais en faute	If it's expiation, fine. If it's Satan
Quand il ne faut pas faire bien,	(Always one to accentuate
Veut-il tenter, invisible hôte,	The negative), he's lodged inside me,
Ma patience de chrétien? . . .	Trying my Christian patience hard.
Bah! ce n'est rien. Dieu voit mon zèle	Bah, it's nothing. God knows my thirst for pain.
A souffrir en cet aujourd'hui,	Once dead, my leg'll turn into a wing,

Et ma jambe muée en aile,	And then I'll fly straight up to Heaven
Moi mort, m'essorera vers Lui.	On what it was that was my limb.
	(Verlaine 1999, 283)

The poem fits into the group of Christian poems of which the collection "Sagesse" is comprised; it fits too among the "personal" poems that Verlaine also wrote, personifying a body part. This dimension has several ramifications, however: not simply is the leg a person, but it's a trickster too, deceiving and misleading the poet. As such, the leg acquires a mind of its own, so to speak, and takes the poem, even more than the poet, in its own direction. The illness Verlaine suffered from prevented him from bending his left knee and he complains thus about the "stiff member" that doesn't do his bidding. Of course, Verlaine could also have complained of the willfulness of another member that led him in directions he later regretted following. Further, the leg will, he claims, serve as a wing to bring him closer to God, following the cliché of the hidden benefits of suffering. This mutation of a recalcitrant member into a wing with which to fly to God has an antecedent: Plato's *Phædrus*, to be exact, where, in love, the stump of the soul's wing swells before the beauty of the beloved,[19] and an erotic meaning comes in question. Under these conditions, it would be all too easy to allegorize this wayward member as a phallus, a signified which gets more than its fair share of signifiers, and which, more importantly, tends to simplify rather than complicate reading.

Here the search to understand "jambe" produces biographical, textual, philosophical, and profane readings simultaneously. What is important to understand is that following any one of these meanings will lead to the others, and consequently, will produce something other than independent, individual readings. To take the word "jambe" first: if one accepts that it refers to the poet's leg (this reading can be embellished with biographical detail, if desired), the poem consists in a complaint against a member of the body; however, by virtue of the reference explicitly acknowledged in the last stanza ("Ma jambe muée en aile"), two things occur: the poet is consoled for his suffering, and "jambe" is transformed, first to "aile," but secondly and just as inevitably, into "penis" (unmistakable in the *Phædrus*). Once this reading is acknowledged, the poem must be reread with another, erotic meaning coming to the fore, but as it does so, the meaning of "jambe gauche" changes, via the etymological link between "iambe" and "jambe," from "left leg" to "awkward verse." Here too, a new meaning imposes itself, for when one attempts to read the poem—quite plausibly—as a complaint about the troubles brought about by the poet's verse, one returns, through the Devil/ God alternative proposed in the fourth and fifth stanzas, back to the Platonic image of the feathered wing, which once again initiates an erotic movement.

What becomes increasingly apparent is that there is no denotation in the poem, no literal meaning, a conclusion reinforced by the poem's title. One cannot say that the poem is any more "about" the poet's leg than it is "about" his poetry, no more "about" about a dragging foot than a wayward member, no more "about" the body than the ideal. What is apparent is that as the poet attempts to speak of any one of these things, he speaks inevitably of another, and this inevitability structures the poem.

"Et tout le reste est littérature." The phrase could be used as the catchword of this volume, which illustrates how the temptation to avoid reading has informed texts from the romantic moment onward. Writers are always on the lookout for procedure that would enable them to communicate more directly, more immediately and without the complexities of codes, and whenever they find one, they bring it to the forefront. There is more to these procedures than what meets the eye, and less to them as models of literature. So Verlaine is absolutely right to say that the "rest" is literature: once rules, symbols, reality-effects, and things are discarded, what remains is indeed literature, and that can only be read.

Art Criticism's Narratives

While critics of Baudelaire's *Le Peintre de la vie moderne* disagree about almost everything else, they do agree that its subject is not what it appears to be. This is strange, for unlike a poem or a novel, an art-critical essay would seem to possess a nominal subject, a subject that can be determined with some precision: the real works of a real artist. One might think or hope that such referentiality would guarantee at least some common ground for criticism. The contrary, however, seems to be the case. Pierre-

Georges Castex, for example, resists the notion that Baudelaire, the great poet, and, he hopes, the prophetic critic, could have chosen a minor illustrator as the subject of his most influential essay: "The complete painter of modern life cannot be identified with a fashion-artist, even an inspired one." However suggestive the works of Constantin Guys might be, or however stimulating he might have been to Baudelaire's thought, it is unfortunate that the essay wasn't about a greater artist: "No doubt Baudelaire could have found a richer material, if not for an analysis of modernity in the sense in which he understood this notion, at least for an analysis of the modern genius of painting, in the works of Édouard Manet" (Castex 1969, 74; author's translation). But it is hard to imagine what a "richer material" would have contributed to an essay which, by all accounts, is a seminal formulation of modernist æsthetics, and, by all accounts, an essay worthy of careful study and close reading, whatever its subject might be. For Castex, Baudelaire's value as critic depends on his ability to single out great artists before wider recognition, and his value as theoretician depends on his ability to formulate a notion—modernity—that will capture the preoccupations of the greatest artists of his day. This contention—from 1969—has had a significant following,[1] its most notable instances being in the field of art history, where both Anne Coffin Hanson and Timothy Clark have used the essay as the starting point of analysis of recognized painters, Manet in the case of Hanson (Hanson 1977), Manet and Monet in the case of Clark (Clark 1984).

The difficulty of defining the subject of *Le Peintre de la vie moderne* has little to do with schools of criticism and everything to do with art-critical writing: not that the essay is confused or contradictory, but it puts forward a concept of the sign as deictic or pointer which itself initiates the uncertainties surrounding the essay, and of which the debate over its subject is just one. The repeated and insistent use of deictics in the essay indicates the importance of their place there, but so does the argumentative thrust of an essay which takes up this aspect of the written sign and calls it "modernity." Since the written "here" and "now," which subtend any effort to designate either a here or a there, a now or a then, lose their point of reference when written, efforts to catch or represent the here and now, even if they are doomed to failure, become "modern." This concept of "modernity," so closely linked to the very nature of the sign, is inscribed everywhere in *Le Peintre*, even in the textual problems surrounding the essay: when was it written, where, what was it written about, and so forth.

This generalization of a property of the sign is not particular to *Le Peintre de la vie moderne*; in the *Salon de 1859* (written just prior to Baudelaire's first mentions of Guys), comparable generalizations and comparable interest in the deictic properties of the sign are at work. The circumstances of the *Salon*'s composition are every bit as problematic as those surrounding the Guys essay. The first to note is that for the first half of 1859, Baudelaire was living with his mother at the *maison joujou* in Honfleur, across the estuary of the Seine from Le Havre. He had moved there for a combination of reasons, among them the desire to escape from creditors and publishers who were hounding him for money and texts, but he also moved out of a desire for the peace necessary to compose a number of important pieces on which he was working.[2] He returned to Paris briefly in early March and again in late April, shortly after the opening of the yearly "Salon" in the Exposition Hall on the Avenue Montaigne, built for the "Exposition universelle" of 1855. What he says about his April visit is what must be noted: to his friend Nadar on May 14, 1859, he writes:

> Je suis vraiment fort en peine; avant de publier mes *Curiosités*, je fais encore quelques articles sur la peinture (les derniers!), et j'écris maintenant un *Salon* sans l'avoir vu. *Mais j'ai un livret.* Sauf la fatigue de deviner les tableaux, c'est une excellente méthode, que je te recommande. On craint de trop louer et de trop blâmer; on arrive ainsi à l'impartialité. (Baudelaire 1973, 1:575)

> [I am in considerable difficulty; before publishing my *Curiosités*, I am doing some articles on painting (the last ones!), and I'm now writing a *Salon* without having seen it. *But I do have a catalog.* Excepting the tiring job of guessing what the paintings look like, this is an excellent method, which I recommend to you. You're afraid to praise too much or to criticize too much, and you arrive thus at impartiality. (author's translation)]

And two days later, still to Nadar, he writes:

> Quant au Salon, hélas! je t'ai un peu menti, mais si peu! J'ai fait une visite, UNE SEULE, consacrée à chercher les nouveautés, mais j'en ai trouvé bien peu; et pour tous les vieux noms, ou les noms simplement

connus, je me confie à ma vieille mémoire, excitée par le livret. Cette méthode, je le répète, n'est pas mauvaise, à la condition qu'on possède bien *son personnel*. (Baudelaire 1973, 1:578)

[As to the Salon, alas!, I lied a bit to you, but so little! I did make a visit, A SINGLE ONE, devoted to finding novelties, but I found very few, and as for the old names, or simply the known names, I rely on my old memory, which I spur on with the catalog. This method, I repeat, is not bad, on condition that you know *your roster* well. (author's translation)]

Sounding like a student proud of having written a paper without reading the book, Baudelaire effectively destroys any understanding one might have of his visit(s) to the Salon, a problem which becomes all the more acute when one finds that the pages of the *Salon* itself tend to present theory (parts I-IV), or descriptions of works not visible at the Salon. And even when the works discussed were in fact to be seen, descriptions of them are based instead on citations from literary works. So much so that it would appear that little of what he says is indebted to the *Salon*, which is a curious state of affairs for a work of æsthetics. By definition, such a work privileges sensory experiences, but it appears in this case that there might not have been one. Was he ever there? If he was there, were the works there? If both he and the works were there, why doesn't his text indicate that coincidence, but rather slip away into a text from elsewhere and about still another place? The instability of place associated with the *Salon de 1859* resembles the referential uncertainties associated with *Le Peintre de la vie moderne*.

One of the places where Baudelaire's text betrays no debt to the *Salon* is his discussion of the faculty of Imagination, a faculty nowhere to be seen in the works of the exposition and presumably absent in their authors. "Discrédit de l'imagination," he writes, "mépris du grand, amour . . . presque exclusive du métier" (Baudelaire 1975-6, 1:612) ["Discredit of the imagination, disdain of the great, love . . . of technique" (Baudelaire 1965, 148)]. Imagination was not present at the *Salon*, and was not present in its artists: not there, one could say, "pas là." Imagination itself is the capacity to postulate, or to create what isn't there, while photography, the unimaginative process *par excellence*,[3] fails because it is nothing more than the reproduction of what is there.

And thus the essay by the writer who wasn't there, about the works which weren't there, invokes a concept of imagination that wasn't there because the artists didn't have it.

The pattern of "not there" shows up again when Baudelaire discusses the works of a distinctly imaginative painter, Eugène Delacroix. Two paintings by the artist interest the critic: the "Descent to the Tomb" and "Ovid among the Scythians." Baudelaire's account of the "Descent to the Tomb" concentrates on the loss expressed by the grieving figures of Mary and the holy women, grief over the loss of Jesus, who is "not there," and who has been replaced by a cadaver. Further, citing a text by Chateaubriand, Baudelaire declares that, at the end of time, this tomb alone will have no body to resurrect: the cadaver shown in the painting will not be there.[4]

Or take "Ovide en exil chez les Scythes," which receives extensive, if second-hand commentary in 1859 (figure 3): Baudelaire begins his discussion of the landscape without even mentioning its title, or, for that matter, the name of its central figure, and asks instead about Ovid's future: Will his exile ever end? Will he return to Rome? He quotes Chateaubriand's epic *Les Martyrs*, to evoke the landscape, its solitude, its calm charm. Another quote

Figure 3. *Ovid among the Scythians*, London, National Gallery, Eugène Delacroix

from Chateaubriand, this time from *Les Natchez*, serves to suggest the beauty of the painting, and finally, a quote of Delacroix's own catalog description of the work indicates how the subject has been conceived. Baudelaire has done the impossible: he has described the painting with citations, or, rather, he has evoked it without recourse to description. Description, the very basis of art critical discourse, is lacking.

Absence also marks the works of Eugène Boudin and Charles Meryon: after a discussion of landscape where he faults its lack of imagination ("Oui, l'imagination fuit le paysage") (Baudelaire 1975–76, 2:665) ["Yes, imagination certainly avoids landscape!" (Baudelaire 1965, 199)],[5] Baudelaire introduces two artists whose works were not even displayed at the *Salon*, the former a painter of seascapes, the latter, an engraver of cityscapes. While there is no doubt that the presence of Boudin's paintings and pastels at the *Salon* would have made a significant contribution to its quality, what strikes Baudelaire about them is what they too lack. They lack finish, to start: Boudin's pastels are notes, preparatory drawings for completed paintings that Baudelaire is sure will come (figure 4). Secondly, they lack human subjects, which would center the compositions, and whose absence Baudelaire notes but

Figure 4. Pastel, Musée Eugène Boudin, Honfleur, Eugène Boudin

does not regret: "il ne m'arriva pas une seule fois . . . de me plaindre de l'absence de l'homme" (Baudelaire 1975–76, 2:666) ["never once . . . did I think to complain of the absence of man" (Baudelaire 1965, 200)]. And what they do include is enigmatic: "Ces études . . . croquées d'après . . . ce qu'il y a de plus inconstant, de plus insaisissable dans sa forme et dans sa couleur, d'après les vagues et les nuages, portent toujours, écrits en marge, la date, l'heure, et le vent: ainsi, par exemple, *8 octobre, midi, vent de nord-ouest*" (Baudelaire 1975–76, 2:665) ["On the margin of each of these studies, . . . sketched from the waves and the clouds . . . he has inscribed the date, the time, and the wind: thus, for example, *8th October, midday, North-West wind*" (Baudelaire 1965, 199)]. Baudelaire seems to accept an amorphous, indescribable, indeterminable object in place of the "positive" representations and reproductions offered by the unimaginative artists of the *Salon*. And this elusive object—resembling nothing so much as the subject of *Le Peintre de la vie moderne*—is what makes Boudin's pastels so attractive.

In the case of Meryon, the etchings were not visible, nor does Baudelaire make any effort to indicate where they could be seen: thus his account of them is hardly æsthetic criticism, judgment based on sensation. Instead, he offers a composite description of Meryon's *œuvre*, and as before, evokes it with a citation, this time from Victor Hugo's 25-year-old poem "À l'arc de Triomphe" in *Les Voix intérieures*. And here, the poem has literally nothing to do with the pictures of an old and sinister Paris overwhelmed by monuments and official buildings. Instead, in order to suggest the beauty latent in the then-new Arc de Triomphe, Hugo evoked a moment far in the future, when the Arc alone will survive to recall France's bygone glory, much as ruins now evoke ancient Rome. What Hugo appends to the arch is what Baudelaire seeks in Meryon's engravings: a sense of loss due to a hyperbolic narrative of time's passage, time, which in Hugo's view, makes all things beautiful. Two features, of which Baudelaire was no doubt aware, further engage the poem in the play of absences Baudelaire has started: The poem was written, it was commonly claimed, to recommend James Pradier as sculptor for the Arc's crowning decoration, perhaps a chariot drawn by four horses: "À ta beauté royale il manque quelque chose" (Hugo 1985, 4:819) [Your royal beauty lacks something]. And then, of course, the entire collection of *Les Voix intérieures* was dedicated to the memory of Hugo's father, whose name was omitted from those inscribed on the Arc: "À Joseph-Léopold-Sigisbert, Comte Hugo, ... non inscrit sur l'arc de l'Étoile. Son fils respectueux, V.H." (Hugo 1985, 4:800) [To Joseph-Léopold-Sigisbert, Count Hugo, ... not inscribed on the Arc of the Étoile. His respectful son, V.H.].

A final example in this enumeration: Baudelaire concludes by stating that he misses romantic landscape: "Je regrette encore ... le paysage romantique" (Baudelaire 1975–76, 2:667) ["In still regretting the landscape of Romanticism" (Baudelaire 1965, 200)], a genre characterized by ruins, deserts, castles, and fortresses. All these things are necessary, but like God are perhaps absent: "enfin tout ce qu'il faudrait inventer si tout cela n'existait pas!" ["everything, in short, which would have to be invented if it did not already exist!" (Baudelaire 1965, 202)]. Baudelaire expresses nostalgia for works of his generation, which are in turn works about the disappearance of things, that is, expressions of nostalgia.

At this point it is possible to characterize Imagination, the concept for which this *Salon* is famous, as a representation of time, and the critic's pleasure on experiencing it as nostalgia. Baudelaire subordinated his descriptions of the works of the *Salon* to the principle of imagination, using this concept as his criterion for judgment; imagination, as all of the *Salon*'s critics have noted, was called *la reine des facultés*. While Baudelaire offered many examples of imagination's effects, he offered no definition *per se*, and that definition must be inferred. Two examples should suffice: "Que dit-on d'un guerrier sans imagination? Qu'il peut faire un excellent soldat, mais que, s'il commande des armées, il ne fera pas de conquêtes" ["What would be said of a warrior without imagination? that he might make an excellent soldier, but that if he is put in command of an army, he will make no conquests" (Baudelaire 1965, 156)]. And, a few lines later, "D'un savant sans imagination? Qu'il a appris tout ce qui, ayant été enseigné, pouvait être appris, mais qu'il ne trouvera pas les lois non encore devinées" (Baudelaire 1975–76, 2:621) ["Of a scholar without imagination? that he has learnt everything that, having been taught, could be learnt, but that he will never discover any laws that have not yet been guessed at" (Baudelaire 1965, 156)]. Imagination is the door to the future, but more precisely, it requires the perception of time: neither the soldier's present competence, nor the scholar's command of past discoveries can be called imaginative; what is imaginative is the ability to perceive a temporal dimension around the present, the present's debt to the past, or the present's own pregnancy with possibility. And if so, one can identify imagination without fail as narrative.

Time becomes apparent, Augustine writes, when the present is distinguished from the past and the future and when these moments are related (Warner 1963, 267–68). It is this relation of present to future that constitutes the imagination of the conquering general, the successful scholar, the rich peasant, and the artists absent from the *Salon*. Alternatively, it is their inability to escape from the present, their fascination with and by the present, that condemns the *Salon* artists to their unimaginative status. Thus the critic praises Delacroix not for what he shows, but for what he doesn't show, and does so not by showing, but by relating other writers' accounts; he praises Boudin for his unfinished representations of time and weather, as if the painter were representing not a moment or an atmospheric condition, but the very process of painting. He compares Meryon to a poet who foretells the destruction of the city, and he likens all the artists he praises to the vanished romantics, whose rendering of what was not and cannot be is matched only by their own absence from mid-century artistic expositions. In all cases, Baudelaire finds a reason to praise in what has disappeared, what is not present. Baudelaire here is nostalgic.

Here too, Baudelaire's hatred for photography and his contempt for progress coincide: photography, which reproduces, he believes, the way things appear, celebrates the present; and progress, the doctrine according to which the present is the *telos* of past history, likewise poses the present as the culmination of past events, something worthy of celebration. This celebration, Baudelaire writes, is vain and self-congratulating. In 1855, Baudelaire writes: "Cette idée grotesque, qui a fleuri sur le terrain pourri de la fatuité moderne, a déchargé chacun de son devoir, délivré tout âme de sa responsabilité, dégagé la volonté de tous les liens que lui imposait l'amour du beau" (Baudelaire 1975–76, 2:581) ["This grotesque idea, which has flowered upon the rotten soil of modern fatuity, has discharged each man from his duty, has delivered each soul from its responsibility and has released the will from all the bonds imposed upon it by the love of the Beautiful" (Baudelaire 1965, 126)[. And in 1859, a similar condemnation of photography, couched in a familiar moralistic tone, is to be found: "À partir de ce moment [the invention of photography], la société immonde se rua, comme un seul Narcisse, pour contempler sa triviale image sur le métal. Une folie, un fanatisme extraordinaire s'empara de tous ces nouveaux adorateurs du soleil. D'étranges abominations se produisirent" (Baudelaire 1975–76, 2:617) ["From that moment our squalid society rushed, Narcissus to a man, to gaze at its trivial image on a scrap of metal. A madness, an extraordinary fanaticism took possession of all these new sun-worshippers. Strange abominations took form" (Baudelaire 1965, 152–53)].

Such an account of Baudelaire's criticism and his *Salon de 1859* can obviously be defended but poses a significant problem when taken in the larger context of his other essays; while it confirms the theoretical thrust of the 1855 article on the *Exposition universelle*, it is at odds with *Le Peintre de la vie moderne*, whose explicit argument is that the representation of the present is a worthy endeavor, and here, of course, Baudelaire is not nostalgic, but modern. Instead of simply dismissing the contradiction between the two essays as an instance of Baudelaire's oft-invoked *droit de se contredire*, it should be worthwhile to look for some principle underlying the apparent contradiction between them.

In his infamous essay on Baudelaire, Sartre qualified the poet as unable to look forward: even when he goes forward, it is reluctantly, and he walks backwards into the future: "avancer à reculons" (Sartre 1963, 206) [to go forward by backing up]. From the moment Narcisse Ancelle was appointed his *conseil judiciaire*, Baudelaire is fixated on a vanished past: perhaps a pre-œdipal moment with his mother or the brief moment of freedom and wealth he knew in his early twenties. And he henceforth appreciates experience only after he has completed it: there is no sense of anticipation, of discovery. Baudelaire thus tries to capture the past, his dreams perhaps or his youth, and does so with a sense of longing and regret. But this effort is every bit as paradoxical as that of Guys, who tries to capture the present; it is no more possible to capture the past than it is to capture the present moment: both elude possession.

In the case of the *Salon de 1859*, as in that of *Le Peintre de la vie moderne*, the language of the essay is inflected by this preoccupation, or perhaps this inflection repeats the thematic and argumentative concerns of the essay. The concept of absence, or, more precisely, that of non-presence, echoes insistently through the *Salon*. Imagination consists in rendering what is not present; Baudelaire describes works of exile or departure, and does so not by describing them but by employing absent texts. He invokes absent artists to advance his thesis. Over all these examples, however, hangs another form of non-presence: narrative. Instead of using description, which would entail present-tense verbs, Baudelaire arranges his accounts of works as stories: *Ovide en exil* is not a scene, but two stories, one of the Latin poet's fall from grace, the other of the reception of his poetry. Boudin's pastels are not snapshots but markers on the way to full-blown paintings. Meryon's engravings relate the story of his madness and that of Paris's eventual decline. While art criticism tends to use the present tense to the exclusion of others, Baudelaire's accounts use the *passé composé* and the future: For *Ovide*: "Ses grands amis de Rome, sauront-ils vaincre la rancune impériale? Retrouvera-il un jour les somptueuses voluptés de la prodigieuse cité? Non . . . ici il vivra, ici il mourra" (Baudelaire 1975–76, 2:635) ["Will his noble friends in Rome be able to quell the emperor's spite? Will he one day know again the luxurious pleasures of that prodigious city? No: . . . here he is to live and to die" (Baudelaire 1965, 169)[. "Tout ce qu'il y a dans Ovide de délicatesse et de fertilité a passé dans la peinture de Delacroix; et, comme l'exil a donné au brillant poète la tristesse qui lui manquait, la mélancolie a revêtu de son vernis enchanteur le plantureux paysage du peintre" (Baudelaire 1975–76, 2:636) ["All the delicacy and fertility of talent that Ovid possessed have passed into Delacroix's picture. And just as exile gave the brilliant poet that quality of sadness which he had hitherto lacked, so melancholy has clothed the painter's superabundant landscape with its own magical glaze" (Baudelaire 1965, 170–71)]. As for Meryon, the narrative couldn't be clearer: starting in the pluperfect, it continues in the *passé composé*: "Il y a quelques années, un homme puissant et singulier, un officier de marine, dit-on, avait commence une série d'études à l'eau-forte. . . . Mais un démon cruel a touché le cerveau de M. Meryon; un délire mystérieux a brouillé ces facultés qui semblaient aussi solides que brillantes . . . Et depuis lors nous attendons toujours avec anxiété" (Baudelaire 1975–76, 2:666–67) ["Some years ago a strange and stalwart man—a Naval Officer, I am told—began a series of etched studies. . . . But a cruel demon has touched M. Meryon's brain; a mysterious madness has deranged those faculties which seemed as robust as they were brilliant . . . And from that moment we have never ceased waiting anxiously" (Baudelaire 1965, 200–201)].

It should come as no surprise that the narrative aspect of this essay has been eclipsed by studies of the theory of imagination. Indeed, studies of the chapters on imagination are far more numerous than those of the other, "descriptive" parts of the *Salon*. This is in part due to Baudelaire himself (or at least to his editors) who tried later to reduce the narrative dimension of the essay by replacing terms like "fuit" with "fait," and stating, perhaps truthfully, that he did in fact visit the exposition. The resistance to narrative is, however, due mainly to the desire to see criticism as systematic, stable, static, and true, rather than as narrative and of course fictitious. If in a novel it suffices to interrupt a narrative with a description for readers to jump ahead, skipping over the "unimportant" passage, criticism uses narrative to flee to theory and avoid denotation.

The End of Citation in Baudelaire's Art Criticism

> En France, on me trouve trop peintre. Ici, on me trouve trop littérateur.
> —Baudelaire
>
> (In France, they think I am too painterly; here I'm too literary.)
> (author's translation)

Art criticism is a field like no other insofar as freedom is concerned: the art-critical judgment is one that refers to no concept, follows no rules, expresses the free play of the imagination before a sense perception. For Charles Baudelaire, who was stripped of some of his most precious rights when Narcisse Ancelle was appointed his *conseil judiciaire* in 1844, the field of art criticism appeared as the one where he retained the majority he had lost everywhere else. Here he could display a maturity, an authority, and abilities that exceeded those of the other citizens of the July Monarchy, even if before the law he had been relegated to the status of a minor. And so in 1846, two years after the appointment of the *conseil judiciaire*, and a year after his first *Salon* and his attempted suicide, Baudelaire returned to art criticism with a proclamation inaugurating a new method: "Je crois sincèrement que la meilleure critique est celle qui est amusante et poétique. . . . Ainsi, le meilleur compte rendu d'un tableau pourra être un sonnet ou une élégie" (Baudelaire 1975–76, 2:418) ["I sincerely believe that the best criticism is that which is both amusing and poetic: . . . Thus the best account of a picture may well be a sonnet or an elegy") (Baudelaire 1965, 44)]. This statement has launched numerous investigations into Baudelaire's art criticism, but also into his poetry: "Les Phares," "Danse macabre," "Le Masque," "Lola de Valence," "Sur 'Le Tasse en Prison' d'Eugène Delacroix," and other poems that do not explicitly refer to plastic works of art.[1] What is striking about it is that "Les Phares," by far the most read of Baudelaire's art-poems, barely echoes his 1846 challenge (not a sonnet, not an elegy, not about a painting, not about a painter, and emphatically not a *compte rendu*), and that those that do (the sonnet "Sur 'Le Tasse en Prison,'" for example) hardly elicit interest beyond perfunctory comparisons with the works supposed to be their nominal inspiration. The great promise of art criticism seems to have eluded Baudelaire.

If one looks at "Les Phares," its differences from the model proposed nine years earlier are striking, and these are not restricted to the superficial ones just mentioned. The feature of the poem that has occasioned the most commentary is the sequence of the first eight stanzas, each one mentioning a great artist and evoking his works. How well these stanzas perform the second function will not be discussed here, as the question has been amply treated elsewhere.[2] What does cause some concern, however, is that the poem goes far beyond the task Baudelaire set for criticism in 1846. If the first eight stanzas depict artists' *œuvres* in terms permitting scholars to debate their accuracy, the last three echo only a garbled despair regarding art's abilities: its message is reduced from ecstasies, tears, and prayers to a single, repeated, imperative cry repeated over leagues and centuries, only to die before it reaches its destination—"Et vient mourir au bord de votre éternité!" (Baudelaire 1975–76, 1:14) [And comes to die at the edge of your eternity!].

The poem seems thus to be ambivalent about the future of art, and implicitly of art criticism. On the one hand, artists make works and critics describe them, and both work and description are worthy of consideration centuries after they are created. On the other, what strives to reach God is just an echoed cry, a sign where the work was an image, an order to do something where an artist had represented a world. This loud, uninformative, imperative discourse at odds with art itself is an evident figure of aesthetic judgment: summary statements demanding assent while remaining unable to supply justification for that demand. The academy is surrounded by gatekeepers and sentinels who shout: "Who goes there?" If "Les Phares" expresses a hope in art's ability to communicate over the centuries, it also expresses a naked distrust of the canon formation that enables it to do so.

When his poetry strayed from the way he traced in 1846, Baudelaire's art criticism also gave the lie to its founding principle of freedom. Certainly the poet voices opinions *envers et contre tous*, as well he might: he roundly condemns Ingres, Vernet, Girodet, and other darlings of the Académie des Beaux-Arts, praising in their place lesser luminaries such as Catlin, Haussouillier, Boudin, Meryon, and Guys. The virulence of his departure from canonical doctrine in the case of Ingres even resulted in the rejection of his 1855 essay on the painter by *Le Pays* and Baudelaire's subsequent choice of publishing it in the relatively obscure *Le Portefeuille*. But for all his freedom, Baudelaire's judgments and his arguments remain quite orthodox. Baudelaire presents, for example, his praise of Delacroix as though the painter were undiscovered or the victim of systematic neglect by the Academy. Such a situation had existed perhaps in 1820, but by the time Baudelaire started writing art criticism, Delacroix was a member of the Académie des Beaux-Arts and the beneficiary of numerous government and church commissions. And when he praises Delacroix, Baudelaire justifies his opinions, as though needing permission to praise the painter: for this Œdipus, Laius is still very much alive. Despite his proclamations of independence, Baudelaire needs authority and amasses references and quotations to reinforce his statements. His use of citation in particular is disconcerting. Starting his career as art-critic in 1845, he uses it quite predictably and with great circumspection: few citations punctuate his *Salon de 1845*, but notable among them are a couple from Stendhal's criticism. In his *Salon* of the following year, however, he makes abundant use of citation: long quotes from Auguste Thiers, Stendhal, and Dante interrupt his discussion of Delacroix; in 1855, his discussion of Delacroix includes both long and short quotations of Théophile Gautier, a short quote from Balzac, and quotes from Baudelaire's own works ("Les Phares").

In 1859, for a *Salon* he admits to having visited only briefly and for which he might plausibly have needed extra material to meet his editor's requirements, he quotes Crowe, Thiers, Hugo, Chateaubriand (quoting Ovid), and Delacroix, as well as his own poetry. Finally, his 1863 obituary article of Delacroix consists in a virtual patchwork of previously-used texts: long quotes from his 1855 *Exposition universelle* and his *Salon de 1859* flesh out an essay that also includes several quotations of the painter's words. What is surprising here is not that Baudelaire used quotation so frequently, but that he used it so often to praise Delacroix, the painter one might think in whose case the poet would want to produce new formulations. Further, if aesthetic pleasure is indeed at the root of his appreciation of Delacroix, it should be supported with personal considerations in order to be supported at all; if, conversely, the approbation Baudelaire voices for Delacroix requires a quite literal reference to authority, it follows that he does not deem his personal reaction a sufficient basis for the praise he confers.[3] In a very real sense, his vituperations concerning Ingres are a purer form of art criticism than the encomia he proposes for Delacroix: the former, excessive and Œdipal though they may be, at least uphold his famous assertions earlier in his *Exposition universelle* that he was "contenté de sentir; [il est] revenu chercher un asile dans l'impeccable naïveté" (Baudelaire 1975–76, 2:578) ["content to *feel*; [he] returned to seek refuge in impeccable *naïveté*" (Baudelaire 1965, 123)].

In point of fact, Baudelaire does not restrict his use of citation to description, for it informs judgment, biographical detail, and theoretical analysis, and serves to convey information while giving their due to those who formulated the statements used. Nor does Baudelaire restrict it to art-critical texts: his literary criticism uses it extensively. His three long articles on Poe, for example, include snippets of popular songs, slogans, and aphorisms, long quotes from other critics, and long quotes from Baudelaire's own translations of Poe's works. It cannot be excluded that these are the expedients of a writer paid by the line, but other considerations demand attention too: citation interrupts the text, multiplies the authors of any given text, and, in cases where the author cited is an authority, authorizes a text where authority might be lacking.[4] It abounds especially in the obituary "L'Œuvre et la vie d'Eugène Delacroix," where Baudelaire extensively re-uses passages from earlier accounts of the painter's works in an essay whose aim is not so much to depict paintings as to venerate them, and which, more than any other, merits apposition to the phrase from *Mon Cœur mis à nu*: "Glorifier le culte des images (ma grande, mon unique, ma primitive passion)" (Baudelaire 1975–76, 1:701) [To glorify the cult of images (my great, my only, my earliest passion)]. In this respect, like "Les Phares," "Le Masque," "Danse macabre," and other solemn poems professing the "cult of images," it endows the text with reverence. This introduction of religion, however, causes as many problems as it resolves.

Certainly aesthetic judgments demand support, but they cannot refer to a concept and thus, as we have already seen, must "often enough to put up with a rude dismissal of [their] claims to universal validity" (Kant 1952, 54). The sincerity of Baudelaire's religious beliefs can be doubted; the fact remains however that he proclaimed his Catholic faith until the very end of his life, and even if he lapsed in one area or another, his use of the word "culte" when talking of images invites religious considerations, first among which is the fifth commandment: "Vous ne ferez point d'image taillée, ni aucune figure de tout ce qui est en haut dans le ciel, et en bas sur la terre, ni de tout ce qui est dans les eaux sous la terre. Vous ne les adorerez point, et vous ne leur rendrez point le culte *souverain*" (Jacquet 1846, 1:82) ["You shall not make for yourself a graven image, or any likeness of anything that is in heaven above, or that is in the earth beneath, or that is in the water under the earth; you shall not bow down to them or serve them" (May 1973, 92)].

Baudelaire worships images so explicitly that one could consider his art-critical and verse accounts of Delacroix's works as part of his Satanism, and perhaps the prime element thereof. Indeed, his "Don Juan aux enfers" is often paired with paintings by Delacroix, notably *La Barque de Dante*.[5] Baudelaire uses citation in his art criticism, not simply for the prestige it confers or for the reality-effect it produces, but to authorize it in the most profound sense: without citation, his text is sinful, unauthorized, and a dubious expression of the freedom intrinsic to art criticism.

Literary-critical essays where Baudelaire eschewed citation are infrequent too. He intended to publish his 1861 essay on Victor Hugo in an anthology including several poems by the author; one would expect such an essay to cite at least some of the poems of the anthology. Instead, Baudelaire concentrates on one poem not on the list of poems designated for the anthology, "La Pente de la rêverie," and fails to quote from the poem even once: since his essays on Poe, and those on other poets among his "contemporaries" freely cite their subjects, the absence of citation here is significant. Indeed here too several of the qualifications of Hugo's writing have been taken in a much more general sense: like Ezekiel, Hugo eats the dictionary only to vomit forth a melodious, colorful book of the world; his poetry is speculative, not didactic; universal, not particular (Baudelaire 1975–76, 2:133). Reluctant to cite Hugo, Baudelaire tropes him instead: citation, with its connotations of truth, authority, and perfect signification, is incompatible with either allegory or metaphor. Where Baudelaire uses citation, he remains literal; where one finds figure—metaphor or the allegories essential to theory—citation is absent. One need only compare this essay to the nearly-contemporary *Salon de 1859*, where Baudelaire does cite Hugo (a citation which he sent, imbedded in its context, to Guernesey, for the author's approval), but which contains no qualifications of Hugo's work: where citation is present, figure perishes; where citation is expelled, figure springs up.[6]

Thus when Baudelaire chooses not to use citation he is making a substantial innovation in his art-critical practice. *Le Peintre de la vie moderne*, often singled out because of the relative obscurity of its subject and the seemingly endless applicability of its theoretical pronouncements to fields other than the visual arts, stands out in this regard too. Alone among Baudelaire's longer pieces of art criticism, it includes virtually no citation, and for that reason it can be considered a mature work, unworried about the stature of its subject, feeling no need to justify either the choice of Guys or its author's judgment, and seeking above all to advance a new conception of art. Further, this essay repudiates the authority of the canon as well as the authority of rules: venturing for the first time to examine an unrecognized artist, Baudelaire for the first time follows to their logical end the implications of his 1855 pronouncement "Le Beau est toujours bizarre" (Baudelaire 1975–76, 2:578). If beauty is truly bizarre, it can no more reside in the canon than in rules, nor is it any more likely to be discovered by an æsthete than by a philistine.

While recourse to authority abounds in Baudelaire's criticism, instances of pure judgment are correspondingly rare. One figure of such judgment is absent, the figure consistently used to express convincing illusionism. This is the metaphor of "resurrection," which figures the effect of the painter on his subject, the painting on the viewer, or that of criticism on the reader. This metaphor, so easily and so often invoked, is lacking almost entirely in Baudelaire's art criticism, occurring nowhere in his obituary of Delacroix (where it would be especially appropriate), but appearing conspicuously in his essay on Constantin Guys. Narrating the sequence of perception, recollection, and drawing that characterizes Guys's representations of modern life, Baudelaire qualifies the moment of recollection as a resurrection:

> Ainsi, dans l'exécution de M. G. Se montrent deux choses: l'une, une contention de mémoire résurrectionniste, évocatrice, une mémoire qui dit à chaque chose: "Lazare, lève-toi!"; l'autre, un feu, une ivresse, de crayon, de pinceau, ressemblant presque à une fureur. (Baudelaire 1975–76, 2:699)

> [Thus two elements are to be discerned in Monsieur G.'s execution: the first, an intense effort of memory that evokes and calls back to life—a memory that says to everything, "Arise Lazarus"; the second, a fire, an intoxication of the pencil or the brush, amounting almost to a frenzy. (Baudelaire 1995, 17)]

The closest Baudelaire comes to the metaphor in the Delacroix obituary are his comments on engraving: tellingly, he refers to this quasi-mechanical reproduction of the painter's works as "translation" and underlines Delacroix's sadness not to have had his works distributed to the larger audiences afforded to the print medium:

> il citait avec envie les anciens maîtres, qui on eu presque tous le bonheur d'être traduits par des graveurs habiles, dont la pointe ou le burin a su s'adapter à la nature de leur talent, et il regrettait ardemment de n'avoir pas trouvé son traducteur. (Baudelaire 1975–76, 2:769)

> [he would enviously cite the old masters, who almost all of them had the good fortune to be translated by skilful engravers whose needle or burin had learnt to adapt itself to the nature of their talent, and he keenly regretted that he had not found his own translator. (Baudelaire 1995, 68)]

Already Poe's translator, Baudelaire's desire to be Delacroix's translator too appears here, but something prevents him from making that claim and he concedes that Delacroix died untranslated.

In the case of Guys there is no such admission of defeat: if Guys can recall scenes to life, Baudelaire's representations of those drawings are just as effective: "Le spectateur est ici le traducteur d'une traduction toujours claire et enivrante" (Baudelaire 1975–76, 2:698) ["The spectator becomes the translator, so to speak, of a translation which is always clear and thrilling" (Baudelaire 1995, 15)].[7] As he makes this claim, a dimension to *Le Peintre de la vie moderne* opens, one lacking in the other essays. While nominally about a minor illustrator, the essay has consistently been read otherwise: as an apology of impressionism, as an anticipation of Manet's work, as a theory of modernity, as allegory of writing.[8] With such a number of readings proliferating in a field where specification is the rule,[9] *Le Peintre* must possess a feature not found in the other essays, and while it is fascinating indeed to speculate on what the "true" subject of the essay might have been, it is perhaps more productive to state that the essay unites an allegorical structure with its descriptive content, thus opening it to multiple readings, but just as importantly, achieving the standing that Baudelaire had not found in his other essays.

To take an example: in chapter XII of *Le Peintre de la vie moderne*, "Les Femmes et les filles," Baudelaire traces a path from the "beau monde" to the "demi-monde," going from "des jeunes filles du meilleur monde" (Baudelaire 1975–76, 2:718) to "la femme révoltée" (Baudelaire 1975–76, 2:720) ["young women of the most fashionable society" (Baudelaire 1995, 35); "woman in revolt" (Baudelaire 1995, 35)]. That he should present static images as a study in sociology, that the study should be arranged as a narrative going from good to bad, that words such as "dernier degré de la spirale," and "lumière infernale" (Baudelaire 1975–76, 2:719) and "pointes sataniques" (Baudelaire 1975–76, 2:721) ["last lap of the spiral" (Baudelaire 1995, 38); "hellish light" (Baudelaire 1995, 36); "satanically pointed shadow" (Baudelaire 1995, 38)] constitute so many allusions to Dante, mentioned so frequently in other essays. That, at the end of the chapter, the narrator should play Dante to Guys's Virgil by condemning the vices shown in the images only makes his choice not to cite more apparent. In chapter III, he refers to Poe's "Man of the Crowd" but fails to designate the author by name. As he develops his concept of the crowd, he picks up and leaves behind key terms from Poe's story: convalescence, mystery, the erotic dimension of the crowd, the desire to possess it. But nowhere does he actually quote from the story whose translation he published in 1855, an omission that allows him to pursue his account of Guys's day into the evening at the illustrator's home, where he composes his pictures from memory. At this point, the poet imagines Guys at his work table, eyeing his sheet with the same look with which earlier, he looked at the world, only now, instead of receiving impressions, he is leaving traces in ink on the paper before him.

> celui-ci est penché sur sa table, dardant sur une feuille de papier le même regard qu'il attachait tout à l'heure sur les choses, s'escrimant avec son crayon, sa plume, son pinceau, faisant jaillir l'eau du verre au plafond, essuyant sa plume sur sa chemise, pressé, violent, actif, comme s'il craignait que les images ne lui échappent, querelleur quoique seul, et se bousculant lui-même.[10] (Baudelaire 1975–76, 2:693)

> [Monsieur G. is bending over his table, darting on to a sheet of paper the same glance that a moment ago he was directing towards external things, skirmishing with his pencil, his pen, his brush, splashing his glass of water up to the ceiling, wiping his pen on his shirt, in a ferment of violent activity, as though afraid that the image might escape him, cantankerous though alone, elbowing himself on. (Baudelaire 1995, 11)]

More to the point still, there is another intertext to mention: Hugo's "Pente de la rêverie," glossed by Baudelaire in the chapter on Hugo in *Réflexions sur quelques-uns de mes contemporains* (Baudelaire 1975–76, 2:137–39), and whose title appears, ghostlike, as a dismembered anagram in the title of the essay on Guys.[11] There is more than a play of the signifier to *Le Peintre*'s echo of *La Pente*. Both texts describe the artist's effort to grasp a fleeting, trembling impression, a memory for Baudelaire, a hallucination for Hugo, but in both cases writing's effort to account for the non-written and the non-linguistic is the deeper subject. The descending spiral may come from Dante, to be sure, but if it does so, it is via Hugo and his attempt to account for the written word. That Baudelaire should describe this attempt by a dimly visible chain of references to prior texts suggests how for him writing succeeds best at evoking when it denotes the least. Thus Baudelaire chooses here to speak without the benefits of authority, having put aside the tool he used elsewhere to ensure assent.

In narrative terms, Baudelaire's account of Guys's actual composition simply follows the passage on the crowds, as recollection follows experience. It is only when shielded from sensation that Guys can compose the drawings based on the day's experiences; it seems that it is only when shielded from textual influences that Baudelaire can go beyond authoritative criticism and begin something else. But as he goes beyond citation, its reference, and authority, he produces allegory: his depiction of Guys dueling with his images, his use of pen and paper for his compositions, his eye not a receptor but a projecting organ, his use of his shirt to clean his brush and his fear that his "images" will escape his grasp, all these features invite interpretation as features of a more generalized creativity. Certainly, these traits are applicable to writing, but their violence and energy also suggest predation, play (such as dueling), and sex. Guys's method of composition possesses many of the features of the subjects he depicts.

As Baudelaire describes Guys's composition, he is aware of his freedom as critic: not simply free do declare Guys comparable to the canon visible at the Louvre—"un Titien ou un Raphaël" (Baudelaire 1975–76, 2:683)—but free also to explain his mode of composition. And since the only mode of composition available is writing, his explanation of Guys's composition must be an allegory of writing; at such moments reading begins, and Baudelaire's reading of Guys is an evident allegory of writing: inspired, rushed, possessed.

> C'est la peur de ne pas aller assez vite, de laisser échapper le fantôme avant que la synthèse n'en soit extraite et saisie; c'est cette terrible peur qui possède tous les grands artistes et qui leur fait désirer si ardemment de s'approprier tous les moyens d'expression, pour que jamais les ordres de l'esprit ne soit altérés par les hésitations de la main (Baudelaire 1975–76, 2:699)

> [It is the fear of not going fast enough, of letting the phantom escape before the synthesis has been extracted and pinned down; it is that terrible fear which takes possession of all great artists and gives them such a passionate desire to become masters of every means of expression so that the orders of the brain may never be perverted by the hesitation of the hand. (Baudelaire 1995, 17)]

In *Le Peintre de la vie moderne*, Baudelaire uses the metaphor of resurrection to account for a stage in the creative process: it renders Guys's recollection into memory of perceptions from the previous day; the painter will subsequently transfer these recollections to paper. In other accounts,[12] the metaphor is used to describe the entire process of painting: the painter brings his subject "back to life"; a painting that fails to do so is not a good painting, rendering only a "ghost." Still other accounts[13] use "resurrection" to describe the critic's activity: the critic's description "brings to life" the painting or sculpture (which in turn brought a man or an animal back to life). That one metaphor can account for memory, painting, and writing is due to the mimetic structure of each of these activities. Each one represents an absent object, and when pushed to hyperbole, as it inevitably is in criticism, the most extravagant claim that can be made for representation is that its object has been restored: that's as good as representation can get. If the object was once alive, whether landscape or sitter, it must live again or be resurrected. Further, since mnemonic representation, artistic representation, and critical representation share the same mimetic structure, it is almost impossible not to use the metaphor: a critic using the metaphor may praise his subject, to be sure, but also implicitly will confer on himself the divine prerogative of recalling someone or something from the dead.

It is tempting to say that Baudelaire resurrects the metaphor of resurrection: certainly, within his critical works, this is the case; Diderot is one critic known to Baudelaire to have used it; it was the stock-in-trade of Gautier's art criticism.[14] But whatever the historical significance of Baudelaire's use of the metaphor, its significance within his criticism cannot be overestimated. Allowing the work to reflect its production, or the work to reflect another work, the specular structure of the metaphor invites and even compels the allegorizing tendency characteristic of readings of *Le Peintre de la vie moderne* and which has been taken as indicative of its success. That in *L'Œuvre et la vie d'Eugène Delacroix*, Baudelaire should have abandoned this metaphor, abandoned allegorical construction, and most importantly, abandoned his resistance to authority and its army of citations, indeed underlines the discouragement of his last years, when not simply did his hero die but he himself went into exile. But their absence also suggests that in *Le Peintre de la vie moderne* he glimpsed something that he did not wish to admit: the arbitrariness of aesthetic judgments.

It does not suffice to use the metaphor of resurrection for criticism to achieve the literary status of *Le Peintre de la vie moderne*. Baudelaire's reluctance to use citation in this essay has been indicated; it should also be pointed out that the body of work discussed in this essay, as well as Boudin's pastels and Meryon's engravings discussed in the earlier *Salon de 1859* were not on display. Recall that a *Salon*, or, as Baudelaire himself put it in 1845, "ces utiles guide-ânes qu'on nomme comptes rendus de Salons" (Baudelaire 1975–76, 2:351) ["those useful handbooks which go by the name of Salon-reviews" (Baudelaire 1965, 1)], was a guidebook, to be consulted as one wandered through the exposition halls, and which would identify, describe, and evaluate the works on the wall. There is thus a strong deictic element to any *Salon*, and such pointing is at odds with with its aesthetic ambitions. Roland Barthes condemned denotation as a tool of the *doxa*: "chaque fois que je crois à la vérité, j'ai besoin de la dénotation" (Barthes 1975, 71) ["each time I believe in the truth, I have need of denotation" (Barthes 1977, 67)]; by inference, denotation serves to present truisms and tautologies. By contrast with such literal-mindedness, the 1859 passages on Boudin and Meryon, and the essay on Guys were explicitly evocative: the works were not there, and the critic's self-appointed task was to summon them to the reader, stimulating memory if they had ever been seen and stimulating the imagination if they had not. It is no accident that Baudelaire's longest and most enthusiastic texts from the *Salons* described only moments of loss: a *Pietà* (1846), an *Entombment* (1859), *Ovid in Exile* (1859): when language is reduced to a pointing function, it cannot help but lament its loss of evocative power. When, on the other hand, Baudelaire theorizes the imaginative power of language, he finds himself obliged to describe artists absent from the 1859 *Salon*, and even, in the later case of Guys, absent from the reader's canon, so that some potential of language may be realized.[15]

What that potential might be comes forward forcefully in a major poem from 1859, having tangentially to do with Constantin Guys, "Rêve parisien," and contributes significantly to any understanding of this rather atypical poem. Most readings of the poem take the word "rêve" in a positive sense and interpret the dreamed cityscape of part I as the world as the poet would like it to be. By contrast, the dark, rainy surroundings of the poet as he "wakes" from his dream in part II represent an unpleasant reality, from which the dream appears as an escape.[16] Sartre's comments on Baudelaire's love of artifice are apposite here: the cityscape, entirely lacking in vegetation and consisting of stone structures, stairways, and channeled water rising in fountains and coming down once more in metal waterfalls, is a repudiation of nature.[17] The poet, this reading would have it, wishes to live in a world of artifice such as the one depicted in the poem; this world is one accessible only through art and is perhaps the world of painting. A salient characteristic is the absence of time: the first part of the poem exists in the present-in-the-past of the imperfect tense; by contrast, the second part introduces the punctual, measurable time of the *passé composé*. Here too the sequence of parts I and II invites interpretation as a fall: the fall into temporality from some sort of heavenly atemporality.

Except for the allusion to painting,[18] however, this reading ignores completely the dedication "À Constantin Guys." The painter's world is one of dusty soldiers, bourgeois families on Sunday strolls in city parks, prostitutes in brothels; it is also qualified as "life," for Guys is "le peintre de la vie moderne." In terms of method, it ignores the acute awareness of time required by Guys's composition, which is characterized by urgency, furor, and fear. Finally, the poet qualifies the "paysage" of the first part with the word "terrible," which certainly troubles any interpretation of this world as an object of desire.

Further, aside from the word "rêve" in the title, nothing in the poem, not even in the long first part, establishes the splendid city as a dream, nor is there anything more to waking in the second part than the opening of the poet's eyes. "Le végétal irrégulier" is indeed banished from the first part, but so indeed is all life: there are no people, no animals, no sounds in this city. If the poet is present, it is not as a participant but only as an all-seeing eye, hardly as an organic being whose needs and actions might destroy the beauty of the scene. Should one then not read the "awakening" of the poet—"rouvrant mes yeux pleins de flamme"—as a return to life rather than as a return to consciousness?

If part II is a return to life, the cityscape of the poem cannot be a city at all but must be a cemetery: this world of marble colonnades, fountains, and silence resembles no metropolis so much as a necropolis, and that there should be no plants here simply instantiates the absence of any life at all. The "terrible landscape" of the dream attenuates the "horror" of his garret, and forces one to ask which of the two visions is worse: a lifeless, if beautiful, spectacle, or a horrible world where worries persist, clocks strike, and time flows relentlessly on.

It helps to consider here "Le Cygne" from the previous year, another poem critical of a marble, monumental city, and yearning for another, dustier and more organic Paris. Based largely on Walter Benjamin's comment that allegory in Baudelaire is a mode of alienation (Benjamin 1999, 10), readings of the verse "Tout pour moi devient allégorie" have insisted on its pathos. Like the swan, like the "négresse," like Andromache, the poet is exiled in modern Paris, but worse off than the others, he lives in a condition of permanent exile arising from his condition as poet where, because he uses perceptions from daily life to feed his poetry, everything becomes grist for the allegorical mill and leaves him nowhere to call home. This reading, however, assimilates Baudelaire's poetic identity with Baron Haussman's urban renewal; both exile the poet, but the former exile is of the poet's choosing and could even be a response to the latter one. Baudelaire would have every reason to prefer a world of allegory to one where *Les Fleurs du mal* was condemned, where he was not allowed access to the money he had inherited, while the debts he had contracted eighteen years earlier remained as pressing as ever. Exile in allegory is hardly an unalloyed delight, but it might not be as painful as Benjamin suggests. And certainly, the new Paris of fountains, marble façades, and monuments was not the one in which Baudelaire yearned to live.

While the disappearance of images of a marble city might be a "loss," narrative also springs from that loss, even if only to recount stories of debt, obligation, and regret. Narrative enables the representation of time: without it, no understanding of time is possible.[19] And criticism, to the extent it evokes what is not there, is both imaginative and poetic but it can only take place when it is not consumed by the need to point.

It follows that life in his "hovel" (*taudis*) could easily be preferable to non-life in the "terrible landscape" of "Rêve parisien," and this, because the poet wakes from his dream, and because wakefulness allows him to construct narratives. These narratives—or readings, to name them by what they do—are what make life worth living, what make Guys's art comparable to that of the old masters, and what make Baudelaire's essay on Guys so rich for present-day readers.

Baudelaire's new-found appreciation for the narrative mode reappears in his short essay on painting and etching of 1862, "Peintres et aquafortistes." As in his essay on Guys, Baudelaire here promotes visual artists working in a print medium, albeit etching rather than engraving, and here, Édouard Manet is explicitly mentioned. While he qualifies Manet's works as "un goût pour la réalité, la réalité moderne" (Baudelaire 1975–76, 2:738) [a taste for reality, modern reality] and justifies claims that he anticipated Manet's later fame,[20] Baudelaire reserves his most extensive comments for the etched medium itself and appeals to its capacity for bringing older works back to life. The medium of printed images (both etching and engraving) has fallen into discredit, Baudelaire argues, and the occasion for his writing the essay is the publication of a volume of etchings that will, he hopes, renew the public's appreciation for it. A play of past and present begins once again, with engraved and etched representations serving as link between the two moments. Manet, etching, engraving: all three promise to bring something back from the dead, whether it be the reality of the present moment, the printed medium, or the works of Old Masters.

Here too, Baudelaire promotes the works of Charles Meryon, whom he included in his *Salon de 1859*. Although he cites almost verbatim his passage from the *Salon*, Baudelaire does not acknowledge that he is doing so, for no quotation marks set the passage off for special consideration. Nor does he include any reference to Victor Hugo or a quotation from "À l'arc de triomphe." Not spent in references to authority, the passage develops a narrative dimension, echoing the preoccupation with decline that frames it while suggesting an apocalyptic future for etching and the printed arts more generally. This apocalyptic future of course implies a last judgment and a resurrection, where images will recall their subjects to life, where descriptions will be as complete as pictures, and where critical prose will vie with its objects for the attention of museum-goers and readers. The implied narrative of criticism, in sum, which will continue until it has fulfilled its own promise.

Baudelaire's art criticism fleshes out the complaint he made in his final years, in *Pauvre Belgique!*: the art critic in particular and the poet more generally must try to account for something, whether it be a sitter, a landscape, a loved one, or a text. But such references, even when they are doubtful, have an undeniable effect: they inhibit signification. Baudelaire's critical discourse teeters on a tightrope, referring abundantly in his early years (to works, to authorities, to rules), while abandoning such reference in his late *Peintre de la vie moderne*. Certainly, *Le Peintre* is the most successful of his critical essays, but perhaps for the wrong reason: the most literary, it has elicited the most enthusiastic response, at the expense perhaps of its nominal subject, Constantin Guys. Baudelaire was aware that *Le Peintre de la vie moderne* represented a departure from his earlier model of criticism. It would seem, because *Le Peintre*'s innnovations can be found in the earlier Salon de 1859 and in the later essay on engravings, Baudelaire understood this new model to be successful. Why then, in 1863, did he revert to his older practice for his Delacroix obituary?

If *Le Peintre de la vie moderne* attempted to evoke life and presence, Baudelaire's obituary of Delacroix, *L'Œuvre et la vie d'Eugène Delacroix* emphatically designates opposing terms: absence and death. And if *Le Peintre* is an article of criticism, *L'Œuvre et la vie d'Eugène Delacroix* is not: Baudelaire abandons any pretense of judgment here and offers encomium in its place. It is because *L'Œuvre et la vie d'Eugène Delacroix* is an obituary that Baudelaire declines to follow up on the insights of *Le Peintre*: he makes no attempt to bring Delacroix back to life, and since he does not judge, he cannot celebrate. Nor is there narrative here; in its place Baudelaire offers citation, abundant citation. He quotes proverbial wisdom, Stendhal, and Emerson, but above all, he quotes Delacroix and Baudelaire. Instead of describing Delacroix's painting of *Apollo and the Python*, he cites the painter's catalog entry; he offers samples of Delacroix's conversation and reproduces verbatim nine pages of earlier articles of his on the painter. He does not try so much to evoke the painter or his work as to preserve him in scattered parts, like organs in canopic jars next to the mummy in its tomb.

It is in this essay, further, that Baudelaire advances his most tantalizing thoughts on translation: how Delacroix's copies of works by Old Masters were faithful (careful, exact, slavish) translations of the originals, and how Delacroix failed ever to find a translator (into a printed medium) of his own works. His juxtaposition of extensive quotation of his own printed descriptions with an account of Delacroix's expression of a desire for a translator leaves no doubt: Baudelaire is offering his services to fill the gap created by Delacroix's death. That a permanent record of Delacroix's works should survive is a consolation; at the same time, that it should return to a past irrevocably lost implies that for criticism, citation is a dead end.

Claiming Painting for Literature:
Fromentin and Claudel

In July 1875, just a year short of his death, Eugène Fromentin left Paris for a month-long trip to the Low Countries, where he visited the museums, galleries, and churches of Belgium and Holland. On his return he compiled and published the reflections recorded during the trip as *Les Maîtres d'autrefois*. Aside from a chapter dealing with characteristics of contemporary French painting, *Les Maîtres d'autrefois* is indeed about the works by the old masters that Fromentin had just seen for the first time, works by van Eyck, Memling, Rubens, Rembrandt, and so forth. It is not a guidebook, not a history, not even an elaboration of Fromentin's æsthetic principles; instead, it is a loosely connected set of appreciations of the works and scenes that happen to have struck Fromentin during the four weeks of his trip (Christin 1985, Schapiro 1949). It nevertheless contains several comments about painting generally and some painters in particular that have elicited lively debate, as much because of what they say as because of who said them.

Of particular interest have been Fromentin's comments on Dutch painting of the seventeenth century, which he distinguishes both from French or Italian painting and from its Dutch precursors. Following Taine, he ascribes this difference to the wars and political struggles that occurred in the Low Countries at the time that this painting evolved (Fromentin 1984, 1572; Taine 1869, 67). One comment in particular has attracted attention and no doubt will continue to do so. Stating how painting changed to accommodate a new political situation and a new public, Fromentin writes:

> Il s'agit de rendre à chaque chose son intérêt, de remettre l'homme à sa place et au besoin de se passer de lui.

Le moment est venu de penser moins, de viser moins haut, de regarder de plus près, d'observer mieux et de peindre aussi bien, mais autrement. (Fromentin 1984, 660)

[The problem now was to give everything its own interest and standing, to put man back into his place, and, if necessary, to do without him.
  The moment was come to think less, to aim less high, to look at things closer, to observe better, to paint just as well but differently. (Fromentin 1948, 98)]

In these lines, Fromentin eschews the subject, especially the human subject, in favor of a simpler, more modest painting. Man must be "put in his place," or even eliminated from painting. Instead of painting man, the Dutch painters that Fromentin admires chose to "observe better," to "paint . . . differently." Most significantly, these renunciations are described as "thinking less": painting is not a matter of thinking, but of doing. No choice, no synthesis, no embellishment or ennobling of the subjects, just plain depiction.

The argument Fromentin puts forward in support of this conclusion is worth dissecting:

1) Dutch art differs from Italian in the relative importance granted to nature and man; in Italian art, "Tout se rapportait plus ou moins à la personne humaine, en dépendait, s'y subordonnait et se calquait sur elle. . . . Il en résultait une sorte d'universelle humanité ou univers humanisé, dont le corps humain . . . était le prototype. . . . La nature existait vaguement autour de ce personnage absorbant" (Fromentin 1984, 659) [Everything was related, more or less, to the human personality, depended on it, was subordinate to it and copied closely from it. . . . There resulted from this a sort of universal humanity or humanized universe, of which the human body . . . was the prototype. . . . Nature existed vaguely around this absorbing personality (Fromentin 1948, 98)].

2) The fundamental gesture of Italian art was thus different from Dutch: its job was not to represent what it found, but to select what it was to represent. "Tout était élimination et synthèse" (Fromentin 1984, 659) ["Everything was elimination and synthesis" (Fromentin 1948, 98)].

3) Thus, when Dutch art arose and chose to reassess the relative value of man and nature, it came to a new conclusion: "de remettre l'homme à sa place, et au besoin de se passer de lui" (Fromentin 1984, 660) ["to put man back into his place, and, if necessary, to do without him" (Fromentin 1948, 98)].

4) Accordingly, this art chose a different method: not to select or eliminate, indeed, not even to think, but to observe: "penser moins, viser moins haut, regarder de plus près, observer mieux, peindre aussi bien, mais autrement" (Fromentin 1984, 660) ["to think less, to aim less high, to look at things closer, to observe better, to paint just as well but differently" (Fromentin 1948, 98)]. "Le but est d'imiter ce qui est, de faire aimer ce qu'on imite, d'exprimer nettement des sensations simples, vives et justes" (Fromentin 1984, 662) ["The object is to imitate that which *is*, to make what is imitated loved, to express clearly one's simple, strong, deep feelings" (Fromentin 1948, 100)].

5) Now, if painting is to observe rather than to select, no preconceived model shall be imposed on the subject: "Quant à embellir, jamais; à ennoblir, jamais; à châtier, jamais; autant de mensonges ou de peine inutile" (Fromentin 1984, 660) ["As for embellishing, never; ennobling, never; punishing, never; all that is so much untruth or useless trouble" (Fromentin 1948, 99)].

6) And if no model is sought, what already exists is adequate: "le plus petit pays scrupuleusement étudié devient un répertoire inépuisable, aussi fourmillant que la vie, aussi fertile en sensations que le cœur de l'homme est fertile en manières de sentir" (Fromentin 1984, 660) ["the smallest country, scrupulously studied, becomes an everlasting field of discovery, as crowded as life, as fertile in sensations as the heart of man is fertile in ways of feeling" (Fromentin 1948, 99)].

7) This æsthetic is indistinguishable from a moral outlook: "Si vous ôtiez de l'art hollandais ce qu'on pourrait appeler la probité, vous n'en comprendriez plus l'élément vital, et il ne serait plus possible d'en définir ni la moralité ni le style" (Fromentin 1984, 662) ["If you take away from Dutch art that which might be called probity, you will no longer understand its vital element; and it will no longer

be possible to define either its morality or its style" (Fromentin 1948, 100–1)].
8) Since clarity, both pictorial and moral, is valued by Dutch art, that art will be linear: "La base de ce style sincère et le premier effet de cette probité, c'est le dessin, le parfait dessin. Tout peintre hollandais qui ne dessine pas irréprochablement est à dédaigner" (Fromentin 1984, 662) ["The basis of this sincere style and the first effect of this honesty and goodness of heart is the drawing—the perfect drawing. Any Dutch painter who does not draw irreproachably is not worthy of consideration" (Fromentin 1948, 101)].
9) Further, such painting is formally centered, just as art is morally centered: "Toute peinture hollandaise est concave; je veux dire qu'elle se compose de courbes décrites autour d'un point déterminé par l'intérêt, d'ombres circulaires autour d'une lumière dominante"(Fromentin 1984, 664) ["Every Dutch painting is concave; I mean that it consists of curves described round a point determined by the interest of the picture—of circular shades around a dominating light" (Fromentin 1948, 103)].
10) In view of this æsthetic, some painters, Rembrandt especially, must be accounted for: according to Fromentin, Rembrandt is always and everywhere to be considered an exception "Rembrandt, qui fait exception chez lui comme ailleurs, en son temps, comme dans tous les temps" (Fromentin 1984, 662) ["Rembrandt—an exception in his own country and everywhere else" (Fromentin 1948, 100)].

Intercalated with the reflections on Dutch art are comments on contemporary French Art, and in particular, on Corot and Théodore Rousseau. When he speaks of such art, Fromentin makes many allusions to French literature, especially that of the Romantics and pre-Romantics. Jean-Jacques Rousseau is singled out, with Senancour and others, as one of those who founded the contemporary appreciation of Nature. While Fromentin's comments are suffused with a reverence for nature, especially as a pictorial subject, his assertions that man should be "put in his place" or "eliminated altogether" from painting also relate him to the "scientific" mentality that Voltaire embodied.

Such statements are certainly intended to qualify Dutch painting but also could amount to a more contemporary æsthetic, both in painting and elsewhere. Fromentin's own paintings of street scenes in Algeria and Morocco,[1] for example, respond to the thrust of his Dutch thesis, and it is in spite, or perhaps because of this preference, that he is drawn to Rembrandt, whom Fromentin must, given his renunciation of history, drama, narrative, and subject, qualify as an exception. But further still, such statements could amount to a program of criticism (which Fromentin of course also practiced) consisting in analysis and enumeration of the aspects of the work under consideration. No embellishment, no figuration, no dramatization of the work: just an account of what meets the eye.[2] It would seem that Fromentin embarked on the paradoxical project of talking simply about painters who painted the world simply. But if their simple paintings are simple records of simple observations, what need could there be of a commentary, even a simple one, of these simple works?

Perhaps then to assess these comments it would be best to turn to an author who also has commented on Dutch painting, Paul Claudel, whose 1935 "Introduction à la peinture hollandaise" in *L'Œil écoute* quotes Fromentin *in extenso*, and in which the author claims to have gone to Holland *because* of Fromentin's book. Of particular interest to Claudel are Fromentin's assertions that there is no "subject" in Dutch painting, that the painting does not "think," that it does not have a message or a rhetoric. On the contrary, Claudel insists that Dutch painting, and Rembrandt's in particular, does have a meaning, and it is that meaning, not the painting's style or technique, that distinguishes it. This thought, if not dramatic or narrative in nature, expresses "sentiment." Further, this art which Fromentin qualifies as an art of "observation," is richly symbolic, signifying a meaning that differs from what it represents. Not the products of mere observation, Dutch paintings are the combined work of memory and sensation. In this regard, Rembrandt, far from being the exception among Dutch painters, is typical, the themes and subjects found in his works are representative of those found elsewhere in Dutch painting, and if his paintings are allegories of reading or contemplation, so are those of his compatriots.

In many respects, Claudel's article is a point-by-point rebuttal of Fromentin's assertions:

1) "et ici je mets un point d'interrogation" (Claudel 1946, 16–17) ["and here I put a question mark" (Claudel 1950, 12)],

just after Fromentin asserts that Rembrandt is an exception, always and everywhere.

2) After Fromentin states that the moment has come to "penser moins," he writes that "Par moments un grain de sensibilité plus chaleureuse fait d'eux des penseurs, même des poètes" (Claudel 1946, 17) ["From time to time, a grain of warmer sensibility makes thinkers of them, even poets" (Claudel 1950, 12)]. Thereupon, Claudel asserts "Un grain, c'est beaucoup" ["A grain is, after all, considerable"]: there *is* thought in Dutch art.

3) More explicitly still, this thought is propositional: "Il n'en [of the old masters' paintings] est aucune qui à côté de ce qu'elle dit tout haut n'ait quelque chose qu'elle *veuille dire* tout bas. C'est à nous de l'écouter, de prêter l'oreille au *sous-entendu*" (Claudel 1946, 17) ["There is not one which, along with what it says out loud, does not contain something that it *wishes* to whisper. It is for us to listen, to lend an ear to the undertones" (Claudel 1950, 13)].

4) The subject of Dutch painting is indeed man: "eux-mêmes [landscape and laymen], sont devenus le tableau" (Claudel 1946, 18) ["they alone have become the picture" (Claudel 1950, 15)].

5) Dutch artists do select their subjects: "l'artiste hollandais ne va pas à la chasse de ses sujets, . . . au gré du hasard et de la fantaisie. . . . On dirait que pour eux la poudre n'a jamais parlé, qu'ils n'ont jamais regardé une chaumière qui brûle" (Claudel 1946, 19) ["the Dutch artist does not engage in a hunt for his subjects" (Claudel 1950, 15)]. "Ils (his clients) demandent au peintre quelque chose et pas autre chose. L'art de la Hollande, comme celui des autres Ecoles, répond à un parti pris. Et ce parti pris, nous l'avons vu, n'est pas du tout le culte, l'exploration et l'inventaire de la réalité pour elle-même. Le poète vient simplement y choisir des thèmes et lui emprunter les éléments de sa composition. Il n'en prend que ce qui lui convient" (Claudel 1946, 20) ["They ask the painter for one thing and not another. Dutch art, like that of the other schools, is based on prejudice. And this prejudice, as we have already seen, is not the cult, exploration and summing up of reality for its own sake. The poet comes simply to choose themes from it and to borrow

from it the elements of his own composition. He only takes what suits him" (Claudel 1950, 16)].
6) Dutch painters do not represent actions or anecdotes, but they do represent something: "ils veulent représenter non pas des actions, non pas des événements, mais des sentiments" (Claudel 1946, 20) ["they wish to represent neither actions nor events but sentiments" (Claudel 1950, 16)].
7) But finally Claudel concludes that Dutch art has direction, focus, and center: "le paysage hollandais a toujours une direction: plus sûrement encore dirions-nous que la composition de ces intérieurs a un centre, un centre de gravité, un foyer" (Claudel 1946, 22) ["the Dutch landscape always has a direction; it would be more exact to say that the composition of these interiors always has a focal point, a center of gravity, a hearth" (Claudel 1950, 18)].

In sum, Fromentin and Claudel differ radically in their assessment of Dutch painting: they disagree regarding the rôle of man in Dutch painting, Claudel saying that it has not eliminated man as a subject as much as it has selected different men engaged in different occupations. Nor is Dutch painting a simple recording of what is to be seen: the very banality of what is represented is a choice, for Dutch artists could easily have recorded the scenes of war and destruction that were everyday sights. Finally, they disagree over the rôle to assign to Rembrandt: was he the exception, as Fromentin maintained, or was he typical?

There are nevertheless some points of convergence that mysteriously arise between the two critics who seem to disagree on most matters of interpretation and appreciation. They agree that Dutch painting was "poetic," or at least was so on occasion, that it was the product and vehicle of a very specific moral and religious outlook, and that it communicated feelings, corporeal in the case of Fromentin (*sensations*), emotional in the case of Claudel (*sentiments*). They also agree the Dutch art is centered. Especially, though, they agree that the paintings they see should be judged.

Where the differences between the two authors become most acute is in the content of the judgments they pronounce regarding specific works, and, in particular, regarding Rembrandt's *Night Watch,* the painting which Fromentin wanted most to see: "Je n'ai point à le cacher, cette œuvre, la plus fameuse qu'il y ait en Hollande, une des plus célèbres qu'il y ait au monde, est le souci de mon voyage" (Fromentin 1984, 734) ["I need not conceal the fact that this work—the most famous in Holland, one of the most celebrated in the world—is the object of my journey" (Fromentin 1948, 177)]. He approaches it with reservations, wondering whether any painting can live up to the reputation of this one. His analysis is critical, detailed, and technical: he demythologizes its subject, and asserts that even taken as a group portrait, its merit is dubious. In fact, Rembrandt, a visionary, was a singularly inappropriate choice for a painting that demanded exact resemblance: "Rien dans cette composition d'apparat ne convenait précisément à son œil de visionnaire, à son âme plutôt portée hors du vrai" (Fromentin 1984, 735–36) ["Nothing in this parade composition precisely suited his visionary's eye, his soul apt to wander from the true" (Fromentin 1948, 179)]. Further, even as a visionary work, the painting does not please: "la *Ronde de nuit* n'a aucun charme.... Elle étonne, elle déconcerte, elle s'impose, mais elle manque absolument de ce premier attrait insinuant qui nous persuade, et presque toujours elle a commencé par déplaire" (Fromentin 1984, 739) ["the 'Night Watch' has no charm whatever.... It astonishes and disconcerts, it obtrudes itself upon us, but it absolutely lacks that primary insinuating attraction which convinces and persuades us, and nearly always at first sight it displeases" (Fromentin 1948, 182)]. Its composition is not particularly good: "La composition ne constitue pas, on en convient, le principal mérite du tableau" (Fromentin 1984, 741) ["The composition does not constitute, it is agreed, the principal merit of the work" (Fromentin 1948, 185)], nor is it a particularly accurate representation: "Ainsi nulle vérité, et peu d'inventions pittoresques dans la disposition générale" (Fromentin 1984, 742) ["So there is no truth and little pictorial invention in the general disposal" (Fromentin 1948, 186)]. As the work of a colorist, it is atypical: "... vous n'apercevez rien dans cette toile incolore et violente qui rappelle la palette et la méthode ordinaire d'aucun des coloristes connus" (Fromentin 1984, 749) ["you can see nothing in this colourless and violent canvas which recalls the palette and the ordinary method of any of the known colourists" (Fromentin 1948, 192)]. The *Night Watch* is not even an example of *clair-obscur*; instead, it is the work of a *luminariste*, someone who seeks to "éclairer une scène vraie par une lumière qui ne le fût pas, c'est-à-dire donner à un fait le caractère idéal d'une vision"

(Fromentin 1984, 759) ["to illumine a real scene by a light that was not real; that is to say, to give a fact the ideal character of a vision" (Fromentin 1948, 302)].

For Claudel, the painting is also the aim of the trip, but precisely because of Fromentin's comments: "C'est elle, [the *Night Watch*] . . . à qui je m'étais promis, il y a bien longtemps, depuis la lecture tantalisante du livre de Fromentin, d'aller rendre visite" (Claudel 1946, 44–45) ["this was what I had promised myself to visit a long time before, in fact ever since I had read Fromentin's tantalizing book" (Claudel 1950, 44)]. The painting represents an action, and what Claudel responds to is the motion that is about to take place, especially on the part of the two principal figures; he even hears the sound of the gun as he sees the movement of the figures: "il me semble même que j'entends le coup de fusil" (Claudel 1946, 45) ["I even seem to hear the sound of a shot" (Claudel 1950, 45)]. The painting is thus related to the Dutch still life generally, that is, "un arrangement qui est en train de se désagréger, . . . quelque chose en proie à la durée" (Claudel 1946, 46) ["an arrangement in imminent danger of disintegration . . . something at the mercy of time" (Claudel 1950, 48)]. This is the key to Claudel's reading of the *Night Watch*: "Toute la composition d'avant en arrière est faite sur le principe d'un mouvement de plus en plus accéléré, comme d'un talus de sable qui s'écroule" (Claudel 1946, 46) ["The entire composition from front to back is arranged on the principle of an ever increasing movement like a sandbank beginning to crumble" (Claudel 1950, 48)], and "c'est l'ébranlement vers une aventure dont on voit bien qu'elle comporte des dangers" (Claudel 1946, 47) ["the start forward on adventure which, as one very well sees, will bring dangers with it" (Claudel 1950, 49)]. For Claudel, this spatial movement is sufficient to explain the glory of the painting: the theme appeals to all and stimulates the imagination. And this "literal" reading leads to another, one suggested by Claudel at the close of his article: "C'est une page psychologique, c'est la pensée elle-même surprise en plein travail au moment où l'idée s'y introduit et y pratique une brèche qui détermine l'ébranlement de tout l'ensemble" (Claudel 1946, 50) ["It is a page of psychology, thought herself at work, surprised at the very moment when the idea enters and forces a breech that causes the whole edifice to totter" (Claudel 1950, 50)].[3]

Differences of method, differences of judgment, differences of

3: LITERARY ACCOUNTS OF THE VISUAL ARTS 159

interpretation: the two authors could hardly disagree more. Where Fromentin procedes analytically, distinguishing the elements of the painting and assessing them individually, Claudel assumes that the painting is a whole whose totality is visible even before its elements can be perceived. Where Fromentin sees a portrait, Claudel sees a story. Where Fromentin sees confusion and uncertainty of purpose or meaning, Claudel sees a meaning so apparent that his interpretation is entirely subordinate to it. Where Fromentin sees a series of failures, Claudel sees a single triumph. And where Fromentin sees a representation, Claudel sees an allegory. These differences can be traced back to the first comments Fromentin made regarding Dutch paintings: "penser moins," he said, and in response, Claudel asserted, "Il n'en est aucun qui à côté de ce qu'elle dit tout haut n'ait quelque chose qu'elle *veuille dire* tout bas." Claudel detects literary structures and propositional meaning in Dutch painting, while Fromentin considers it only an art of recorded perception; on the one hand a fiction, on the other, a list.

But even where Fromentin and Claudel disagree most, the judgment to pronounce regarding the *Night Watch*, they share a metaphor. According to Fromentin, if Rembrandt's painting is a failure, it is because it fails to give life back to, to resuscitate, the figures it represents:

> D'ordinaire, il excelle à rendre la vie, il est merveilleux dans l'art de peindre les fictions, son habitude est de penser, sa faculté maîtresse est d'exprimer la lumière; ici, la fiction n'est pas à sa place, la vie manque, la pensée ne rachète rien. . . . Ici deux des figures principales perdent leurs corps, leur individualité, leur sens humain dans des lucurs de feux follets. (Fromentin 1984, 759)

> [Generally he is excellent in rendering life, he is marvellous in painting fictions, his habit is to think, his master faculty is to express light; here fiction is not in its place, the life is lacking, the thought makes up for nothing. . . . Here two of the principal figures lose their corporality, their individuality, their human significance in the glimmer of an *ignis fatuus*. (Fromentin 1948, 203–4)]

And according to Claudel, if the painting is a triumph, it is because it brings its subjects back to life: "il y a des présences, ce sont tous ces gens debout et qui ne se sont pas décidés encore" (Claudel 1946, 50) ["there are presences, dominating the whole and contemplating the undertaking—all these people standing there and unable to make up their minds" (Claudel 1950, 51)]. Still more generally, beautiful paintings always bring something or someone back to life: "ce n'est plus un visage seul qui monte vers nous à travers l'ombre, c'est toute une compagnie à la fois de ces concitoyens de l'Erèbe, ranimant par une réciprocité de visages et d'attitudes cette heure dans le temps que jadis ils se sont partagée" (Claudel 1946, 28) ["it is no longer one face alone that moves toward us through the shadow; it is a whole company at once of the inhabitants of Erebus, bringing back to life, by a mutual communion of faces and attitudes, that hour in time that formerly they enjoyed together" (Claudel 1950, 25)]. But how can painting "bring back" to life what it represents?

The notion of "rendering" has been for some time the subject of close scrutiny. In his "Restitutions," Jacques Derrida explores an exchange of letters between the art historian Meyer Schapiro and the philosopher Martin Heidegger regarding a painting of shoes by van Gogh, suggesting that the use of the verb "rendre" to designate pictorial representation is central to the debate: "Pourquoi dire toujours de la peinture qu'elle rend? qu'elle restitue?" (Derrida 1978, 295) ["Why always say of painting that it renders, that it restitutes?" (Derrida 1987, 258)[. In particular it is responsible for the insistence with which the two writers each asserted that the shoes belonged to a peasant (Heidegger) or a city-dweller (Schapiro). Whose shoes did van Gogh paint? Whose painting was it? Whose interpretation was the right one? Whose argument was best? etc.: To which Derrida responds: "Posons en axiome que le désir d'attribution est un désir d'appropriation. En matière d'art comme partout ailleurs. Dire: ceci (cette peinture ou ces chaussures) revient à X cela revient à dire: ça me revient par le détour du 'ça revient à (un) moi'" (Derrida 1978, 297) ["Let us posit as an axiom that the desire for attribution is a desire for appropriation. In matters of art as it is everywhere else. To say: this (painting or these shoes) is due to [*revient à*] X, comes down to [*revient à*] saying: it is due to me, via the detour of the 'it is due to [a] me,'") (Derrida 1987, 260). The use of the verb "rendre" is thus predicated on a number of presuppositions, each of which defines a proprietary relationship, and each of which is indefensible.[4] And indeed, the concept of property similarly permeates Fromentin's book: from determining whose likeness is represented, to determining whether a work is indeed typical *of* such-and-such an artist, to the often noted insistence on the part of Fromentin on specifying exactly the technique used. In the case of Claudel, the question is what phrase one should use to describe Holland, what intention to ascribe to a person represented, what word best labels what is happening in the painting.

As is usually the case with Derrida, it would be hard to overestimate the significance of the concept discussed. It certainly would be at the heart of discussions of attribution, and presumably at the heart of discussions of connoisseurship. And inasmuch as huge stakes are involved in attribution—ownership, authorship, identity, interpretation—it is not a problem that will go away soon.

But finally, this argument over attribution has to do with the very gesture of naming: to say that one can name something correctly is just as fallacious, Derrida argues, as to assert that an essential relation exists between an owner and a possession: "Les discours d'attribution, les déclarations de propriété, les performances ou les investitures du type: ceci est à moi, ces chaussures ou ces pieds sont à quelqu'un qui dit 'moi' et peut du coup s'identifier, elles appartiennent à du nommable" (Derrida 1978, 331) ["the discourses of attribution, declarations of property, performances or investitures of the type: this is mine, these shoes or these feet belong to someone who says 'me' and can thereby identify himself, belong to the domain of the nameable" (Derrida 1987, 288–90)]. In other words, the truth-values of naming and telling are not radically distinct and there is no less fiction in getting something's name "right" than there is in telling its story. And thus, no difference of method between Fromentin and Claudel.

But there is another dimension to the verb "rendre" that has not been elucidated, but which seems to be central to art-critical discourse. *What* must be given back (*rendu*), Fromentin and Claudel agree, is specifically *life*: the job of the painter is to figure life, to represent it, to present it convincingly, to preserve in his painting the life of the subject represented. Success in this ambition produces a "life-like" resemblance, and a good painting is said to have captured the "life" of its subject: it is not dead. This quality is what Fromentin sought in Rembrandt's *Night Watch*, and what he did not find. It is the thing the absence of which brought him to qualify the painting as a failure, as a-typical of the artist, etc. By extension, the judgments a critic makes bring a painting to life, bring it back to life from the death where it lingers, animate or reanimate it in some way. In a word, if the art historian tells fictions about art, the critic resurrects it, and it would be hard for any critic, literary or artistic, to resist the seductions of that claim. Here, Claudel is of course in complete agreement with Fromentin, even to the point of saying that the subjects of Dutch painting generally are brought back to life by critical contemplation:

> Derrière ces lèvres humides, ces joues vivifiées par le sang, ces yeux qui ont cessé de vivre mais non pas d'interroger et de répondre, nous sentons ce qui par-dessous produit, nourrit et compose tout cela, la plénitude d'une âme qui s'adresse à la nôtre et qui la provoque à l'entretien, quelqu'un qui offre son visage. (Claudel 1946, 28)

> [Behind these moist lips, these ruddy cheeks, these eyes that have ceased to live but not to question and to answer, we feel underneath, what produces, nourishes, composes all that: the plenitude of a soul that speaks to ours and provokes a response, someone who offers his face. (Claudel 1950, 25)]

Claudel and Fromentin might differ as to the subjects they perceive in Dutch painting and the interpretation that must be made of the paintings; they certainly disagree over the value to grant to the paintings they consider. But they do agree that painting can preserve life, keep the living from dying, and that criticism restores the life painting preserves. In this respect, the differences that separate them seem superficial, while their common project takes on greater importance. This would explain why Fromentin, after saying that Dutch painting lacks a "subject," is nevertheless able to talk about its morality, and conversely, why Claudel, after enumerating many different aspects of a painting's subject, is nevertheless able to say that its composition is what strikes one first. In all cases, they postulate a "life" behind a painting's forms, stating that it is the painter's job to preserve that life and the critic's to find it.

More generally one could say that the illusion of difference between Claudel and Fromentin illustrates a little-noticed feature of art-critical discourse, made all the more apparent by the fact that the superficial differences between the two writers are so plain: the concept of returning, of giving back, inhabits the discourse of painting, both in terms of its æsthetic ambition, and in terms of art-criticism's historical origins. If art-criticism derives ultimately from connoisseurship, it betrays that heritage in a proprietary attitude towards the (valuable) objects it discusses. This is what Jacques Derrida argued so pointedly in *La Vérité en peinture*. But what is also true, and what Derrida did not point out, is that just as generally, what is "rendered" by both painting and criticism is "life," and the metaphor of choice is "resurrection." This might explain the reverence bordering on the religious that accompanies art-critical discourse. Art criticism does not simply "render," it resurrects; it is not only about the ownership it claims to determine, but about life it claims to give; its fictions are not just identifications, but the narratives of its own purpose, and even when it tries to be like painting and to "think less," it cannot avoid becoming complicated and becoming literature.

SARTRE AND TINTORETTO: THIS SIDE OF WORDS

> Le moment est venu de penser moins, de viser moins haut, de regarder de plus près, d'observer mieux et de peindre aussi bien, mais autrement.
> —Fromentin

> ["The moment was come to think less, to aim less high, to look at things closer, to observe better, to paint just as well but differently"]

> ... whereas we have been accustomed to reading literature by analogy with the plastic arts and with music, we now have to recognize the necessity of a non-perceptual moment in painting and music, and learn to *read* pictures rather than to *imagine* meaning.
> —de Man

Sartre's reflections on the art of painting are not numerous: several pages from *La Nausée* give a satirical picture of a provincial museum; a very short piece from the same period, published in *Verve*, provides views on official portraiture; an essay from 1961 on the abstract painter Lapoujade, a 1954 essay on Giacometti's paintings, an essay from 1960 on works by André Masson, and a preface to an exposition of the works of Paul Rebeyrolle from 1970 furnish the sum of his completed works on painting.[1] But even together these works are much less extended than a never-to-be completed work on Tintoretto published in fragments between 1957 and 1981: according to Simone de Beauvoir, two essays from 1957 and 1966 were to be united with other works in a book-length study of the Venetian painter's life and work, *Le Séquestré de Venise*. But, "dissatisfied with its style," Sartre put it aside after writing the 55-page essay first published in *Les Temps Modernes* (and later, in *Situations, IV*), the 25-page article first published in *L'Arc* (and later, in *Situations, IX*), and the posthumous 100-page (to approximate what the *Obliques* essay would give in the unillustrated *Situations* format) chapter published by Michel Sicard in the collection entitled *Sartre et les arts*.[2] In sum, almost two hundred pages on Tintoretto alone, most of which became available only after Sartre's death.

While the fragments on Tintoretto could not be said to comprise the totality of the book alluded to by Simone de Beauvoir, they do give an idea of what its broad outlines would have been:

I Le Séquestré de Venise (55 pp.)
   A Les Fourberies de Jacopo
   B Les Puritains du Rialto   *Les Temps Modernes* (1957)
   C L'Homme traqué
   D Une Taupe au soleil

II "Saint Marc et son double" ("Le Séquestré de Venise")
   A (Introduction) (24 pp.)   *Obliques* (1981)
   B Le Parti pris (75 pp.)
   C L'Obsession (11 pp.)

III Saint-Georges et le dragon (25 pp.)   *L'Arc* (1966)

A situational analysis (I) of the painter, describing the nature of his conflict with his city, explains why Tintoretto painted as he painted, why so many paintings, why only for Venice, why he accepted the difficult conditions imposed on him, etc. Analysis of paintings (II and III) would have elucidated the fundamental devices used by Tintoretto and how these devices unfailingly produced the results he obtained (I). The significance of these devices would have been assessed and related to deliberate choices on the part of the painter (II B). These choices would have been linked to the frenzy Tintoretto showed as he painted, how he rationalized painting into an industry simultaneously capable of producing variety, originality, and vast numbers of paintings. It does seem plain that the 1966 essay on *Saint George and the Dragon* is a concluding chapter: it returns to themes developed at some length in "Saint Marc et son double," and adds to that list. While it is hardly prudent, given the length of Sartre's other critical works, to say that one can now read most of *Le Séquestré de Venise*, and hence speculate on the conclusion of the book, it is possible to determine some of its major theses and determine the sources of Sartre's fascination with the visual arts, and thence to suggest that the reason that the book never came to light was not "dissatisfaction with its style" but a more fundamental reason that has to do with the relation of Sartre's argument both to his own writing and to the language of art criticism.

What is perplexing is the very choice of painting, and among painters, Tintoretto, for a prolonged critical essay. To take painting, especially representational religious painting, with its implications of stasis, with its implicit denial of temporality, with its assurance of what Yves Bonnefoy calls *l'image*,[3] would seem to be at odds with Sartre's other writings, where he seeks out choice and movement, and eschews celebrations of things as they are or as they should be.[4] This is all the stranger as Sartre, when he analyzes painting, remains very much at the level of what is represented, talking of persons and their actions rather than of colors, brushstrokes, or of geometry.[5] So why painting? Why Tintoretto? What did Sartre gain from this critical study? And why did it not see the light of day?

Painting is indeed central to Sartre's æsthetics, and Tintoretto is central to his reflections on painting. Significantly for this argument, Sartre's first mention of Tintoretto occurs not in his essay on the painter, but ten years before, in his famous essay on the novel, *Qu'est-ce que la littérature*? There, seeking to show how prose differs from other forms of writing and other arts as well, he describes just how it is that a painting means:

> Cette déchirure jaune du ciel au-dessus du Golgotha, le Tintoret ne l'a pas choisie pour *signifier* l'angoisse, ni non plus pour *la provoquer*; elle *est* angoisse, et ciel jaune en même temps. Non pas ciel d'angoisse, ni ciel angoissé; c'est une angoisse faite chose, une angoisse qui a tourné en déchirure jaune du ciel et qui, du coup, est submergée, empâtée par les qualités propres des choses, par leur imperméabilité, par leur extension, leur permanence aveugle, leur extériorité et cette infinité de relations qu'elles entretiennent avec les autres choses; c'est-à-dire qu'elle n'est pas du tout lisible, c'est comme un effort immense et vain, toujours arrêté à mi-chemin du ciel et de la terre, pour exprimer ce que leur nature leur défend d'exprimer. (Sartre 1948, 61)

[Tintoretto did not choose that yellow rift in the sky above Golgotha to *signify* anguish or to *provoke* it. It is anguish and yellow sky at the same time. Not sky of anguish or anguished sky; it is an anguish become thing, an anguish which has turned into a yellow rift of sky, and which thereby is submerged, and impasted by the qualities peculiar to things, by their impermeability, their extension, their blind permanence, their externality, and that infinity of relations which they maintain with other things. That is, it is no longer *readable*. It is like an immense and vain effort, forever arrested half-way between sky and earth, to express what their nature keeps them from expressing. (Sartre 1988, 27)]

The passage is justly famous, distinguishing painterly from literary meaning,[6] while at the same time using images that make painting exemplary of man's condition. It is characterized by the very specific vocabulary found elsewhere in Sartre's works: *aveugle, effort immense et vain, submergée, empâtée*, etc. In a word, painting *is* not; it exists. Further, it should be noted that painting is not legible (*lisible*), nor does it signify; there is a fundamental difference here between literary meaning, and painterly meaning. More generally, reading, where signs efface themselves before their meaning, is at odds with a philosophy that places existence prior to essence, and thus painting, not literature, should be *the* paradigmatic art. Painting is a central metaphor in Sartre's æsthetics, exhibiting more clearly perhaps than any other art form the tension between the æsthetic dimension and the signifying function, and this tension is strikingly similar to that of existence and essence that Sartre uses elsewhere. But it is far from evident just what Sartre means here: the passage has been quoted many times, but it would seem that it still needs elucidation. How can a yellow sky be a yellow sky and anguish at the same time? "Anguish" is not its meaning, nor is it an attribute. Certainly "yellow" can "be" yellow pigment and represent yellow sky at the same time—that is Sarte's argument from *L'Imaginaire*, but how can a single patch of pigment also *be* (Sartre's word; I read: "represent") two different things at once, and if so, how does this happen? What does this conflation mean? Sartre claims both here and elsewhere that painting does not deal in "signs," but in "things." In his early *L'Imaginaire* Sartre concedes that paintings are not what they seem, for the real pigments arranged on a canvas or panel give rise to an "unreal," and thus are one thing while meaning another, and while not of any great theoretical sophistication, that distinction should suffice to qualify them as rudimentary signs. But Sartre still contends that paintings, music, etc., unlike prose, are not signs:

> L'écrivain peut vous guider et s'il vous décrit un taudis, y faire voir le symbole des injustices sociales, provoquer votre indignation. Le peintre est muet: il vous présente *un* taudis, c'est tout: libre à vous d'y voir ce que vous voulez. Cette mansarde ne sera jamais le symbole de la misère; il faudrait pour cela qu'elle fût signe, alors qu'elle est chose. (Sartre 1948, 62)

> [The writer can guide you and, if he describes a hovel, make it seem the symbol of social injustice and provoke your indignation. The painter is mute. He presents you with *a* hovel, that's all. You are free to see in it what you like. That attic window will never be the symbol of misery; for that, it would have to be a sign, whereas it is a thing. (Sartre 1988, 27)]

Here Sartre appeals to one level of meaning so simple and so evident that he does not bother to say "cette représentation d'une mansarde"; this level he calls "la chose." In language, there is a second level of meaning, built on the first, where ideology enters the discussion; this he calls "le signe." By "signe," Sartre understands here what linguists call connotation, while by "chose," he understands denotation. Thus, what Sartre argues is of some considerable theoretical significance: that in painting, there are not two levels of meaning, one—which uses things—requiring no interpretation, and another—using signs—requiring interpretation. Only one level exists, la "chose," or denotation. While in language, a word can have a meaning (denotation) and a symbolic function (read connotation) at the same time, no such possibility exists in painting: "cette mansarde ne sera jamais le symbole de la misère." Looking at paintings allows thus a freedom ("libre à vous") from signifying codes and constrictive signification that is not to be found in prose: this would explain Sartre's fascination with this medium.

To make this point, it might be best to invoke a counter-example: in his "Portraits officiels" of 1936, Sartre describes the way in which an official portrait signifies; the argument is repeated in the passage on Olivier Blévigne in *La Nausée*. To understand the functions of official portraiture, Sartre writes, it is necessary to oppose the experience of seeing a man to that of seeing his portrait. In the first case, a man appears with all his defects and ambiguities and is only later identified with a name and a title; in the second, name, title, attributes, and official character appear well before the face itself. "Le badaud voit un gros homme et pense: 'Il paraît que c'est Napoléon.' Mais s'il regarde le portrait, c'est le Premier Consul ou l'Empereur qui paraissent d'abord" (Sartre 1970, 43) [The idler sees a fat man and thinks: "That must be Napoleon." But if he looks at a portrait, it's the First Consul or the emperor who first appears (author's translation)]. The painter of official portraits hides the face and body among signs of office. Why? the office is the message, it is what the painting communicates, well before any likeness of its occupant. But the occupant cannot disappear entirely: there is a difference between an official portrait and, for example, a presidential seal, where only the office is signified, and which remains unchanged from president to president. A gulf exists then between the man and his position, and the strategy of any official portrait is thus to associate the office and the man, to suggest that the office belongs to the man, in short, to introduce a specific ideological claim: "le portrait officiel vise à justifier. Il s'agit de suggérer par l'image que le gouvernant a le droit de gouverner" (Sartre 1970, 44) [the official portrait aims to justify. It's a question of suggesting by an image that the ruler has the right to rule (author's translation)]. Concurrently, signs of flesh and its concomitant weaknesses must be eliminated, such that the subject's body is less present, less disturbing to the air of authority that the portrait seeks to communicate: "parce qu'il ne veut pas non plus faire montre de la faiblesse, le peintre amenuise discrètement la chair des visages, jusqu'à les réduire à une simple *idée* de chair" [because he also doesn't want to display weakness, the painter slightly reduces the flesh of faces, to the point of making them a simple *idea* of flesh (author's translation)]. The man denoted recedes before the message connoted, and thus disappears behind the signs of office, an office that becomes all the more *his* because *he* is less present. But although the portrait disinforms, communicates a falsified message, it does communicate: one's experience in viewing it is ultimately that of understanding, for connotations require deciphering, and what is deciphered is ideological: "On a compris que le portrait officiel, qui défend l'homme contre lui-même, est un objet religieux" [It is understood that the official portrait, which defends a man against himself, is a religious object (author's translation)].

The difference between the face of the portrait and the face of a living man could not be plainer, for the portrait is a message and a message above all, draped in attributes whose sole purpose is to make it legible and to communicate meaning to us. In the case of official portraits, the portrait communicates the office of its subject well before it even attempts to communicate his likeness, and this choice reveals the predicament of portraiture. Does it denote an individual or does it say something about him? Is it particular or general? If the office were not connoted, the sitter would have to offer himself to perception, and that would be intolerable: kings and emperors are not objects, even for their subjects. But in exchange for their unwillingness to represent individuals, portraits provide a reassuring sense of understanding, for one reads the subject in a context and feels (erroneously, of course), that one has read what is there to be read.

If the connotations of such paintings communicate errors, ideological theses that tend to deny the viewer's freedom, the task of criticism is clear: it must denounce connotations as arbitrary, constructs, ideology, and show what it is that they disguise. What is also plain is that these paintings *connote* their message, and efforts to show that they denote what they mean are correspondingly naïve. While Sartre and Barthes are at different ends of the spectrum here, it is easy to see how Barthes could have used Sartre as a starting-point for his analysis of the rhetoric of the image. In the present case, the office hides the man, the signs hide the thing, knowledge prevents seeing.

The official portrait could not be further from the painting of the "mansarde" where no message, no symbol, no signs are offered: what is presented is a "thing," and it is this manipulation of things that characterizes the work of the painter. The portrait could not be further either from the works of Tintoretto. It goes without saying for Sartre that painters represent things, and it is not how they do this (which is what interests Gombrich), but what they do with these representations that fascinates him. For Sartre there is no difference between Delacroix's and Matisse's depiction of a carpet: "L'artiste, même s'il se préoccupe uniquement de rapports sensibles entre les formes et les couleurs a précisément choisi un tapis pour redoubler la valeur sensuelle de ce rouge" (Sartre 1940, 365) ["Even if the artist is concerned solely with the sensory relationships between forms and colors, he chooses for that very reason a rug in order to increase the sensory value of the red" (Sartre 1948, *Situations II*, 276)].

But why does Sartre (like Barthes) short-circuit his analysis of painting to the point where (like Hegel!) he assumes that the "thing" and the representation of the thing are interchangeable?

Beyond the personal and practical reasons that dictate the creation of a work of art, there are other concerns, specifically those of the medium chosen. Here Sartre distinguishes between the arts along a continuum of signification. Writing, and especially the writing of prose, is a question of meaning: the writer wishes to communicate something to someone, and the thing-like qualities of language recede behind its meaning. By contrast, a poet considers words things foremost, and signs secondarily:

> L'homme qui parle est au delà des mots, près de l'objet; le poète est en deçà. Pour le premier, ils sont domestiques; pour le second, ils restent à l'état sauvage. Pour celui-là, ce sont des conventions utiles, des outils qui s'usent peu à peu et qu'on jette quand ils ne peuvent plus servir; pour le second, ce sont des choses naturelles qui croissant naturellement sur la terre comme l'herbe et les arbres. (Sartre 1948, *Situations II*, 64)

> [The man who talks is beyond words and near the object, whereas the poet is on this side of them. For the former, they are domesticated; for the latter they are in the wild state. For the former, they are useful conventions, tools which gradually wear out and which one throws away when they are no longer serviceable; for the latter, they are natural things which sprout naturally upon the earth like grass and trees. (Sartre 1988, 29)]

In this respect, the poet is more like the painter than the novelist: his fascination with the thing-like qualities of words likens him to sculptors and musicians: "l'empire des signes, c'est la prose; la poésie est du côté de la peinture, de la sculpture, de la musique" (Sartre 1948, *Situations II*, 63) ["The empire of signs is prose; poetry is on the side of painting, sculpture, and music" (Sartre 1988, 28)]. Significantly, painters and sculptors are at the extreme end of a continuum from writer to artisan: they work with things, not with meanings: the objects of their efforts are not signs, but matter. It is here that the reasons for Sartre's interest in painting come to the fore: the face, the portrait, the painter, the writer: the thing, the sign. In each case, Sartre privileges the concrete, material pole and devalues the idealistic or ideological one. Painters like Tintoretto are materialists.

It is hardly surprising that Sartre, who chose to analyze artists whose relation to their society was uneasy (if not one of mutual rejection), should choose to write about Tintoretto: as a Venetian-born artisan, he was both a member of Venetian society and excluded from that society. But what is surprising is that Sartre should find examples not simply in the painter but in his paintings, that is, in static images (and largely religious, to boot), where freedom and choice are not altogether obvious. And yet, even his analysis of commissioned religious images supports Sartre's view of Tintoretto as a proto-materialist, whose intuition of Newtonian physics put him at odds with the rulers of his city and forever denied him the favor they granted so generously to less gifted and more conventional painters.

It is this attribute of painting—its stasis—that accounts for Sartre's returns to the subject and especially for his choice of Tintoretto: his most extended treatment of painting, the *Obliques* essay "Saint Marc et son double," contains an early allusion to Cézanne: "un juge inattaquable l'a depuis longtemps absout: Cézanne l'appelait 'le Peintre': voilà ce qu'il est" (Sartre 1981, 174) [an unassailable judge absolved him a long time ago: Cézanne called him "The Painter": that's what he is (all translations of "Saint Marc et son double" are by the author)]. If Sartre cites Cézanne, the painter's painter, calling Tintoretto "The Painter," it can only mean that for Sartre, Tintoretto, first among painters, best exemplifies the painter's art, and if painting best exemplifies the tension he discusses, Tintoretto must illustrate this predicament best. It is also because Tintoretto was the painters' painter that his life in Venice was so difficult; what is perhaps more significant is that it was Tintoretto's painterliness, not his social class or his Venetian origin or his *chutzpah*, that brought Venice's rulers to favor others (especially Veronese) over him. Sartre's discovery of just how painting itself could subvert social institutions was the spark that lighted the second essay.

The early essay hardly mentions Tintoretto's painting; indeed, its subject is not his painting, but his exclusion from the society of his native city. Tintoretto could be any artist at odds with an oligarchy; the names of those who received in his stead the recognition that he strove to obtain just happen to be Titian, Veronese, and Caliari, and that is perhaps why this fragment was published. For Tintoretto (the pariah) is like Sartre's other artist-heroes: Baudelaire, Genet, and Flaubert. Sartre relates Vasari's implausible story of Tintoretto's expulsion from Titian's studio; the public reception of his first scandalous work, *The Miracle of Saint Mark*; his price-cutting, his unceasing efforts to increase market share (and thus, his competitors' enmity), his "gifts" to potential patrons, his sly deals to obtain commissions (especially from the Scuola san Rocco). Sartre also describes the political and moral climate of Venice, a city whose economic and strategic decline had been underway for some time, but whose artistic decline had been forestalled by Titian's presence and surprising longevity. Yet alone among his competitors Tintoretto was the Venetian, painting for his city, and only for it. Sartre concludes that Tintoretto, an artisan from a family of artisans, saw painting as the only way open to him to win respect from a society whose doors were closed to all but the aristocracy. It is here that Sartre's turn to Tintoretto's paintings, first the *Miracle of Saint Mark*, then the *Visitation*, then the *Presentation*, serves to promote a materialist vision of art. With each analysis he shows how Tintoretto tries to bring in an element that had been excluded from the idealizing painting of the period, and how the presence of this hitherto excluded element caused a revolution in painting. The 1548 *Miracle* is paradigmatic of Tintoretto's method; it is also the first painting to be described by Sartre in "Saint Marc et son double," and the painting that revealed Tintoretto's differences with the orthodoxy of his time (figure 5). It caused a scandal then, and still does, even if it depicts an entirely orthodox event, one of the miracles attributed to the patron saint of Venice. What is told is the story recounted by Jacopo da Voragine in the *Golden Legend*, how a slave, guilty only of having visited without permission the remains of the saint, is to be tortured by his enraged master: but the instruments of torture—nails, hatchets, pincers—break, soften, or become dull and useless, and all through the intervention of the saint.[7] The master repents and with his slave thereupon visits the remains of the saint. Of course, this story does not make for a good painting (how does one show metal softening?), so what Tintoretto paints is quite different: a crowd of turbaned pagans surround a dazed figure lying naked on the ground, looking at him and the debris of various tools surrounding him, while one, the torturer, holds a broken hammer up for the master to see.

Figure 5. *Miracle of Saint Mark*, Gallerie dell'Accademia, Venice, Jacopo Tintoretto

Above all this, a haloed Saint Mark is suspended, head down, feet up, as he swoops over the scene. The scene is one of confusion, explicable only by the miracle that is to be inferred from the title: one might think, for example, that it shows Mark bringing some tools and is entitled "The Miracle of the Hammer."

This reading is erroneous of course, but the point is to indicate what a difference there is between what the painting shows and what it means. Its subject, the meaning it was commissioned to convey, is confirmed by the torturers' stupefaction, the ostentatious placement of some broken tools, the passivity of the slave: these tell of the intervention of the saint to those who know the story. What they show is less coherent. Even the saint's intervention is difficult to assess: what one sees is a bearded man dressed in robes, suspended with no visible means of support above an amazed crowd: is he crashing down upon them? is he flying? is he hovering? Is the book he holds the book of judgment or the gospel that says that he is Saint Mark? All of these questions can be answered, but only by reference to the story.

Further, Tintoretto's language is at odds with the conventions of painting: the saint is foreshortened, depicted head down (as he swoops in to save the slave), his foot, closest to us, almost pokes out of the canvas: in a word the conventions holding that divinity never be distorted, always be dignified (and implying that dignity is always divine) have been ignored, and in their place Tintoretto has put a muscular, but thoroughly human saint. Sartre's own language hardly dignifies Mark: he is a *dix-tonnes* (ten-ton truck), a *superman* (Sartre 1981, 177). Whatever the words, though, Tintoretto has repudiated the conventions so respected by his elder, Titian, and thus has implicitly rejected the political and social orders they subtend. Sartre's argument is thus that the simple depiction of the saint as a man sufficed to cause a scandal, to question the social hierarchy, and to brand Tintoretto as a trouble-maker.

But nothing is simple. The pull of gravity and the laws of physics that the saint obeys as he intervenes are inferred, not given. Granted, these intuitions did put Tintoretto (and Copernicus, Galileo, etc.) at odds with the orthodox thought of the moment, but gravity and inertia are no more visible than grace or eternity: they are connoted, they are signified. Gravity becomes an obsession with Tintoretto in later works, and its influence is found in all aspects of his compositions, from the exaggeration of architectural forms to the depiction of male anatomy. In the *Presentation of the Virgin*, for example, the conventional two or three steps leading to the temple become a mountain, the better to suggest the effort Mary must make to fight gravity: "Jacopo veut représenter un perron et nous montre le Matterhorn" (Sartre 1981, 187) [Jacopo wants to represent a portico and shows us the Matterhorn]. And the only use his male nudes ever have for their bulging muscles is to stand up:

> Ils ne portent qu'eux-mêmes et c'est assez: voilà des kilos de viande surnuméraire dont chacun s'épuise à porter les autres tout en augmentant la charge qu'ils ont à porter: le mal infecte le remède et Robusti fait mesurer la gravité de l'infection à l'importance des moyens qui doivent en guérir: cette force hyperbolique se dépense toute entière à préserver le patrimoine de l'homme, la station debout. (Sartre 1981, 183)

> [They carry only themselves, and that's enough: here are kilos of surplus meat each one of which is exhausted by carrying the others, all

the while adding to the weight they carry: the illness infects the cure, and Robusti makes us measure the seriousness of the infection by the strength of the remedies that should cure it: this hyperbolic strength is used exclusively to preserve the human legacy: upright stature.]

All of this effort is shown to make one feel gravity, even if one cannot see it, but there is another dimension too: if it is felt without being seen, it never becomes knowledge, it is never signified. Thus Tintoretto strove to make gravity felt, not read, a denotation, not a connotation: "Tant que la pesanteur peinte se fera voir au lieu de nous sauter à la gorge, la machinerie folle du Tintoret continuera de tourner à vide" (Sartre 1981, 186) [As long as weight is only seen, instead of grabbing us at the throat, Tintoretto's mad machinery will continue to spin without result]. In other works (such as the *Visitation*), Tintoretto used a new device to produce the visceral effects he sought: lowering the point of view, he made his viewers look up at his subjects. The effect is immediate: one feels awe or respect or fear before these people, admirable or dangerous, well before one understands why.

> Dans les films noirs, par exemple. N'est-il jamais arrivé que vous vous sentiez doucement étouffer—mettons: au bout de vingt minutes? Pourtant, rien ne s'est produit, on attend encore le premier sang . . . On aura déjà compris la raison de cet émoi: le détective nous en impose parce qu'on a commencé par nous l'imposer. Physiquement. Par ses muscles, bien sûr, par sa belle gueule féroce—mais ce ne sont que des images: en fait ce type nous domine parce qu'on nous agenouille devant lui; il suffit pour cela de placer la caméra au niveau de sa ceinture en le renversant un peu. . . . Bien joué. Mais quel que soit l'art du cinéaste, il pense trop à nous émouvoir et transforme en rhétorique de mélo un procédé vieux de quatre siècles et mis au jour par le Tintoret. (Sartre 1981, 184)

[In noir films, for example. Hasn't it happened to you to feel like you're slowly suffocating—say, after about twenty minutes? But nothing has happened, you're still waiting for the first bloodshed . . . You've already understood the reason for this emotion: the detective is imposing because he has been imposed on us. Physically. By his muscles, of course, and by his handsome, ferocious face—but these are only images: in fact this guy dominates us because we have been made to kneel in front of him. To do that it's just necessary to put the camera at the level of his belt and to tilt it up a bit: well done. But whatever the artistry of the film-maker, he's trying too hard to move us and uses a four-centuries-old gimmick developed by Tintoretto to create a melodrama.]

What has happened is that the painter has put the reader in a position not occupied since childhood; she is an "enfant rabougri" looking at grown-ups.

> Le premier qui s'est avisé de creuser une fosse devant ses personnages et d'y descendre, c'est Jacopo. En fait, la fosse est imaginaire, il s'est contenté de surélever ses figurines de cire. N'importe: il a refusé la convention du plain-pied et, pour nous persuader qu'elle s'appuie sur nous, il invente de prendre la jeune Géante en contre-plongée. (Sartre 1981, 184)

> The first one to think of digging a ditch in front of his characters and going down into it was Jacopo. In fact, the ditch is an imaginary one; he was happy just to elevate his wax figures. No matter: he refused the convention of frontal composition, and, in order to persuade us that she is leaning on us, he thought of looking up to paint the young Giantess.]

Again, the immediate and the physical overshadow what is known or understood: Tintoretto's denotations short-circuit conventional signification, so that one feels before one sees, and one sees before one reads. The result is an almost material painting that through the eyes addresses the other senses, especially balance, inertia, and weight. Before his paintings, one unconsciously registers bodies in states of disequilibrium, masses over one's head, trajectories that will intersect one's own position, and reacts to them with unease. The viewer is aware of Tintoretto's paintings as if they were real bodies and not mere images in some idealized world that will never come in contact with her own. And indeed, according to Sartre, that is Tintoretto's point: not allowed to say that the Aristotelian worldview is false, he can nonetheless expose its failings. Instead of transmitting an ideology, he assimilates it to a physics and transmits that; instead of saying that saints are ordinary, he shows them subordinate to laws of gravity and inertia, just like us; instead of saying that rulers are one's superiors, he shows them subject to the same natural laws. Further, Sartre posits in his readers the ability to feel without understanding:

faute de déchaîner contre nous l'ennemi, il est réduit a *trop* le montrer, comme un Alcide de foire, croisant les bras pour faire ressortir ses biceps. avec qui voulez-vous lutter? Robusti a déplu, en 48, par un exhibitionnisme de la pesanteur: s'il nous oblige à la *sentir*, il peut la cacher à nos yeux. (Sartre 1970, 186)

[unable to unleash the enemy against us, he has been reduced to showing it *too* much, like a fair-ground Hercules, crossing his arms to display his biceps: who do you want to wrestle with? Robusti displeased, in 1548, by his display of weight: if he forces us to *feel* it, he can hide it from our eyes.]

These comments on painting can be readily inscribed in Sartre's general project of refuting essentialism: matter (pigment) takes priority over spirit (subject); physics over metaphysics, situation takes precedence over intention and depiction takes precedence over meaning. Sartre did seek to show in his works—philosophical, biographical, critical, fictional and dramatic—the pitfalls of essentialism. While the portrait of Olivier Blévigne intends to connote authority, power, justice, etc., the painting actually shows a tiny man easy to laugh at; where the official portrait seeks to justify the occupant's tenure of the office in a world governed by law, the man himself is only a "fat man"; where Tintoretto's paintings were commissioned to celebrate the ideology of their time, they actually show the discoveries of physics.

But when he claims, as he must when he speaks of Tintoretto's works, that contrary to the ideology of his day the painter "just showed" things as they are, Sartre is lapsing into another ideology, positivism, for pictures never "just show" things as they are or any other way. Depth, distance, relative size, relative illumination are all inferences, connotations, not denotations. The same color can "show" light or shadow depending on its placement relative to other colors; a figure of a given size can "show" one distance or another, depending on other factors; a figure of a given color can "show" local color or some modification thereof by distance, atmosphere, shadow, etc. In other words, the most basic devices of representational painting employ multiple signs and multiple codes which together produce single, more general signifieds, such as "depth," "shadow," "distance," and "size." Sartre himself furnishes one of the best examples of the distinction in

L'Imaginaire, where he opposes the devices used to the effect they produce:

> Chaque touche de pinceau n'a point été donnée *pour elle-même* ni même pour constituer un ensemble *réel* cohérent. ... Elle a été donnée en liaison avec un ensemble synthétique irréel et le but de l'artiste était de constituer un ensemble de tons *réels* qui permissent à cet irréel de se manifester. Ainsi le tableau doit être conçu comme une chose matérielle *visitée* de temps à autre ... par un irréel qui est précisément *l'objet peint*. (Sartre 1940, 364)

> [Each stroke of the brush was not made *for itself* nor even for the constructing of a coherent real whole. ... It was given together with an unreal synthetic whole and the aim of the artist was to construct a whole of *real* colors which enable this unreal to manifest itself. The painting should then be conceived as a material thing *visited* from time to time ... by an unreal which is precisely the *painted object*. (Sartre 1948, *Psychology*, 274)]

The object seen is an inference deduced from more primitive signs such as color, brushstroke, and placement, just as ideology is deduced from simpler representations. But what is troubling here is that perception of the object painted or its component elements flickers from one to the other; the brushstrokes and the image can never be seen at the same time:

> Il en est ici comme de ces cubes qu'on peut voir à son gré cinq ou six. Il ne conviendrait pas de dire que lorsqu'on les voit cinq, on *se masque* l'aspect du dessin où ils paraîtraient six. Mais plutôt on ne peut pas les voir *à la fois* cinq et six. (Sartre 1940, 362–63)

> [The situation here is like that of the cubes which can be seen at will to be five or six in number. It will not do to say that when they are seen as five it is because at that time the aspect of the drawing in which they are six is *concealed*. (Sartre 1948, *Psychology*, 274)]

There is no progression from colors and brushstrokes to the image; it is either one or the other that one sees, and to read pictures one uses a language that is so effective that learning it has been forgotten. Pictures, as Saussure's example showed, are often used to exemplify denotation; in fact, they are examples *par excellence* of connotation.

In official portraits, the iconography of office that accompanies the portrait of a man connotes his just occupation of that office. In the case of Olivier Blévigne, the trick perspective that made him appear large connotes his importance. And so, likewise, does the lowered vantage point of the Visitation imply the divinity of Mary and Elizabeth. Whether the sign is the icon of an office, or the choice of a perspective, or the occupation of a particular vantage point, painting uses signs, and its "visceral" effects always pass through understanding.

Two things must be said here: no matter how well one knows that pictures must be read, deciphered by appealing to learned codes, one tends in the last analysis to think of them as transparent indicators, signifying more directly than does language. Secondly, this error inhabits art criticism and causes characteristic problems in that discourse. In that regard, art criticism is paradigmatic of the efforts of literature to discuss fields like history, biography, sociology, and philosophy.

The essay on the National Gallery's *Saint George and the Dragon* is of particular significance: published in 1966, it differs from *Le Séquestré de Venise* in that it engages a single painting which it both describes and analyzes; it also happens to be the last statement Sartre was to make on Tintoretto. Originally appearing in *L'Arc*, it was accompanied by a black-and-white reproduction of the painting, cropped to remove much of the sky and to make the action represented more apparent (figure 6). This reproduction did not accompany the essay when it was republished in *Situations, IX*, and both its cropping and its absence from the more widely-available edition of the essay have been criticized:[8] How can Sartre speak of the importance of action in a painting if the very reproduction of the painting to which he refers has been cropped to increase the apparent importance of the action represented? The subject was set: the slaying of a Dragon by Saint George, patron saint of the Dalmatian Brotherhood. Such a painting should reassure: Saint George is there to protect the innocent, just as the rulers of Venice protect their city, just as God protects the faithful. Further, this protection may not be questioned: no doubts should arise in the minds of those protected as to the abilities of their protectors. Finally, the protectors should know whom to protect, and should do so. And thus Carpaccio, when he painted the scene, chose to portray the slaying so decorously that it would seem that the saint was only playing with the dragon, and that, for the amusement of the virgin he saved.

Figure 6. *St. George and the Dragon*, National Gallery, London, Jacopo Tintoretto

But there is no such reassurance in Tintoretto's version of the events. Sartre's reading starts with the observation that pathos dominates mimesis: the virgin flees the dragon with no hope of rescue, while Saint George's conquest of the dragon is relegated to the background, diminished by perspective into a small anecdote whose outcome is of no interest. The virgin's fear is nevertheless extreme: crazed with terror, she flees she knows not where, without hope, forever. The painting is thus not about a conquest, but about an emotion, an emotion felt as soon as one sees the painting, and here, as in the *Miracle*, Sartre substitutes an immediate reaction (emotional as well as physical, this time) for a decoded understanding. Further, the conquest, such as it is, of the dragon by the saint, is not the triumph related by other painters: Tintoretto's George is the mere agent of another's action, the vehicle of the laws of physics:

Humain, trop humain, il se cramponne à sa lance. Ce n'est pas lui qui porte le coup, c'est son cheval: le soldat n'a qu'à profiter de la vitesse acquise, on ne lui demande que de serrer les cuisses et de se coucher sur le col de sa monture pour amortir le choc en retour. (Sartre 1970, 208)

[Human, all too human, he clings to his lance. It will not be him who will take the blow, it is his horse: the soldier needs only to take advantage of the accumulated speed, he is asked only to clamp his thighs on the neck of his steed to deaden the coming shock.]

Unlike Carpaccio's Saint George, whose sainthood was such that he could kill a dragon easily and ostentatiously, directing his lance with one hand over the neck of his mount, Tintoretto's must use all of his strength, all of his horse's strength, and the inertia they both have acquired to shove the lance into the monster. George here is a worker; his labor is evident; he sweats as he kills. Further, the virgin is not saved; her adversary is indeed dead, but she is by no means safe: abandoned by the town that set her out to die, she cannot return there. She flees thus towards us, away both from the monster and the town. "Pour le militaire et la princesse, l'affaire doit se régler dans le désert, sans le secours des hommes: il faut tuer ou mourir" (Sartre 1970, 211) [For the soldier and the princess, business must be taken care of in the desert, without the help of men]. And the sky, unlike the vaporous Venetian sky of innumerable painters, is closed, heavy, leaden: the only light is at the horizon, distant, inaccessible. That light, Sartre maintains, is the light of Venice, for it represents, among many other figures, Tintoretto's despair of ever being recognized in his own city.

> Plus loin, beaucoup plus loin, au-dessus de l'horizontale, voici Venise, tendre gerbe d'incandescences, rose des vents: elle s'ouvre, tous les plaisirs du vol à voile nous attendent. Ils nous attendront jusqu'au Dernier Jugement: l'homme doit gagner ou perdre son procès sous les bitumes d'un ciel fermé. (Sartre 1970, 216)

> [Far away, much farther away, beyond the horizontal line, lies Venice, a tender bouquet of incandescent lights, the rose of the winds: she is open, all the pleasures of gliding await us. They will wait for us until Judgment Day: man must win or lose his case here under the asphalt of a closed sky.]

Finally, the composition is dominated by curves, curves that order the painting's elements in gracious geometric shapes, but which serve above all to remove the anecdote from the painting's center, to push it into a corner, and thus, to make it difficult to find and the painting irritating to look at:

> le spectateur s'indigne: on lui bouffe son temps, et pour quoi faire? Pour le gaspiller sans compter. Quel coulage! Le duel de l'Homme et de la Bête serait depuis longtemps terminé si le peintre n'avait arrondi les mouvements, remplacé partout les directs par des moulinets, obligé ses créatures à téléphoner leurs coups, à les suspendre, et même à prendre des temps. (Sartre 1970, 220–21)

> [the spectator becomes angry: they are wasting his time and to do what? To spend it without counting. What a waste! The duel of Man and Beast would have been over long ago if the painter hadn't rounded off the movements, hadn't replaced jabs with rabbit-punches, hadn't obliged his creatures to telegraph their blows, to suspend them, to take time-outs.]

Thus action, that quality so dear to heroes such as George, is minimized even in a painting that represents an heroic deed; instead, one witnesses the terror of a woman put out to die, and whose death has merely been postponed by the action of the saint. Sartre's argument is hence unusual: he declares that action—Saint George's slaying of the dragon—loses significance before the reaction it produces:

> On connaît son but à présent: laisser, au sein de l'enchaînement le plus rigoureux, une indétermination calculée, *ne pas peindre* le fait d'armes, figurer une éclipse d'action en l'occultant par les corps mêmes qui sont censés la produire, faire de l'acte un secret. *Le* secret de la toile. Exiler cette absence au plus loin, du côté de tous les autres exils, des remparts pâlissants, du ciel en fuite. (Sartre 1970, 225)

> [We know his aim now: to leave, at the very middle of the most rigorous causal chain, a calculated indeterminacy, *not to paint* the armed combat, to eclipse the action by hiding it with the bodies that are supposed to be producing it, to make a secret of the act. *The* secret of the canvas. To exile this absence far away, over there with all the other exiles, there by the pale ramparts and the fleeing sky.]

The virgin's flight, her fear, her abandonment of the city away from which she runs, all of these features of the painting, Sartre argues, are figures of Tintoretto's own reaction to Venice, the city to which he wished passionately to belong, but which, in turn, would never allow him to be one of her citizens. Tintoretto thus painted one thing, while claiming to paint another, denoting a human predicament while connoting divine intervention. This kind of duplicity, Sartre argues, is especially characteristic of painting, where painters must paint what their patrons wish to see, but where also, precisely because the patrons wish to see something, the painters may paint something else, and here, that something is the intuition that man is alone on earth and has no hope of salvation.

But here too Sartre argues that the painting can be grasped without reading: one senses the virgin's fear and her plight; the city's distance, the Virgin's corresponding abandonment, are both felt, not understood. "Regardez au loin," writes Sartre, as if there were such a thing as distance in painting, "cette ville blême de peur" (Sartre 1970, 211) [Look in the distance . . . that city livid with fear]: both distance and emotion are perfectly evident here and do not require interpretation. And whether Sartre speaks of George's difficulty in slaying the dragon, the virgin's hope of ever finding safety, or Tintoretto's desire to be recognized in the city where he was born, he does so by telling stories about the painting. Jacques Leenhardt has argued that Sartre narrativizes and dramatizes Tintoretto's painting, a painting more properly characterized by suspense than by the flow of time.[9] In Sartre's own terms, he *irrealizes* the painting, much as a historical novelist irrealizes historical figures by setting them in a story he has invented. The point though is that in order to tell such stories, he must accept the figures as if they were given, as if they existed, as if they were simply denoted and he ceases correspondingly to read, if by reading one understands the deciphering of connotations; conversely, if figures are denoted, they can be irrealized, and such irrealization is yet another example of connotation. And all these unreals—stories, dramas, narratives—are not in the painting; rather they evade it just as all other connoted meanings evade it.

Sartre thus claims that Tintoretto invented situations where God's presence is particularly doubtful, and selects phenomena—insisting on gravity and the laws of physics—where the failures of Aristotelian physics were particularly acute. Further, Tintoretto rejected conventions of composition (frontality, head-superior positions, dignity of the person represented) that support hierarchies derived from the religious structure. Certainly the thesis is appealing, for it assimilates Tintoretto to more modern artists and makes of him a prophet, an artist who, like Galileo, intuited if not understood the discoveries of physics that were to change the metaphysics of his own world. At the same time, Sartre reads Tintoretto's paintings in a new light and confers on them the sacrilegious, even blasphemous interpretations implied by his thesis.

But this thesis hinges on a materialist Tintoretto and a materialist theory of painting. To look at the different dimensions of the question: Sartre opposes Tintoretto to Titian as Venetians, the pariah to the invited guest, the artisan to the ennobled painter, such that Tintoretto becomes a working-class hero. As an artist, Tintoretto is the committed painter, opposed to Michelangelo, whose desire above all was to be a poet, an artist whose work did not dirty his hands. As a thinker, Tintoretto, the Venetian, is opposed to the Florentines, as materialists are opposed to idealists. They represent a beautiful world, a world as it should be, where the order of things goes unquestioned. Tintoretto's frequent ugliness, his upside-down and topsy-turvy representations preclude any Florentine idealism. And as a painter, Tintoretto insisted on the materiality of his medium, where other painters tried to forget it: thus Tintoretto modeled wax figurines to experiment with different compositions, thus Tintoretto was ever mindful of weight, inertia, and statics and did not allow his painting to forget these concerns. No floating bodies in Tintoretto's paintings, no ethereal figures: his saints incarnate Newton's laws, even when, for the purpose of performing a miracle, they must ascend, descend, or fly. Watch out: don't get in their way. Even the illusion of depth is subject to these laws, for the viewer of Tintoretto's works cannot simply take in foreground and background; she must arduously work out the spatial construction and push her way into a resisting depth that is only to be inferred, never given, only read, never shown.[10]

Showing. It would seem that in his discussion of painting, Sartre believes that truth can be shown. It does not have to be interpreted, nor to be inferred or deduced; it can be shown, and the very subjects Sartre chooses, the interpretations he constructs, prove his adhesion to this ideology. His discussion of *Saint George* is predicated on an opposition of what is thought and what is painted: what is painted is evident, even if what is thought is not. "Ce n'est pas ce qu'il pense? D'accord. C'est ce qu'il peint" (Sartre 1970, 219) [That's not what he thinks? OK. It's what he paints].

And finally, his detection of a scientific revolution in Tintoretto's works relies equally on showing: Tintoretto shows gravity and its effects in his paintings, and thus refutes the Aristotelian world-view. But one does not (or can not) *show* gravity any more than one can show the rotation of planets about the sun. One can only show behavior of bodies that does not correspond to their inherent divinity, or planets that do not follow the paths defined by Ptolemy. Any statement beyond that, as Karl Popper and Thomas Kuhn after him have argued, requires the establishment of a new paradigm, equally dependent on the interpretation of facts as its predecessor, and equally subject to refutation by simple observation.

It is this reliance on denotation, or showing, that distinguishes Sartre's art criticism from his other works. When he denounces the failures of Proustian subjectivism, he does so dialectically, by elaborating the opposed idea of "intentionality"; when he criticizes François Mauriac's narrative interventions, it is by contrasting their effect to a notion of "liberty"; but when he sides with Tintoretto against the ideology of his time, it is by simply designating bodies in motion subject to the laws of gravity, as if painting, or pictures more generally, were somehow easier to understand and communicated more directly, relieving one of any need to acknowledge their codes, to specify the context that gives them meaning, to read them. And this is the fallacy of art criticism, a discourse haunted by the hope of denoting, simply and without any possibility of error, what a painting represents, even if, as is almost invariably the case, that denotation is played off against a more sophisticated connotative reading. Art criticism acknowledges this hope indirectly, by ascribing to pictures the ability of denoting their meanings, winking at its readers: since I recognize denotations in pictures, won't you recognize them in my writing?

For Sartre, painting, more than writing, exemplifies the tension between existence and essence that he describes elsewhere: while words always signify an elsewhere, paintings do not necessarily do so, and it is possible to appreciate paintings for what they are, rather than what they mean. Because of this aspect of painting, Sartre concludes that paintings possess two modes of signification: simultaneously things and signs, they both denote and connote. While their denotations are apparently simple, their connotations are charged with an ideology that it is their duty to transmit. Sartre resists this function and, in his analyses, plays the denotation off against the connotation, the thing against the sign, claiming that things or denotations transmit messages that signs or connotations refuse to allow. Such an analysis allows him to debunk many connoted messages and to dramatize a critique of ideology, but it relies on a dubious presupposition: that denotation exists in more than a limited number of special cases, and is clearer, simpler, more trustworthy than connotation. In fact, neither pictures nor words habitually denote anything, and if denotation exists, it is only in the very precise cases of denomination and citation, where signifier and signified converge. Thus Sartre claims to replace ideological messages with some kind of truth—to show, for example, how Tintoretto undermined the Aristotelian world view with paintings that represented the discoveries of modern science—but instead replaces one ideology (theology, in the example) with another (e.g., science). This trust in denotation is not characteristic of Sartre, nor is the apparent fear of ideology. But what does seem to be the case is that art criticism more generally relies on denotation: just as paintings "denote" their objects, so also does art criticism "denote" its own. One could call this the denotative fallacy: as he became aware of it, rather than aware of some stylistic flaw, Sartre abandoned his effort to account for the near side of words.

Epilogue

"RIEN N'EST JAMAIS *DÉNOTÉ*" (BARTHES 1982, 129) ["NOTHING IS ever denoted" (Barthes 1985, 138)]. It is hardly fair to take Barthes's comment on Giuseppe Arcimboldo's paintings out of context and in a more general sense than what that context allows. And yet, this is the direction of Barthes's thought, the asymptote towards which he drew forever nearer. In the early *Éléments de sémiologie*, following Saussure, Barthes conceived of denotation as the model of all signification, a simple sign by contrast with which connotations appeared as complicated, perhaps needlessly so. Very soon afterwards, in "Rhétorique de l'image," he modified this position, portraying connotation as a relatively free mode of signifying, by contrast with which denotation served to maintain the status quo, the *doxa*: denotation "naturalized" connotations, making them acceptable, deflecting efforts at understanding and reading. By the late '70s, this critique was fully developed: his *Roland Barthes* denounces denotation as the tool of a repressive ideology, an ideology that requires some signs to be "true," "natural," or "as-they-are." Thus, the quote above, taken from the 1978 article on Giuseppe Arcimboldo, merits consideration in far more general terms than an article on a single painter would ordinarily allow.

Where the citation is found is indeed important. It comes in a discussion of the painted allegories done by the sixteenth-century painter Giuseppe Arcimboldo. The painter's fantastic portraits made of vegetables, dead animals, cuts of meat, or kitchen utensils are a far cry from the naturalism that Barthes denounced in his other works and display a playfulness Barthes himself displayed in his last writings. The fact that this essay came late (as did his book on photography, *Camera lucida*) should alert one to the misgivings he doubtless felt regarding these undertakings: it is hard indeed to denounce the illusion of "natural" signification on the one hand, and to study images on the other. Images demand to be understood as "simple" *analoga* of familiar objects and resist the sophisticated decoding Barthes practiced.

In Arcimboldo, however, Barthes found an artist who, while displaying technical proficiency in illusionism, simultaneously put into question the very aims of representational art. For when one sees a portrait by the artist, one sees simultaneously the illusion of a person's face, neck, and shoulders, and the arrangement of fruits and vegetables of which the portrait is supposedly "made." Or, perhaps, one sees one or the other, but not both at the same time. Certainly, both face and plants can be seen, and the relation of these two forms is of course another example of that opposition dear to Barthes, denotation/connotation. Fruits and vegetables are denoted, but the face is connoted from signs that function as signifiers in a "larger" context. The squash, the gourd, the stem function as signs in the portrait, the flesh of the cheek, the curl of hair, the wrinkled skin, but these signs are made of smaller signs: pigments, outlines, perspectival modifications of line and color, and so on. Further, the portraits are in fact allegories. They do not represent individuals but types: the Scholar, the Jurist, Winter, Summer, Spring, or Autumn. Thus the selection of "terms" denoted for the Scholar is taken from a library, while those used for Spring come from a field of flowers, while those for Summer come from gardens or orchards. And just as one learns with amusement to read Arcimboldo's arrangements, so did one learn long ago to read images.

To take the example of "Winter" (figure 7): at first sight, the trunk of a gnarled tree appears, wrapped with a woven mat at its base, topped with bare branches above. Broken branches protrude from the side; fungus grows on the right; some sort of ivy on the left. It quickly becomes apparent, or perhaps it was so all along, that these shapes form a face: broken branches are ears and nose; fungus forms the lips, and so forth. So while it might make sense to say that the painting denotes a tree, it connotes a face, and that face, formed of the bleak materials of December, further connotes Winter. But just as the face, and later, the face of Winter, are inferences, so also are the bark, branches, and plants from which they spring: these too are connoted, from pigments and shapes which denote colors and forms. But if colors are all that pigments denote, this is hardly denotation: pigments *are* colors, they don't represent or signify them. This complexity and this paradox certainly pleased Barthes, and it is a far cry in-

Figure 7. *Winter*, Louvre, Paris, Giuseppe Arcimboldo

deed from Saussure's sign, a sign exemplified, as it happens, by the representation of a tree. It would appear that one of Barthes's contributions to Saussure's concept of the sign was to appreciate its complexities, a sign that was hardly simple to begin with.

This admittedly marginal discourse is one part then of the larger Romantic project, one of the aims of which was to develop, or at least, to promote, a more direct form of communication.

There is no coincidence in the fact that Victor Hugo's first great success was about a work of art and placed the problems of communication in the forefront; conversely, one could say that such a novel's success is hardly coincidental, given the existent preoccupation with direct communication. But what might be surprising is that Hugo explored several modes of simple signification, and exploited them for their greatest effect. Nowhere, however, was he ever persuaded that such a shortcut through reading is ever possible, or that words can mean independently of the texts where they are found.

Notes

INTRODUCTION

1. Any short list would include those mentioned here, as well as Victor Hugo, Eugène Fromentin, Paul Claudel, Marcel Proust, André Malraux, Jean-Paul Sartre, Yves Bonnefoy, Roland Barthes, and Michel Butor.

2. Here one can cite Honoré de Balzac, Gustave Flaubert, Marcel Proust, and Yves Bonnefoy.

3. In *La Gloire de Victor Hugo*, Pierre Georgel, basing his conclusions on the numbers of copies of Hugo's works printed and sold over the century since his death, determined that for the nineteenth century, Hugo was both *a* poet and *the* poet, editions of his poetry outstripping by far those of any one of his fellow poets, as well as editions of his own novels. In the twentieth century, by contrast, editions of *Les Fleurs du mal* outnumber those of any other poet or collection of poetry, while Hugo's novels, with *Notre-Dame de Paris* and *Les Misérables* in the lead, outsell any of his other works.

4. *N.B.* Translations by the author will be marked as such in the text. Concerning the translations used: in the case of Hugo's poetry, where published translations tend to be mellifluous and the author's, pedestrian, the choice of the latter was dictated by semantic considerations. Cognates, titles, *incipit*, and such are left untranslated. It will be noted in many cases that published translations simply avoid the word or words analyzed: an indication of their borderline status.

5. I am indebted to David Carrier for this term, which he uses to describe the art-critical texts of Baudelaire, Proust, and others. See his *Artwriting* (Carrier 1987).

HUGO'S DATES: THE FUNCTIONS OF CHRONOLOGY

1. As example of this calendar-consciousness, see John Frey's account of the events central to the chronology of *Les Contemplations:* Ash Wednesday, 1843, Léopoldine's wedding day (February 15, 1843), and the date of her drowning, September 4 (Frey 1988, 1–5).

2. Thus, from *La Légende des siècles*, poem VI, ii is entitled "1453"; three of its chapters are entitled "Seizième Siècle—Renaissance Paganisme," "Dix-septième Siècle—Les Mercenaires" and "Vingtième Siècle"; his last novel was of course *Quatrevingt-treize*.

3. With the exception of II, 1, "Premier mai," dated "Saint-Germain 1ᵉʳ mai . . ."

4. See, for example, the concordances in the Pierre Albouy (Albouy 1973) and Jean Gaudon (Gaudon 1985) editions of the work. Peter Cogman points out how Hugo altered the dates of *Aujourd'hui* to produce a more compelling symmetry between the work's two parts (Cogman 1984, 21).

5. Poems I, 23; II, 25; V, 25; and V, 23, dated 10 août 1830, juin 1830, 26 août 1852, and 16 août 1870, respectively, are from 1859, 1836, 1875 and 1876.

6. The word "trauma" describes Hugo's reaction to the news of Léopoldine's death, and "neurosis," his response to it: the ritualistic observance of the anniversary has all the hallmarks of a "repetition compulsion" whose purpose is "to master the stimulus retrospectively, by developing the anxiety whose omission was the cause of the traumatic neurosis" (Freud 1972, 60). The same structure, and presumably, the same cause, hold true for his observance of the anniversary of his first night with Juliette, as if here too Hugo had to master retrospectively an overpowering and unexpected stimulus.

7. Harold Bloom defines the trope thus: "The trope . . . is the unsettling one anciently called metalepsis or transumption, the only trope-reversing trope, since it substitutes one word for another in earlier figurations." See Harold Bloom, *Poetry and Repression* (1976, 19–21). Indeed, Hugo is one of a very few French authors whom Harold Bloom has characterized as "anxious," a particularly apt characterization here.

8. "On peut dire que le respect que l'on a pour les héros augmente à mesure qu'ils s'éloignent de nous: *major e* longinquo reverentia. L'éloignement des pays répare en quelque sorte la trop grande proximité des temps" (Rat 1960) ["We may say that the respect that we harbour for heroes increases in proportion to their distance from us: *major e longinquo reverentia*. The distance in place makes up in some sort for the too great nearness in time" (Racine 1967, 2:5)].

LIMITS OF PERFORMATIVE LANGUAGE IN HUGO'S THEATER

1. Some indications of the frequency of the single expression "je jure": 8:135 (*Cromwell*); 8:734, 743 (*Marion Delorme*); 8:1019 (*Lucrèce Borgia*); 8:1126, 1127, 1129, 1134, 1136, 1142 (*Marie Tudor*, 8:1234, 1263), (*Angelo Tyran de Padoue*, 9:64, 138), (*Ruy Blas*).

2. Tellingly, the Emperor responds "En effet, j'avais oublié cette histoire" (Hugo 1985, 8:641); ["I had quite forgotten this history" (Hugo 1995, 97)], when it is also the fact that Hernani has forgotten his pledge.

3. Over each of these reversals hovers a boast made by the queen at the moment of her pact with Gilbert: "Nous ne sommes pas la reine pour rien" (Hugo 1985, 8:1126), where the royal "we" troubles even further identity of the speaker.

4. Other examples can be found: Ruy Blas's sarcastic wish, lacking any authority, "Bon appétit! messieurs!" (Hugo 1985, 9:75) ["I wish you joy! (Hugo 1995, 278)] to the assembled Counsellors of Spain; Don Alphonse's promise of clemency to Gennarro in *Lucrèce Borgia* (Hugo 1985, 8:1022).

5. There is yet another complication: written performatives record the deed

they accomplish and thus blur any distinction between performative and constative language one might hope to make.

PEOPLE, PLACES, AND APOSTROPHE IN "TRISTESSE D'OLYMPIO"

1. No sooner had Victor Hugo written his famous "Tristesse d'Olympio" than questions arose about his intentions. Was the name "Olympio" a mask worn by Hugo? Was the poem "for" Juliette? Was it "about" their trysts in Bièvre two years previously? Hugo seems to have answered these questions (or, perhaps, to have elicited them) by dedicating a manuscript of the poem to Juliette Drouet: since then, readings of the poem have turned in orbit around this question of origin: was Hugo generalizing a particular experience (Levaillant)? Was Juliette right to think that the poem was not really "hers" (Souchon)? Was her preference for "Quand tu me parles de gloire . . ." an error (Souchon)? And "was" Hugo Olympio?

2. Hugo's stays in Bièvre began in 1831, before Hugo met Miss Drouet, when Louis-François Bertin invited the poet and his family to spend the summer months in his Château des Roches, close to the village of Bièvre outside of Paris. The experience was repeated in the summer of 1832, on which occasion, it seems, Mrs. Hugo profited from the stay to meet with her lover Sainte-Beuve. In January 1833, of course, Hugo met Juliette and the following summer he spent only part of the summer at Les Roches with Adèle. When, the following year, Hugo went to Les Roches with his family, Hugo rented a small house for Juliette in the hamlet of Les Metz, where she was also to stay the following year.

3. "Mon moi se décompose en: *Olympio*: la lyre; *Hermann*: l'amour; *Maglia*: le rire; *Hierro*: le combat" (Albouy 1964, 3:1524); [My self is decomposed in *Olympio*: the lyre; *Hermann*: love; *Maglia*: laughter; *Hierro*: battle]. According to Albouy, this famous citation dates from "les premières années de l'exil" [the first years of exile].

4. That Hugo was jealous of Juliette's early lovers seems a logical conclusion to make from Juliette's letters of July 4, 1834, where she vows to return to her state of ecstasy if ever Hugo presents her with the letter in question, and of October 1834, where she speaks of "délivrance" from her "vie passée" (Souchon 1940, 42–43 and 64–65).

5. "And how," writes Levaillant, "can one fail to note the malice of destiny which, in about 1836, took pleasure in piling on disgraces, misunderstandings, taunts, and sorrows, as though to defie the ambition of the poet's soul which, in its magnificent vitality, was tormented by his appetite for glory and his desire for pre-eminence?" (18; author's translation).

6. The paradigmatic use of this poem comes of course from Baudelaire's "Victor Hugo," in *Quelques-uns de mes contemporains*, and the definitive gloss of *"rêverie"* is Jean Gaudon's *Le Temps de la contemplation* (Gaudon 1969).

7. To take the venerable example of St. Augustine, his argument for the existence and the description of time depends on verbal structures, past, future, and present: "a measured confidence in the daily use of language obliges us to say, in a way which we cannot yet explain, that time is . . . But if it is true *that* we speak of time in a meaningful way and in positive terms (will be, was, is), the

inability to explain the *how* of this usage springs precisely from this certainty" (Ricœur 1983, 1:22; author's translation).

8. "to apostrophize is to will a state of affairs, to attempt to call it into being by asking inanimate objects to bend themselves to your desire . . . At this second level, the function of apostrophe is to constitute encounters with the world as relations between subject and object" . . . the third level of reading, at which apostrophe was a way of constituting a poetical persona by taking up a special relation to objects" (Culler 1975, 139, 141, 146).

9. "*Apostrophe*, ordinarily accompanied by *Exclamation*, is this sudden diversion of discourse in which one turns away from one object to address another, whether natural or supernatural, absent or present, alive or dead, animate or inanimate, real or abstract, or, to address oneself" (Fontanier 1968, 371; author's translation).

10. "But what gives rise to *Apostrophe*? . . . it can only be feeling, and only a feeling so excited in one's heart that it bursts and spreads outside, as of its own impulse" (Fontanier 1968, 372; author's translation). Fontanier, of course, refers frequently to Racine, and it might be interesting to note here that while Oreste's speech at the end of *Andromaque* is punctuated by apostrophe as defined by Fontanier, Phèdre nowhere uses the figure: she is lucid throughout the play.

11. "[I]t [prosopopeia] reasserts itself as the central trope of the poetic corpus which, more than any other, is the model for the textual system he [Michael Riffaterre] has so carefully worked out: the corpus of the poetry (and the prose) of Victor Hugo" (de Man 1986, 45).

QUATREVINGT-TREIZE: REVOLUTION AND ÆSTHETICS

1. As indicated, for example, by his use of the word "Claymore" to designate the Royalist corvette: this was the name of a gunship used by the Commune against Versailles in 1871 (Hugo 1985, 3:1105).

2. Jacques Coppenole predicts the Revolution in *Notre-Dame de Paris* (Hugo 1985, 1:822), and Hugo analogizes the events of England in 1650 to those of France in 1789 in *L'Homme qui rit* (Hugo 1985, 3:476).

3. See "L'Explication des faits littéraires" and "Le Poème comme représentation: Une Lecture de Hugo" (Riffaterre 1979, 7:27 and 175–99). For Roland Barthes's analysis, see "L'Effet de réel" (Barthes 1984).

4. For an indication of the kind of knowledge presupposed in the reader, see Riffaterre's "Flaubert's Presuppositions" (Riffaterre 1981, 5–8).

5. For an account of the French importation of Kantian æsthetics see my "Narrative Evasions of Æsthetics: Hugo's Architectural Fictions" (1989).

6. "[A]ll men find pleasure in imitations. The proof of this is what actually happens in life. For there are some things that distress us when we see them in reality, but the most accurate representations of these same things we view with pleasure—as, for example, the forms of the most despised animals and of corpses" (Hardison 1981, 7).

7. This suppression of the "historical" term "marquis de Lantenac" in

favor of a-temporal qualifiers exemplifies the tension between pastoral and historical discourse Petrey analyzes in his *History in the Text* (1980, 67).

POLITICS AND ÆSTHETICS OF RACE IN *BUG-JARGAL*

1. Indeed, Hugo writes that the second *Bug-Jargal* eclipses not only the first, but also the intervening *Han d'Islande*: "Ce livre a donc été écrit deux ans avant *Han d'Islande*. Et quoique, sept ans plus tard, en 1825, l'auteur l'ait remanié et récrit en grande partie, il n'en est pas moins, et par le fond, et par beaucoup de détails, le premier ouvrage de l'auteur" (Hugo 1985, 1:275); ["This book was written two years before 'Hans of Iceland.' Although seven years later, in 1825, the author recast it and rewrote a large portion of it, it is nevertheless in substance and in many details, the author's first work" Hugo 1894, v)]. What has changed, of course, with the second version of *Bug-Jargal*, is that Hugo has started to sign his works, and it is especially significant that he starts to sign works the ideology of which diverges markedly from that of the first *Bug-Jargal*: it is as if he can only sign Hugo when the too-explicit message of the first version has been made to disappear.

2. The slaves of Santo Domingo revolted in August 1791, when the white colonialists refused to apply the decrees of equality promulgated by the National Assembly. In 1800, Toussaint-Louverture, leader of the insurrection, proclaimed Haiti's independence only to be captured by Napoleon's armies two years later and die in prison in France in 1804.

3. In *Ruy Blas*, for example, Ruy Blas and Don Guritan vie for the queen's affections but the queen elevates Ruy Blas to a high position, from which his acceptance of Don Guritan's challenge to a duel appears all the stranger; further, Ruy Blas's *alter ego*, Don César, actually goes about killing Don Guritan. Each character here takes on a different value as it is contrasted with another one.

4. From *Han d'Islande*, *Notre-Dame de Paris*, and *L'Homme qui rit*, respectively.

5. From *Notre-Dame de Paris*, *Ruy Blas*, and *L'Homme qui rit*, respectively.

6. These, Miller argues in *Blank Darkness*, can be summarized in such self-canceling formulations as "virtueless slaves," and have been in use since Herodotus and Aristotle (1985, 27).

7. For a comprehensive study of the æsthetic dimension of *contemplation*, see (Gaudon 1969). Here it is the withdrawal from politics implicit in contemplation that is under discussion. It is worth noticing that Flaubert also shared this æsthetic: Gérard Genette points out in his "Silences de Flaubert" (1966) that Flaubert used the term "amour de la contemplation" [love of contemplation] to justify extended descriptions: here the withdrawal from politics is doubled with a withdrawal from narrative.

8. "M. Victor Hugo laisse voir dans tous ses tableaux, lyriques et dramatiques, un système d'alignement et de contrastes uniformes. L'excentricité elle-même prend chez lui des formes symétriques. Il possède à fond et emploie froidement tous les tons de la rime, toutes les ressources de l'antithèse, toutes les tricheries de l'apposition" (Baudelaire 1975–76, 2:431) ["In all his pictures,

both lyric and dramatic, M. Victor Hugo lets one see a system of uniform alignment and contrasts. With him even eccentricity takes symmetrical forms. He is in complete possession of, and coldly employs, all the modulations of rhyme, all the resources of antithesis and all the tricks of apposition" (Baudelaire 1965, 56)]. In the same *Salon*, Baudelaire praised "political" criticism, albeit without mentioning Hugo: "la critique doit être partiale, passionnée, politique" (Baudelaire 1975–76, 2:418) ["criticism should be partial, passionate and political" (Baudelaire 1965, 44)]. While Hugo is only mentioned much later in the article, it is clear that Baudelaire's rejection of him is due at least in part to what Baudelaire perceives as his apolitical stance.

THE DISCIPLINE OF LETTERS: *LE DERNIER JOUR D'UN CONDAMNÉ*

1. One historian of capital punishment recounts an anecdote regarding Guillotin's promise to the National Assembly: "Messieurs, with my machine I can whisk off your heads in the blink of an eyelid. You won't feel a thing" (Naish, 104).

2. "Le titre seul me fait mal aux nerfs" (Hugo 1985, 1:421) ["The mere title throws me into hysterics" (Hugo 1894, 333)]. "On n'a pas le droit de faire éprouver à son lecteur des souffrances physiques" (Hugo 1985, 1:425) ["No one has the right to force his readers to undergo physical suffering" (Hugo 1894, 341)].

3. It would be useful in this regard to mention the 1834 "Claude Gueux," Hugo's account of the crime and execution of a prisoner of that name: Gueux, in response to "moral provocation" on the part of his jailer, M. D., kills the latter, after deliberation and consultation with the other prisoners, actions that Hugo strives to portray as the equivalent of the judicial steps leading to Gueux's execution. Gueux is more respected in the prison where he is serving five years for petty larceny, and is better obeyed, than the judges and investigators of the state.

4. The Panopticon can also be realized in bureaucracies, surveillance systems, and computer networks as well, in fact in any arrangement where an invisible observer monitors any of many activities or people on permanent display.

5. Pleasure and freedom are key concepts in the first and second moments respectively of Kant's "Analytic of the Beautiful" (Kant 1952).

6. It is also quite simple to see in "autrefois" and "maintenant" a prototype of Sartre's distinction between "pour soi" and "en soi," where, one feels oneself either as a subject (free, capable of moving, capable of appreciating others) or as an object (paralyzed, subject to the judgment of another).

7. Jean Gaudon, describing the conditions under which *Le Rhin* was written, refers to Hugo's prodigious output as "writing's forced labor" (Gaudon 1985, 1:16; author's translation), and Adèle Hugo, the writer's wife, states that Hugo wrote *Notre-Dame de Paris* under conditions approaching those of a prisoner or a monk (Hugo 1985, 483).

Reading and Reference in *Notre-Dame de Paris*

1. Not simply do both authors characterize the media using the same images, but they also suggest ramifications to choices of media so similar to McLuhan's that, were it not for the difficulties of chronology, one might think Proust and Hugo were trying to advance his argument. In particular, the latter's chapter on "argot" and his inclusion of plot developments concerning the role of the King in Church affairs prefigure, respectively, McLuhan's arguments regarding the standardization of language resulting from printing, and the printed page as instrument of nationalism. Indeed, many of McLuhan's contentions concerning the printed word have uncanny echoes in the pages of *Notre-Dame de Paris* and the preface to *La Bible d'Amiens*. McLuhan argues that the introduction of the printing press brought about changes in outlook far greater than those entailed by the wider diffusion of texts. Obviously, the printed page affected institutions of learning, spelling the end of Medieval scholasticism with its emphasis on memory: easily-available texts obviated the need for memory as conceived of since classical times. But it also had effects more remote from the book: the clean, uniform page influenced dress and decorum, and implied a single, sustained "tone" of discourse and behavior that had not previously existed. Since the printed page was the virtual space of a finite number of moveable characters, a new conception of space, independent of the objects occupying it, was born, a space represented by the single-point perspective whose inventor Vasari claimed to be. The printed book was the first mass-produced commodity, detached in a new way both from its author and its maker. Thus when Hugo evokes a bygone world, part of which is an attitude of spontaneity, and another part of which is a generalized lack of decorum, or good taste ("le bon ton"), one can anticipate that this, too, would be ended by the introduction of the printing-press.

2. Alban Krailsheimer glosses the word thus in his translation of the novel: "the word means rather more than the 'fatality' by which Hugo translates it in the novel; 'force', 'constraint', 'necessity', are the basic meanings, but it could also be used for actual torture"(Hugo 1993, 543).

3. It was only in 1832, in the so-called "eighth" edition of *Notre-Dame de Paris*, that the chapters "Abbas beati Martini" and "Ceci tuera cela" were added to the novel; it is in these chapters, and only in them, that Frollo's phrase appears. It has been speculated that the reasons for the delayed insertions were venal (Hugo 1993, ix); however, it hardly can be coincidental that the chapters articulating the power of writing to obliterate earlier monuments are the ones added to the novel and dramatically change its thesis.

4. See "La Mort des cathédrales" in *Contre Sainte-Beuve* (1971), where in his introductory footnote (141), Proust evokes a moment when cathedrals alone will subsist as relics of western civilization, in an apocalyptic landscape reminiscent of Hugo's "À l'arc de Triomphe." What Proust opposes is the "Projet de loi portant sur la séparation de l'Église et de l'État, dont A. Briand était le rapporteur...."

5. "The upper creature on the left is biting something, the form of which is hardly traceable in the defaced stone—but biting he is; and the reader cannot but recognize in the peculiarly reverted eye the expression which is never seen,

as I think, but in the eye of a dog gnawing something in jest, and preparing to start away with it: the meaning of the glance, so far as it can be marked by the mere incision of the chisel, will be felt by comparing it with the eye of the couchant figure on the right, in its gloomy and angry brooding. The plan of this head, and the nod of the cap over its brow, are fine, but there is a little touch above the hand especially well meant: the fellow is vexed and puzzled in his malice; and his hand is pressed hard on his cheek bone, and the flesh of the cheek is *wrinkled* under the eye by the pressure" (Wedderburn 1903-12, 8:217).

6. In a fragment published posthumously, Proust qualifies criticism (and the Dreyfus affair) as an "excuse" for not writing. See "La Création poétique" in *Contre Sainte-Beuve* (Proust 1971, 413).

7. Consider, for example, the repetition of "j'allai" and the insistent quasi-biblical use of "Et" at the beginning of sentences at key points in the passage, most tellingly at moments of "resurrection."

8. Proust of course uses the same device at the end of *La Recherche*, when he bases his conclusion that time can be recaptured on a desire to become a writer.

9. This is what happened to Ruskin at Rouen, and this is what happened to Proust when he found *The Bible of Amiens*. More importantly perhaps, this is the model of discovery for *La Recherche*, where the chance encounter of an object and an intelligence is the key to the recollection with which the novel starts.

10. Ruskin's assessment of *Notre-Dame de Paris* was not favorable: in *Fiction Fair and Foul* he writes that "the effectual head of the whole cretinous school [i.e., French realists] is the renowned novel in which the hunchbacked lover watches the execution of his mistress from the tower of Notre-Dame" (Wedderburn 1903-12, 34:277); and in a letter to F. J. Furnivall (May 22, 1855) Ruskin writes that *Notre-Dame de Paris* is "simply the most disgusting book ever written by man, and on the whole to have caused more brutality and evil than any other French writing with which I am acquainted. . . . for pure, dull, virtueless, stupid, deadly poison, read Victor Hugo" (Wedderburn 1903-12, 36:212). Proust was aware of Ruskin's reaction: see "Journées de pélerinage," in (Proust 1971).

11. One could even deduce a reference to Hugo's claim from the prosody of Proust's slogan: just as Hugo's aphorism is built around two indefinites embracing the verb "tuer," Proust builds his around the second-person pronoun "tu" and the verb "vivre." Each is lapidary, each involves a parallelism, but their senses are diametrically opposed.

READING AND DENOTATION

1. "On peut dont concevoir *une science qui étudie la vie de signes au sein de la vie sociale*; elle formerait partie de la psychologie sociale, et par conséquent de la psychologie générale; nous la nommerons *sémiologie* (du grec *semeîon*, 'signe'). Elle nous apprendrait en quoi consistent les signes, quelles lois les régissent. Puisqu'elle n'existe pas encore, on ne peut dire ce qu'elle sera; mais elle a droit à l'existence, sa place est déterminée d'avance" (Saussure 1972, 33) ["*A science that studies the life of signs within society* is conceivable; it would be part of social psychology and consequently part of general psychology; I shall call it

semiology (from the Greek *semeîon* 'sign'). Semiology would show what constitutes signs, what laws govern them. Since the science does not yet exist, no one can say what it would be, but it has a right to existence, a place staked out in advance" (Saussure 1959, 16)].

2. For Barthes's theoretical works in semiology, one need only consult his *Éléments de sémiologie* and his numerous contributions to *Communications*; as models of cultural studies, however, his *Mythologies*, *Système de la mode*, and *L'Empire des signes* are more frequently quoted. At times, his late *Roland Barthes* is taken as an example of how personal experience can be written into more general social analyses.

3. Saussure pictured the relation of signifier to signified thus, in order of increasing specificity (Saussure 1972, 99 and Saussure 1959, 66–67):

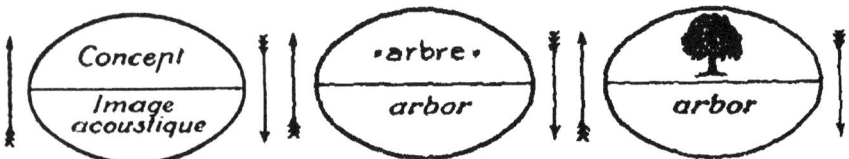

4. Barthes diagrams the relation of connotation to denotation thus (Barthes 1965, 164):

Signifiant		Signifié	(level of connotation)
Signifiant	Signifié		(level of denotation)

Connotation

5. Derrida argues that the linkage of painting to writing is questionable because it tends to make the latter a deferred form of sensation; I would argue instead that the absence specific to writing already structures painting and images generally, making them unassimilable to perception (Derrida 1972, 369–81).

6. "'If this fish shall rise up against you on the last day, and say, "You have certainly given me a body, but no living soul," how are you going to justify yourself against such a complaint?'" (Hegel 1920, 1:58).

7. Janet Wolff makes a comparable claim concerning the relation of art history to the social sciences: "the new art history deals with rereadings of texts, with the decoding of images in relation to social, political, and ideological meanings. This is, of course, a very worthwhile project. . . . My criticism is that it remains at the level of textuality" (Wolff 1992, 708–9).

8. Thus, the linguistic approach precludes the assignation of value (or "pertinence") to variations in the font of most texts: texts are considered the same whether they are printed (or displayed) in Time New Roman or Courier, and this, despite the fact that the choice of font has definite effects.

9. To take just one example of its importance for him, from the late *Roland Barthes*: "Il ne sortait pas de cette idée sombre, que la vraie violence c'est celle du *cela va de soi*: ce qui est évident est violent, même si cette évidence est représentée doucement, libéralement, démocratiquement; ce qui est paradoxal, ce qui ne tombe pas sous le sens, l'est moins, même si c'est imposé arbitrairement: un tyran qui promulguerait des lois saugrenues serait à tout prendre moins violent qu'une masse qui se contenterait d'énoncer *ce qui va de soi*; le 'naturel' est en somme *le dernier des outrages*" (Barthes 1975, 88) ["He could not get away from that grim notion that true violence is that of the *self-evident*: what is evident is violent, even if this evidence is gently, liberally, democratically represented; what is paradoxical, what does not follow of itself, is less so, even if it is imposed arbitrarily; a tyrant who promulgated preposterous laws would be all in all less violent that the masses which were content to utter *what is self-evident, what follows of itself*: the 'natural' is, in short, *the ultimate violence*" (Barthes 1977, 85)].

10. Translated, of course, by Marcel Proust.

11. Proust criticizes this conception of reading in *La Recherche*, when Marcel makes fun of Albertine's essay topics (Proust 1988–9, 2:265–67).

12. Again, there is an appeal to reading: Monet's paintings, Proust informs us, may have subjects that were dictated by reasons of convenience: the painter was called to such-and-such a location in order to deal with family affairs, for example, and yet the paintings appear to the viewer as invested with meaning. The new bridge at Argenteuil, for example, might have "just been there" for Monet, but comes to mean something about progress, technology, and leisure for his viewers (Proust 1971, 177 and Proust 1971, 37).

13. One illustrative example occurs in Renée Riese-Hubert's assessment of Michel Deguy "Art Poétique": "Since the 19th century or more specifically since Verlaine's 'art poétique,' the poetic domain reveals the manifestation of tensions of forces and counterforce, of dialectics. Verlaine's theory and practice of the 'impair' presupposes the existence and the presence of the 'pair' as he threatens its future. Whereas Boolean opposes good poetry to bad poetry, Verlaine opposes poetry to literature, presence to absence" (Riese-Hubert 1979, 172).

14. The many dimensions of Verlaine's irony have already been traced, and in great detail, by Michel Grimaud (Grimaud 1979 and Grimaud 1984), who nonetheless does not go on to interrogate this irony.

15. Pierre Popovic avoids such reductionism, while at the same time supplying all that could be desired in the way of biographical context for the poem (Popovic 1993).

16. The expression *art poétique* suffuses his *Vie, poésies et pensées de Joseph Delorme* (Antoine 1956, 144).

17. "Au lieu du mot vaguement abstrait, métaphysique et sentimental, employer le mot propre et pittoresque" (Antoine 1956, 146–47) [Instead of the vaguely abstract, metaphysical, and sentimental word, employ the proper and picturesque word].

18. Carol Rifelj writes: "there was no such meaning of the word at the time: it is this poem itself which turns *littérature* into a pejorative word" (Rifelj 1982).

19. The relevant passages are *Phædrus* are 246, 251, and 255c; here is 251:

"but when one . . . beholds a godlike face or bodily form that truly expresses beauty. . . a strange sweating and fever seizes him . . . the stump of the wing swells and hastens to grow from the root of the whole substance of the soul" (Plato 1961, 497).

ART CRITICISM'S NARRATIVES

1. For a list of authors who think that Baudelaire ought to have chosen otherwise, see David Carrier's, *High Art* (Carrier 1996, 50–51).

2. Richard D. E. Burton writes thus about Baudelaire's frame of mind immediately prior to his stay in Honfleur: "With his literary reputation, it seemed, definitively besmirched, his brief, botched liaison with Madame Sabatier ending in recrimination and self-disgust and in his day-to-day existence tyrannized by creditors, publishers and the ubiquitous presence of the persnickety and fatuously loquacious Ancelle, Baudelaire was, by the end of 1857, as close to total despair as at any time since the suicide attempt—if such it was—of June 1845" (Burton 1988, 2). As for Baudelaire's creativity during 1859, beyond the *Salon de 1859*, the year is known for the publication of "Le Cygne," "Les Petites Vieilles," "Les Sept Vieillards," "La Chevelure," and several other poems of the first order.

3. This is at least what Baudelaire maintains concerning photography in 1859. He characterizes photography as positive, a reproduction rather than a creation, repetition rather than innovation.

4. One might say that the text of this passage scarcely corresponds to the painting shown at the *Salon*: the painting, currently in the Santamarina collection in Buenos Aires, shows a long staircase winding down to an underground tomb: at the top, in the light, Mary is helped up by the Holy Women; at the bottom, two men carry Christ down the stairs as still others, a woman and two men, light their way. What Baudelaire's text does echo is his description of the *Pietà* described in the *Salon de 1846*, which, of course, was not present in 1859; nor, however, was it present at the 1846 *Salon*: it was already at its definitive location, the church of Saint Denis du Saint Sacrement in the Marais.

5. It is of course typical of this essay and its problems that in its first publication in *La Revue française*, the verb is "fuit," while in the posthumous *Curiosités esthétiques*, the verb is "fait." In the first instance, the sentence runs : "Imagination flees from landscape," implying a story; in the second, it runs "Imagination makes landscape," implying a state of affairs.

THE END OF CITATION IN BAUDELAIRE'S ART CRITICISM

1. For the scope of this bibliography, see pp. 1262–64 of Charles Baudelaire, *Œuvres complètes*, Bibliothèque de la Pléiade, 2 vols. (Paris: Gallimard, 1975-6).

2. See, for example, Jean Prévost's *Baudelaire: Essai sur l'inspiration poétique* (Paris: Mercure de France, 1953).

3. The argument here is evidently Kantian, but it is not necessary to invoke readings of the *Critique of Judgment* by Baudelaire (which of course can't be done) in order to defend its use: the poet's famous assertion that "le beau est toujours bizarre" is entirely consonant with the conclusion of the *Critique*'s second moment: "The *beautiful* is that which, apart from a concept, pleases universally."

4. Citation of course has other effects: in description (as in the Delacroix chapter of the *Salon de 1859*) it produces an illusion of reference: the certain reference of a text to another text is the very model of denotation and confers on the art-critical description a pointing effect that spreads to the areas of judgment and theory (Raser 1993). Reading an art-critical text whose descriptions use citation, one accepts the reference to the painting to be as effective as a reference to a text, and the critic's judgments to be correspondingly accurate.

5. See, for example, Claude Pichois's juxtaposition of the poem to Delacroix's *Barque de Dante* and *Naufrage de Don Juan*, and his assertion that Baudelaire brought Simon Guérin's lithograph of the same title to completion: "Ce tableau, c'est Baudelaire qui l'a réalisé . . ." Baudelaire, *Œuvres complètes* 1:868.

6. The role of figure in art criticism is particularly difficult to assess: while a verbal context permits the determination of "literal" meaning, and by inference inappropriate—thus figural—terms in that context, no such level of literal meaning exists in the description of a work of art. All descriptions, especially those words designating "things" depicted by a picture, are figural: it is by a long process of decoding that one determines that patterns of pigment on a surface represent three-dimensional objects (Gombrich 1969, 279). Conversely, one could consider any description of a work of art to be "literal," there being no linguistic context with which to compare its terms and thereby to decide their appropriateness. Figure lives a precarious existence in art criticism: it must be figural to some degree, but the temptation to authorize its judgments by resorting to citation has an inhibiting effect on figural play.

7. That Baudelaire is one such translating spectator is evident from his comment at the end of part XII: "Elles sont grosses de suggestions, . . . que ma plume . . . n'a peut-être traduites qu'insuffisamment" (from *Œuvres complètes*).

8. See Timothy Clark (Clark 1984), Ann Hanson (Hanson 1977), Robert Jensen, *Marketing Modernism* (1994), and Paul de Man (de Man 1983), respectively.

9. Art criticism springs historically from connoisseurship, the aim of which is to establish provenance, to attribute works to artists or schools, and to distinguish forgeries from authentic works; it follows that it will be more particular, less open to allegory than the more general discourse of literary interpretation.

10. Paul de Man has glossed this passage as an allegory of writing, apposing it to the description of ships' rigging in chapter XIII (de Man 1983).

11. Since Baudelaire's article on Hugo, "La Pente de la rêverie" has been considered a seminal poem for Hugo scholars: Jean Gaudon, for instances, traces the founding concept of "contemplation" to this poem (Gaudon 1969). Yet "La Pente" is just as much about perception and the truth thereof as it is about contemplation or inner vision. In its early moments, it describes the pleasures of the senses, pleasures that are troubled by the simultaneous recollection

of memories, which in turn are troubled by the simultaneous existence of "memories" never experienced, but learned indirectly, through history or logic. In a gesture repeated from Locke to Hegel, Sartre, and beyond, Hugo questions one's knowledge of sense perceptions. To this assertion of the primacy of memory Baudelaire responds that there is a distinct sensory and sensual component to art.

12. For example, Diderot's comments on Greuze in his *Salon de 1765*: he uses the figure of prosopopeia, the very trope of resurrection, and calls the absent milkmaid forth to dialogue with him. See Diderot 1976–83, 2:145–49. More recently, Jacques Derrida has deconstructed the figure in "Restitutions" (Jacques Derrida, "Restitutions de la vérité en peinture," *La Vérité en peinture*, Champs [Paris: Flammarion, 1978)], where rendering back to life is one of many "renderings" demanded of painting.

13. For example, Proust's account of John Ruskin's criticism in his preface to *La Bible d'Amiens*.

14. See, for example, Gautier's comments on Leonardo, in his *Guide de l'amateur au musée du Louvre* (Théophile Gautier, *Œuvres complètes*, vol. 8, 13 vols. [Geneva: Droz, 1978]).

15. Baudelaire sent his description of Meryon's works from the *Salon de 1859* to Victor Hugo in Guernesey, as though it were a poem; he later quoted it *in extenso* in his discussion of etching and Manet's etchings.

16. For example, see Claude Pichois's persuasive account in his comments on "Rêve parisien" in Baudelaire, *Œuvres complètes* 1:1041.

17. This reading builds on Sartre's comments on *Mon Cœur mis à nu* (Sartre 1963, 128–47).

18. And, of course, the world described in the poem is nothing like that of Guys's drawings: Alma-Tadema or some other historian of imperial splendors would be a more consistent choice.

19. If one takes Baudelaire's discussion of Delacroix's *Mise au tombeau* in his *Salon de 1859* as a counter-example, things perhaps become clearer. Here, Baudelaire performs two distinct acts of pointing; on the one hand, he designates a work present at the *Salon*; on the other, in this designation, he designates several texts: Delacroix's catalog description, the passage from Chateaubriand's *Martyrs*, where Eudore discovers Ovid's tomb; another brief text from Chateaubriand's *Natchez*, and finally, two verses in translation from Ovid's *Tristia*. While many different arrangements of the citations can be imagined, from at one pole a chronology of the events depicted (Ovid's exile, Delacroix's description of his arrival, Ovid's complaint about his exile, Eudore's discovery of Ovid's tomb, Chateaubriand's description of the American wilderness) to at the other pole, a chronology of the texts (Ovid's *Tristia*, Chateaubriand's *Natchez*, Chateaubriand's *Martyrs*, Delacroix's description), no story arises from these quotations, and, indeed, the quotations are antithetical to any narrative reconstruction. Baudelaire's text reads like a painting with *pentimenti* under the surface, offering a blurred and self-contradictory image, a reversed narrative of the painting's creation.

20. The prescience of Baudelaire's aesthetic judgment enables Pierre-Georges Castex, for one, to read Manet into Baudelaire's article on Guys.

Claiming Painting for Literature: Fromentin and Claudel

1. See for example two paintings shown at the *Salon de 1859* and commented by Baudelaire: *Audience chez un khalifat* (1860 copy at Schweitzer Gallery, New York) and *Une Rue à El-Aghouat* (Musée de Douai) in Thompson (1987).

2. These comments are of a type that has been familiar since Rousseau: Fromentin expresses a desire for a simpler art, one less dependent on thought, more dependent on sensation, and presupposing the identity of thought and perception. As such, it could be deconstructed quite easily and without too much interest. The comments are also, however, those of a painter turned critic and could just as well describe a program of criticism as well as one of painting: here, Fromentin promotes a criticism based more on analysis, less on speculation; what he seeks is less like fiction and more like simple naming. If one reads his comments as dealing only with painting, Fromentin is promoting genre painting and landscape; if one reads them as an allegory of criticism, then enumeration, with all its attendant perspectives of dreary lists, not narrative, with its attendant interest and drama, seems to be the model he advocates.

Les Maîtres d'autrefois certainly justifies both views: it amply shows Fromentin's fascination with both genre and landscape painting, and his analyses, relying heavily on his painter's knowledge of the terms of the trade, are less metaphorical and less narrative than those of other critics.

3. The thesis here is the contrary of that put forward by Emmanuelle Kaes in her excellent " 'L'Action sourde et comme latérale'." There Kaes sees a movement away from painting and towards literature, from the eye to the ear: "the eye as organ of intellectual conquest and appropriation recedes to the benefit of the ear, the organ of receptivity" (Kaes 1993, 7; author's translation). Claudel continues to appropriate, doing what he sees the Dutch artists doing: "L'artiste hollandais n'est plus une volonté qui exécute un plan préconçu . . . c'est un œil qui choisit et qui saisit" (Claudel 1946, 39–40) ["The Dutch painter is no longer a will that executes a preconceived plan . . .; he is an eye that selects and takes possession" (Claudel 1950, 38)]. One thesis however does not exclude the other: Kaes's article speaks of Claudel's article as an allegory of poetics, which of course it is. Here Claudel's article of course considered art criticism. And it is precisely the contention here that art-critical discourse, as opposed to poetics, involves the proprietary relations and self-representation that are discussed. For another treatment of *L'Œil écoute* as a work of poetics, see Pierre-Yves Bourdil (1993).

4. Derrida writes: "—Je distinguerais trois dogmes dans le credo de Schapiro, quand il spécule ainsi sur l'occasion de ces vieux souliers. Trois dogmes de structures distinctes mais analogues dans leur finalité fonctionnelle. 1. Des chaussures peintes peuvent appartenir réellement et se laisser restituer réellement à un sujet réel, identifiable, nommable. Cette illusion est facilité par l'identification la plus proche entre le détenteur allégué des chaussures et le soi-disant signataire du tableau. 2. Des chaussures sont des chaussures, qu'elles soient peintes ou 'réelles', seulement et simplement des chaussures qui sont ce qu'elles sont, adéquates à elles-mêmes et d'abord adaptables à des pieds. Des

chaussures appartiennent en propre. Elles n'ont pas, dans leur structure de produit remplaçable, dans le standard de leur pointure, dans le détachable de cet instrument de type vestimentaire, de quoi faire dériver toute appartenance et toute propriété *strictes*. 3. Des pieds (peints fantomatiques ou réels) appartiennent à un corps propre. Ils n'en sont pas détachables. Ces trois assurances ne résistent pas à la moindre question. Elles sont aussitôt démontées, en tout cas, par ce qui *se passe*, ce qu'*il y a* dans cette peinture" (Derrida 1978, 357–358) ["I would distinguish three dogmas in Schapiro's credo, when he speculates in this way on the occasion of these old shoes. Three dogmas with structures that are distinct from one another but analogous in their functional finality. 1. Painted shoes can belong really and really be restituted to a real, identifiable, and nameable subject. This illusion is facilitated by the closest identification between the alleged holder of the shoes and the so-called signatory of the picture. 2. Shoes are shoes, be they painted or "real," solely and simply shoes which are what they are, adequate to themselves and in the first place fittable onto feet. Shoes belong properly. In their size, in the detachability of this clothing-type instrument, they do not have what it would take to make all *strict* belonging and propriety drift. 3. Feet (painted, ghostly, or real) belong to a body proper. They are not detachable from it. These three assurances can't stand up to the slightest question. They are in any case immediately dismantled by what *happens* [*se passe*], by what *there is* in this painting (Derrida 1987, 313–14)].

SARTRE AND TINTORETTO: THIS SIDE OF WORDS

1. See *La Nausée* (Sartre 1938, 117–33); "Portraits officiels" (Sartre 1970); "Les Peintures de Giacometti" (Sartre 1954); "Le Peintre sans privilèges" (Sartre 1964); "Masson" (Sartre 1964); and "Coexistences" (Sartre 1972). There is also an allusion to Tintoretto in the essay *Qu'est-ce que la littérature*, where Sartre distinguishes between painting as a medium and the linguistic sign (Sartre 1948, *Situations II*, 60–67).

2. "What is under discussion here is a fragment of a book that Sartre had almost finished, but which he abandoned because he was not satisfied with its style . . . Simone de Beauvoir explains in *La Force des choses*: 'A publisher asked him, for an art series, for a text on a painter. Sartre had always liked Tintoretto: he had been interested, since before the war, and especially since '46, in the way in which he conceived of time and space'" (Contat 1970, 314; author's translation).

3. "This impression of reality finally incarnate, coming to us, paradoxically from words turned away from incarnation, I will call *image*" (Bonnefoy 1983, 32–33; author's translation).

4. The essay on Lapoujade is an exception to this rule, but its brevity only indicates all the better Sartre's preponderant interest in art that represents the human figure.

5. Sartre explicitly states in *L'Imaginaire* that the object of a work of art is not its pigments, brushstrokes, etc. but the "unreal" that arises in the imagination when these elements are perceived together. Sartre argues there that what

is apprehended in a painting is not its material aspect, but what the painting represents, even if what is represented is chosen for its material aspects.

6. It has often been said that Sartre was superceded by more recent writers because he failed to incorporate linguistic theory, especially Saussure's distinction of *signe* and *signifié*, into his works. Instead, he offers what appears to be an antiquated definition of the sign (opposed only to the thing signified, Saussure's referent); there is no distinction here of meaning and referent, no discussion of the arbitrary nature of signification, features of Saussure's analysis that have enabled a theory of linguistics abstracted from problems of reference. And yet, in passages like this one, it is obvious that Sartre has a theory of the sign. Here he opposes sign (*signe*) and referent (*chose*) and states that in the plastic arts, the signifying function is not present, or at least, less than in writing: "Les notes, les couleurs, les formes ne sont pas des signes, elles ne renvoient à rien qui leur soit extérieur" (Sartre 1948, *Situations II*, 60) ["Notes, colours, and forms are not signs. They refer to nothing exterior to themselves" (Sartre 1988, 25)]. This view is of course opposed to that of a semiologist, for example, who would hold that language is the model of any artistic practice. But Sartre's intuition here is undeniable: even if paintings and sculptures are some kind of protolinguistic statements, there is another dimension to them: what could be called (for lack of another word) their "just-thereness": While statements appeal for interpretation, one can always eschew interpretation of a painting, a sculpture, or a piece of music, and appreciate it for what it is, not what it means.

7. "A faithful Christian . . . set out without asking permission, and went to pray at the saint's tomb. . . . his master, much angered, ordered him to have his eyes put out. At once, the slaves, more cruel than their lord, stretched their pious comrade upon the ground, and set about their task of gouging out his eyes with wooden stakes. But their fury was of no avail, because the points broke when they touched his eyes. Then the master commanded the poor man's limbs to be broken with hatchet-blows, but the iron of the axes softened and turned to lead. Next the master ordered his teeth to be smashed with iron hammers. But again the iron forgot its strength and softened, as if dulled by the power of God. Seeing all this, the master . . . repented, begged forgiveness of the slave, and went with him to pray at the tomb of Saint Mark" (de Voragine 1969, 242–43).

8. "It must be admitted that, supported by a careful division of the painting into four close-up details, the fragment that was published in *L'Arc* somewhat forgets the painting as a whole" (Leenhardt 1981, 43; author's translation); "The fact is that Sartre approaches *Saint George* with a head full of fixed ideas and prejudices with regard to Tintoretto" (O'Donohoe 1981, 165; author's translation).

9. "In a passage of this type, the painting becomes history, it becomes a story, there is a diegetization of the painting . . . Whereas the essential characteristic of paintings by Tintoretto is suspense, . . . the discourse used by Sartre reinstalls the a priori conditions of the action by offering a *dramatic* reading" (Leenhardt 1981, 46; author's translation).

10. "Here then is Tintoretto as materialist philosopher, or better, *materialist painter*, the painter of a world stuck in chrematistics and closed in the lonely and impenetrable weights of the Venice that sequestered him" (Leenhardt 1981, 40; author's translation).

Works Cited

Abrams, M. H. *The Mirror and the Lamp: Romantic Theory and the Critical Tradition*. New York: Oxford University Press, 1953.
Albouy, Pierre, ed. *Œuvres poétiques de Victor Hugo*. 3 vols., Bibliothèque de la Pléiade. Paris: Gallimard, 1964.
———, ed. *Victor Hugo: Les Contemplations, Gallimard Poésie*. Paris: Éditions Gallimard, 1973.
Antoine, Gérald, ed. *Sainte-Beuve: Vie, poésies et pensées de Joseph Delorme*. Paris: Nouvelles Éditions Latines, 1956.
Austin, J. L. *How to Do Things with Words*. Cambridge: Harvard University Press, 1960.
Barthes, Roland. "Arcimboldo, or Magician and Rhétoriqueur." In *The Responsibility of Forms*, edited by Éditions du Seuil, 129–48. New York: Hill and Wang, 1985.
———. "Arcimboldo, ou Rhétoriqueur et magicien." In *L'Obvie et l'obtus*, 122–38. Paris: Éditions du Seuil, 1982.
———. "Éléments de sémiologie." In *Le Degré zéro de l'écriture suivi de Éléments de sémiologie*, 77–176. Paris: Gonthier, 1965.
———. "La Rhétorique de l'image." In *L'Obvie et l'obtus*, 25–42. Paris: Éditions du Seuil, 1982.
———. "L'Effet de réel." In *Le Bruissement de la langue*, 167–74. Paris: Éditions du Seuil, 1984.
———. "Rhetoric of the Image." In *The Responsibility of Forms*, edited by Éditions du Seuil, 21–40. New York: Hill and Wang, 1985.
———. *Roland Barthes*. Vol. 96 of *Écrivains de Toujours*. Paris: Éditions du Seuil, 1975.
———. *Roland Barthes by Roland Barthes*. Translated by Richard Howard. New York: Hill and Wang, 1977.
———. *S/Z*. Edited by Philippe Sollers, *Tel Quel*. Paris: Éditions du Seuil, 1970.
———. *S/Z*. Translated by Richard Howard. New York: Hill and Wang, 1974.
Baudelaire, Charles. *Art in Paris 1845–1862*. Translated by Jonathan Mayne. *Landmarks in Art History*. London: Phaidon Press, 1965.
———. *Correspondance*. 2 vols., *Bibliothèque de la Pléiade*. Paris: Éditions Gallimard, 1973.
———. *Œuvres complètes*. 2 vols., *Bibliothèque de la Pléiade*. Paris: Éditions Gallimard, 1975–76.

———. *The Painter of Modern Life, and Other Essays*. Translated by Jonathan Mayne. 2nd ed. London: Phaidon Press Ltd., 1995.

Benjamin, Walter. *The Arcades Project*. Translated by Howard Eiland and Kevin McLaughlin. Cambridge: Harvard University Press, 1999.

Benveniste, Émile. "Analytical Philosophy and Language." In *Problems in General Linguistics*, 231–38. Coral Gables, Fla.: University of Miami Press, 1971.

———. "La Philosophie analytique et le langage." In *Problèmes de linguistique générale*. Paris: Éditions Gallimard, 1964.

Bloom, Harold. *The Anxiety of Influence*. New York: Oxford University Press, 1973.

———. "The Breaking of Form." In *Deconstruction and Criticism*, 1–37. New York: The Seabury Press, 1979.

———. *Poetry and Repression*. New Haven: Yale University Press, 1976.

Bonnefoy, Yves. *La Présence et l'image*. Paris: Mercure de France, 1983.

Boudriot, Jean. *Le Vaisseau de 74 canons*. 3 vols. Grenoble: Éditions des Quatre Seigneurs, 1975.

Bourdil, Pierre-Yves. "Écrire et voir: Pour une poétique philosophique." *Claudel Studies* 20, no. 1 and 2 (1993): 18–44.

Brombert, Victor. *Victor Hugo and the Visionary Novel*. Cambridge: Harvard University Press, 1984.

Bryson, Norman. *Vision and Painting: The Logic of the Gaze*. New Haven: Yale University Press, 1983.

Burton, Richard D. E. *Baudelaire in 1859: A Study in the Sources of Poetic Creativity*. Edited by Malcolm Bowie. *Cambridge Studies in French*. Cambridge: Cambridge University Press, 1988.

Carrier, David. *Artwriting*. Amherst, Mass.: University of Massachusetts Press, 1987.

———. *High Art: Charles Baudelaire and the Origins of Modernist Painting*. University Park, Pa.: Pennsylvania State University Press, 1996.

Castex, Pierre-Georges. *Baudelaire critique d'art*. Paris: SEDES, 1969.

Christin, Anne Marie. "Fromentin critique d'art ou La Rhétorique du vide." *Cahiers de l'Association Internationale des Études Françaises* 37 (1985): 193–212.

Clark, Timothy. *The Painting of Modern Life*. New York: Knopf, 1984.

Claudel, Paul. *The Eye Listens*. Translated by Elsie Pell. New York: Philosophical Library, Inc., 1950.

———. *L'Œil Écoute*. Paris: Éditions Gallimard, 1946.

Cogman, Peter. *Hugo: Les Contemplations*. London: Grant and Cutler, Ltd., 1984.

Contat, Michel and Michel Rybalka, eds. *Les Écrits de Sartre*. Paris: Éditions Gallimard, 1970.

Cousin, Victor. "Cours de philosophie sur le fondement des idées absolues du vrai, du beau et du bien." In *Œuvres de Victor Cousin*. Brussels: Hauman et Compagnie, 1840.

———. *The Philosophy of the Beautiful*. Translated by Jesse Cato Daniel. New York: Daniel Bixby, 1849.

Culler, Jonathan. "Apostrophe." In *The Pursuit of Signs*, 135–54. Ithaca: Cornell University Press, 1975.

da Voragine, Jacopo. *La Légende dorée*. Translated by J.-B. M. Roze. 2 vols. Paris: Garnier-Flammarion, 1967.

de Maistre, Joseph. *Les Soirées de Saint-Pétersbourg*. 2 vols. Paris: Éditions de la Maisnie, 1980.

de Man, Paul. "Hypogram and Inscription." In *The Resistance to Theory*, edited by Wlad Godzich, 27–53. Minneapolis: University of Minnesota Press, 1986.

———. "Literary History and Literary Modernity." In *Blindness and Insight*, edited by Wlad Godzich, 142–65. Minneapolis: University Of Minnesota Press, 1983.

———. "The Resistance to Theory." In *The Resistance to Theory*, edited by Wlad Godzich, 3–20. Minneapolis: University of Minnesota Press, 1986.

de Voragine, Jacobus. *The Golden Legend*. Translated by Helmut Granger and Ryan Ripperger. New York: Arno Press, 1969.

Derrida, Jacques. "La Mythologie blanche: La Métaphore dans le texte philosophique." In *Marges de la philosophie*, 247–324. Paris: Éditions de Minuit, 1972.

———. "Signature événement contexte." In *Marges de la philosophie*, 365–93. Paris: Éditions de Minuit, 1972.

———. "Restitutions de la vérité en pointure." In *La Vérité en peinture*, 291–435. Paris: Flammarion, 1978.

———. "Signature Event Context." In *Margins of Philosophy* 307–30. Translated by Alan Bass. Chicago: University of Chicago Press, 1982.

———. *The Truth in Painting*. Translated by Geoff McLeod and Ian Bennington. Chicago: University of Chicago Press, 1987.

———. "White Mythology." *New Literary History* 6 (1974): 5–74.

Diderot, Denis. *Salons*. 2nd ed. 3 vols. Oxford: Oxford University Press, 1976–83.

Fontanier, Pierre. *Les Figures du discours, Flammarion Champs*. Paris: Flammarion, 1968.

Foucault, Michel. *Discipline and Punish: The Birth of the Prison*. Translated by Alan Sheridan. New York: Vintage Books, 1977.

———. *Les Mots et les choses: Une Archéologie des sciences humaines, Bibliothèque des Sciences Humaines*. Paris: Éditions Gallimard, 1966.

———. "Les Mots et les images." In *Dits et écrits: 1954–1988*, edited by Daniel Defert and François Ewald, 620–23. Paris: Éditions Gallimard, 1994.

———. *Surveiller et punir, Bibliothèque des idées*. Paris: Éditions Gallimard, 1974.

France, Anatole. "Aristos and Polyphilos on the Language of Metaphysics." In *The Garden of Epicurus*, edited by J. Lewis Frederic and May Champion. New York: John Lane Company, 1920.

———. *Le Jardin d'Épicure*. Paris: Calmann-Lévy, 1921.

Freud, Sigmund. *Beyond the Pleasure Principle*. Translated by James Strachey. New York: Bantam Books, 1972.

Frey, John A. *Les Contemplations of Victor Hugo: The Ash Wednesday Liturgy*. Charlottesville: The University of Virginia Press, 1988.

Fromentin, Eugène. *The Masters of Past Time*. Translated by H. Gerson. London: Phaidon Press, 1948.

———. *Œuvres complètes, Bibliothèque de la Pléiade*. Paris: Éditions Gallimard, 1984.

Gaudon, Jean. *Le Temps de la contemplation*. Paris: Flammarion, 1969.

———. "Les Vicissitudes du savoir." In *"L'Homme qui rit" ou La Parole-monstre de Victor Hugo*. Paris: SEDES, 1985.

———, ed. *Victor Hugo: Le Rhin Lettres à un ami*. Edited by Pierre-Georges Castex. 2 vols. *Lettres Françaises Collection de l'Imprimerie Nationale*. Paris: Imprimerie nationale, 1985.

———, ed. *Victor Hugo: Lettres à Juliette Drouet*. Paris: Jean-Jacques Pauvert, 1964.

———, ed. *Victor Hugo: Les Contemplations*. Paris: Le Livre de Poche, 1985.

Gautier, Théophile. *Œuvres complètes*. 13 vols. Vol. 8. Geneva: Droz, 1978.

Genette, Gérard. "Silences de Flaubert." In *Figures*, 223–43. Paris: Éditions du Seuil, 1966.

Georgel, Pierre. *La Gloire de Victor Hugo: Galéries nationales du Grand Palais, Paris, 1er octobre 1985–6 janvier 1986*. Paris: Ministère de la Culture: Éditions de la Réunion des musées nationaux, 1985.

Gombrich, E. H. *Art and Illusion: A Study in the Psychology of Pictorial Representation*. Bollingen Series. Princeton: Princeton University Press, 1969.

Grimaud, Michel. "'Art poétique' de Verlaine, ou De la rhétorique du double-jeu." *Romance Notes* 20 (1979): 195–201.

———. "Questions de méthode: Verlaine et la critique structuraliste." *Œuvres et critiques* 9, no. 2 (1984).

Grossman, Kathryn. *The Early Novels of Victor Hugo*. Geneva: Droz, 1986.

Hanson, Anne Coffin. *Manet and the Modern Tradition*. New Haven: Yale University Press, 1977.

Hardison, O. B., ed. *Aristotle's Poetics: A Translation and Commentary for Students of Literature*. Tallahassee: University Presses of Florida, 1981.

Hegel, Georg Friedrich. *Phenomenology of Spirit*. Translated by A. V. Miller. New York: Oxford University Press, 1977.

———. *The Philosophy of Fine Art*. Translated by F. P. B. Osmaston. 4 vols. London: G. Bell and Sons, Ltd., 1920.

Huas, Jeanine. *Juliette Drouet: Le Bel Amour de Victor Hugo*. Paris: Gaston Lachurié, 1985.

Hugo, Adèle. *Victor Hugo raconté par Adèle Hugo, Collection les Mémorables*. Paris: Plon, 1985.

Hugo, Victor. *Bug-Jargal, to Which Are Added: Claude Gueux and the Last Days of a Condemned*. New York: Little, Brown, and Company, 1894.

———. *By Order of the King*. Translated by A. C. Steele. Chicago: Donohoe, Henneberry and Co., 1900.

———. *The Dramatic Works of Victor Hugo*. Translated by Mrs. Newton; Ives Crosland, George Burnham and Frederick L. Slous. 3 vols. New York: Little, Brown, and Company, 1909.

———. *Ninety-Three*. Translated by Helen B. Dole. Chicago: Donohue, Henneberry and Co., 1900.

———. *Notre-Dame de Paris*. Translated by Alban Krailsheimer, *The World's Classics*. New York: Oxford University Press, 1993.

———. *Œuvres complètes*. Edited by Guy Schoeller. 16 vols. Bouquins. Paris: Robert Laffont, 1985.

———. *Three Plays by Victor Hugo*. Translated by C. Crosland and F. L. Slous Crosland. New York: Howard Fertig, 1995.

Jacquet, M. l'Abbé, ed. *La Sainte Bible traduite en français par Lemaistre de Sacy*. 2 vols. Paris: Garnier Frères, 1846.

Jameson, Fredric. *The Prison-House of Language*. Princeton: Princeton University Press, 1975.

Jenkins, Ernest A. *A History of the French Navy*. London: MacDonald and Company, 1973.

Kaes, Emmanuelle. "'L'Action sourde et comme latérale...'." *Claudel Studies* 20, no. 1 and 2 (1993).

Kant, Immanuel. *The Critique of Judgement*. Translated by James Creed Meredith. Oxford: Oxford University Press, 1952.

Lacan, Jacques. *Le Séminaire, Livre XI, Les Quatre Concepts fondamentaux de la psychanalyse*. Edited by Jacques Lacan, *Le Champ Freudien*. Paris: Éditions du Seuil, 1973.

Leenhardt, Jacques. "Sartre face au Saint Georges du Tintoret." *Revue d'esthétique*, no. 2 (1981).

Leroux, Pierre. "Du style symbolique." In *Œuvres*, 328–38. Geneva: Slatkine Reprints, 1829.

Maurois, André. *Olympio, ou La Vie de Victor Hugo*. Paris: Librairie Hachette, 1954.

May, Herbert G. and Bruce M. Metzger, ed. *The New Oxford Annotated Bible with the Apocrypha*. New York: Oxford University Press, 1973.

McLuhan, Marshall. "The Printed Word: Architect of Nationalism." In *Understanding Media*, 170–78. New York: McGraw Hill Book Company, 1964.

Miller, Christopher. *Blank Darkness: Africanist Discourse in French*. Chicago: University of Chicago Press, 1985.

Naish, Camille. *Death Comes to the Maiden: Sex and Execution, 1431–1933*. New York: Routledge, 1991.

Nash, Suzanne. *Les Contemplations of Victor Hugo: An Allegory of the Creative Process*. Princeton: Princeton University Press, 1976.

O'Donohoe, Bénédict. "Sartre tuant Saint-Georges." In *Sartre et les arts*, edited by Michel Sicard, 163–66. Paris: Librairie Obliques, 1981.

Packard, Vance. *The Hidden Persuaders*. New York: Pocket Books, 1963.

Petrey, Sandy. *History in the Text: "Quatrevingt-Treize" and the French Revolution*. Amsterdam: Purdue University Monographs in Romance Languages, 1980.

Piroué, Georges. "Les Deux Bug-Jargal." In *Œuvres complètes de Victor Hugo*, edited by Jean Massin. Paris: Club du Meilleur Livre, 1970.

Plato. "Phaedrus." In *The Collected Dialogues*, edited by Edith and Huntington Cairns Hamilton, 475–525. Princeton, N.J.: Princeton University Press, 1961.

Popovic, Pierre. "Les Deux 'Arts poétiques' de Paul Verlaine." *Études françaises* 29, no. 3 (1993): 103–22.

Proust, Marcel. *À la recherche du temps perdu*. 4 vols. Bibliothèque de la Pléiade. Paris: Gallimard, 1988–89.

———. *Contre Sainte-Beuve*, Bibliothèque de la Pléiade. Paris: Gallimard, 1971.

———. *On Reading*. Translated by Jean Autret and William Burford. New York: The MacMillan Company, 1971.

———. *On Reading Ruskin*. Translated by Jean Autret, William Burford, and Phillip J. Wolfe. New Haven: Yale University Press, 1987.

Racine, Jean. *Complete Plays*. Translated by Samuel Solomon. 2 vols. New York: Random House, 1967.

Raser, Timothy. "Citation and Narrative in Baudelaire's Art Criticism." *Word & Image* 9, no. 4 (1993): 309–19.

———. "Narrative Evasions of Æsthetics: Hugo's Architectural Fictions." *French Forum* (1989).

Rat, Maurice. *Racine: Théâtre complet*. Paris: Garnier Frères, 1960.

Ricœur, Paul. *Temps et récit*. Edited by Jean Wahl. 3 vols. *Ordre Philosophique*. Paris: Éditions du Seuil, 1983.

Riese-Hubert, Renee. "Michel Deguy's 'Art poétique.'" *Sub-Stance: A Review of Theory and Literary Criticism* 23–24 (1979): 172–76.

Rifelj, Carol de Dobay. "Familiar and Unfamiliar: Verlaine's Poetic Diction." *Kentucky Romance Quarterly* 29, no. 4 (1982): 365–77.

Riffaterre, Michael. "Flaubert's Presuppositions." *Diacritics: A Review of Contemporary Criticism* 11 (1981).

———. *La Production du texte*. Paris: Éditions du Seuil, 1979.

Robb, Graham. *Victor Hugo*. New York: W. W. Norton and Company, 1997.

Rosa, Guy. "*Quatrevingt-Treize* ou La Critique du roman historique." *Revue d'Histoire Littéraire de la France* 75 (1975).

Sartre, Jean-Paul. *Baudelaire, Idées*. Paris: Édition Gallimard, 1963.

———. "Coexistences." In *Situations, IX*, 316–25. Paris: Éditions Gallimard, 1972.

———. *La Nausée*. Paris: Éditions Gallimard, 1938.

———. "Le Peintre sans privilèges." In *Situations, IV*, 364–86. Paris: Éditions Gallimard, 1964.

———. "Les Peintures de Giacometti." *Les Temps modernes*, no. 103 (1954): 2221–32.

———. *L'Imaginaire*. Paris: Éditions Gallimard, 1940.

———. "Masson." In *Situations, IV*, 387–407. Paris: Éditions Gallimard, 1964.

———. "Portraits officiels." In *Les Écrits de Sartre*, edited by Michel Contat and Michel Rybalka, 557–58. Paris: Éditions Gallimard, 1970.

———. *The Psychology of Imagination*. New York: Philosophical Library, 1948.

———. "Saint Georges et le dragon." In *Situations, IX*. Paris: Éditions Gallimard, 1970.

———. "Saint Marc et son double (Le Séquestré de Venise)." In *Sartre et les arts*, edited by Michel Sicard, 169–203. Paris: Librairie Obliques, 1981.

———. *Situations, II: Qu'est-ce que la littérature?* Paris: Éditions Gallimard, 1948.

———. "What Is Literature?" In *What Is Literature? and Other Essays*, edited by Steven Ungar. Cambridge, Mass.: Harvard University Press, 1988.

Saussure, Ferdinand de. *Cours de linguistique générale*. Paris: Payot, 1972.

———. *Course in General Linguistics*. Translated by Wade Baskin. New York: Philosophical Library, 1959.

Schapiro, Meyer. "Fromentin as a Critic." *Partisan Review*, no. 16 (1949): 25–51.

Souchon, Paul. *Olympio et Juliette*. Paris: Albin Michel, 1940.

Taine, Hippolyte. *Philosophie de l'art dans les Pays-Bas*. Paris, 1869.

Thompson, James, and Barbara Wright. *La Vie et l'œuvre d'Eugène Fromentin*. Paris: ARC Édition Internationale, 1987.

Ubersfeld, Anne. "L'Anankè du discours." In *Hugo le fabuleux*, edited by Jacques Séebacher and Anne Ubersfeld, 297–307. Paris: Éditions Seghers, 1985.

Verlaine, Paul. *Selected Poems*. Translated by Martin Sorrell. Oxford World's Classics. London: Oxford University Press, 1999.

Warner, Rex, ed. *The Confessions of St. Augustine*. Mentor-Omega Books. New York: New American Library, 1963.

Wedderburn, Alexander and E. T. Cook, eds. *The Works of John Ruskin*. 39 vols. London: George Allen and Sons, 1903–12.

Wolff, Janet. "Excess and Inhibition: Interdisciplinarity in the Study of Art." In *Cultural Studies*, edited by Cary Nelson, Paula Treichler, and Lawrence Grossberg, 706–18. New York: Routledge, 1992.

Index

Abrams, Meyer Howard, 15
Albouy, Pierre, 40, 45, 193, 194
Ancelle, Narcisse, 202
Arcimboldo, Giuseppe, 108, 188, 189
Aristotle, 26, 30, 49, 57, 176, 196
Augustine of Hippo, 131

Balzac, Honoré de, 16, 94, 136
Barthes, Roland, 16, 17, 18, 52, 100, 107–10, 112, 113, 145, 169, 170, 188–91, 192, 195, 200, 201
Baudelaire, Charles, 13, 19, 49, 69, 123–50, 172, 192, 194, 197, 202–5
Baudrillard, Jean, 108
Beauvoir, Simone de, 164, 206
Benjamin, Walter, 147
Bentham, Jeremy, 79
Benvéniste, Émile, 31, 32, 36
Bertin, Louis-François, 40, 194
Beyle, Henri (Stendhal), 13, 17, 136, 149
Bloom, Harold, 14, 29, 193
Bonaparte, Napoléon, 168, 196
Bonnefoy, Yves, 165, 192, 206
Boudin, Eugène, 128, 129, 131, 133, 136, 145
Bourdil, Pierre-Yves, 205
Brombert, Victor, 50, 51
Brown, John, 62, 69, 71
Bryson, Norman, 106
Buonarroti, Michelangelo, 184
Burton, Richard D. E., 202
Butor, Michel, 192

Carrier, David, 192, 202
Castex, Pierre-Georges, 124, 204
Cézanne, Paul, 171
Chateaubriand, François-René de, 14, 15, 29, 127, 128, 137, 204

Clark, Timothy, 124, 203
Claudel, Paul, 150, 154–56, 158–62, 192, 205
Cogman, Peter, 193
Condillac, Étienne Bonnot, Abbé de, 110
Cousin, Victor, 16, 56, 57
Culler, Jonathan, 46–48, 195

Deguy, Michel, 201
Delacroix, Eugène, 127, 128, 131, 133, 136–38, 140, 141, 144, 149, 169
de Maistre, Joseph, 76, 78
de Man, Paul, 46, 47, 163, 195, 203
Derrida, Jacques, 102, 103, 110, 205, 206
Diderot, Denis, 144, 204
Drouet, Juliette, 22, 23, 25–27, 29, 40–43, 48, 193, 194

Fontanier, Pierre, 46, 48, 195
Foucault, Michel, 79–81, 83, 84, 86, 87, 108
France, Anatole, 100–104
Freud, Sigmund, 193
Fromentin, Eugène, 150–59, 163, 192, 205

Gaudon, Jean, 19, 23, 27, 53, 55, 193, 194, 196, 197
Gautier, Théophile, 136, 144, 204
Genette, Gérard, 196
Georgel, Pierre, 192
Gombrich, Ernst, 94, 110, 112, 169, 203
Grossman, Kathryn, 63, 65, 69
Guys, Constantin, 124, 125, 132, 136–49, 204

216 INDEX

Hanson, Anne Coffin, 124, 203
Hegel, Georg F. W., 14, 89, 100, 111
Heidegger, 160
Herodotus, 65, 196
Heurtelou, 72
Holbein, Hans, 108
Homer, 18
Hugo, Adèle (née Foucher), 40–42, 49, 91, 194, 197
Hugo, Eugène, 91
Hugo, Joseph-Léopold-Sigisbert, 130
Hugo, Victor, 14–16, 18, 19, 21–78, 81–95, 100, 103–7, 129, 130, 137–39, 142, 148, 191–99, 203, 204
Huysmans, Joris-Karl, 13

Jameson, Fredric, 85

Kaes, Emmanuelle, 205
Kant, Immanuel, 56, 57, 60, 68–69, 82, 83, 138, 195, 197, 203
Krailsheimer, Alban, 198
Kuhn, Thomas, 85

Lacan, Jacques, 21, 108
Lamartine, Alphonse de, 41, 42, 94
Lapoujade, Robert, 263, 206
Leenhardt, Jacques, 207
Leroux, Pierre, 14–16, 18, 46, 47
Levaillant, Maurice, 40, 194

Mallarmé, Stéphane, 19
Malraux, André, 192
Manet, Édouard, 124, 141, 148, 204
Martignac, Jean Baptise de, 33
Marx, Karl, 91
Masson, André, 163, 206
Matisse, Henri, 169
Maurois, André, 192
McLuhan, Marshall, 198
Memling, Hans, 150
Meryon, Charles, 128, 129, 131, 133, 136, 145, 148, 204
Michelangelo. *See* Buonarroti, Michelangelo
Miller, Christopher, 65, 66, 196
Musset, Alfred de, 42

Napoléon. *See* Bonaparte, Napoléon
Newton, Isaac, 171, 185
Nietzsche, Friedrich, 85

O'Donohoe, Bénédict, 207

Packard, Vance, 108
Petrey, Sandy, 50–53, 55, 57
Philostratus, 18
Pichois, Claude, 203, 204
Piroué, Georges, 63, 64, 68, 69
Plato, 122, 123, 201
Poe, Edgar Allan, 141
Popovic, Pierre, 201
Popper, Karl, 185
Pradier, Claire, 25, 148
Pradier, James, 129
Proust, Marcel, 90, 94–100, 102–4, 106, 113–15, 185, 192, 198, 199, 200, 204
Ptolemy, 185

Racine, Jean, 14, 15, 28, 193, 195
Rat, Maurice, 28, 193
Rebeyrolle, Paul, 163
Rembrandt. *See* van Rijn, Rembrandt Harmensz
Ricœur, Paul, 194
Riese-Hubert, Renée, 201
Rifelj, Carol de Dobay, 201
Robusti, Jacopo, *called* Tintoretto, 163–66, 169, 171–77, 179–86, 206, 207
Rosa, Guy, 50, 51, 55, 57
Rousseau, Jean-Jacques, 40, 153, 205
Rubens, Pieter-Pauwel, 150
Ruskin, John, 13, 15, 16, 18, 94–100, 104, 106, 113, 198, 199, 204

Sainte-Beuve, Charles Augustin, 42, 119, 194
Sand, George, 16
Sartre, Jean-Paul, 19, 111, 112, 132, 146, 163–87, 192, 197, 204, 206, 207
Saussure, Ferdinand de, 21, 101, 107, 109, 111, 116, 178, 188, 190, 199, 200
Schapiro, Meyer, 150, 160, 205, 206
Senancour, Étienne Pivert de, 153

Sicard, Michel, 164
Souchon, Pierre, 40, 194
Stendhal. *See* Beyle, Henri
Sue, Eugène, 16

Tadié, Jean-Yves, 94
Taine, Hippolyte, 150
Tintoretto. *See* Robusti, Jacopo
Titian. *See*, Vecellio, Tiziano
Toussaint-Louverture, François Dominique, 196

Ubersfeld, Anne, 31, 32, 34, 35

Vacquerie, Charles, 26
van Eyck, Jan, 150

van Gogh, Vincent, 160
van Rijn, Rembrandt Harmensz, 91–93, 150, 153–57, 159, 161
Vecellio, Tiziano, 143, 171, 172, 174, 184
Velazquez, Diego, 108
Verlaine, Paul, 19, 116–23, 201
Veronese, Paolo, 171
Voragine, Jacopo da, 172, 207

Wolff, Janet, 111, 112
Wordsworth, Henry, 14, 15

Zeuxis, 106
Zola, Émile, 13